Mentoring Partnerships

Mentoring Partnerships

A Guidebook for Inclusive Special Education

Tara Mason

ROWMAN & LITTLEFIELD
Lanham • Boulder • New York • London

Published by Rowman & Littlefield
An imprint of The Rowman & Littlefield Publishing Group, Inc.
4501 Forbes Boulevard, Suite 200, Lanham, Maryland 20706
www.rowman.com

86-90 Paul Street, London EC2A 4NE

Copyright © 2024 by Tara Mason

All rights reserved. No part of this book may be reproduced in any form or by any electronic or mechanical means, including information storage and retrieval systems, without written permission from the publisher, except by a reviewer who may quote passages in a review.

British Library Cataloguing in Publication Information available

Library of Congress Cataloging-in-Publication Data

Names: Mason, Tara, 1976– author.
Title: Mentoring partnerships : a guidebook for inclusive special education in the 21st century / Tara Mason.
Description: Lanham, Maryland : Rowman & Littlefield, 2024. | Includes bibliographical references and index.
Identifiers: LCCN 2024008077 (print) | LCCN 2024008078 (ebook) | ISBN 9781538177327 (cloth) | ISBN 9781538177334 (paperback) | ISBN 9781538177341 (epub)
Subjects: LCSH: Special education. | Inclusive education. | School improvement programs. | Teacher turnover—Prevention. | Teacher effectiveness.
Classification: LCC LC3965 .M285 2024 (print) | LCC LC3965 (ebook) | DDC 371.9072—dc23/eng/20240411
LC record available at https://lccn.loc.gov/2024008077
LC ebook record available at https://lccn.loc.gov/2024008078

Contents

Acknowledgments ix
Introduction 1

SECTION I: LAYING A FOUNDATION 7

August 11
Key Learning Goals .16
Part I: Getting Started in Your Mentoring Partnership? 16
Part II: The First-Year Special Education Teacher 23
Suggested Resources .29

September 31
Key Learning Goals .34
Part I: Evidence-Based Practices 34
Part II: Evidence-Based Practices 39
Part III: Evidence-Based Practices 41
Suggested Resources .46

October 48
Key Learning Goals .51
Part I: A Brief History of Special Education 51
Part II: The Individualized Education Program (IEP) 56
Suggested Resources .74

SECTION II: GETTING INTO IT 77

November 79
Key Learning Goals .82
Part I: Universal Design for Learning (UDL) 82
Part II: Assistive Technology (AT) and Curriculum Planning . . .91
Suggested Resources .97

December 99
   Key Learning Goals 102
   Part I: Understanding Special Education Systems. 102
   Part II: Bias, Disproportionality, and Evaluation 107
   Suggested Resources 114

January 117
   Key Learning Goals 119
   Part I: Working with Your Related Service Special Education
       Teams 119
   Part II: Working with Your General Education Teams and
       Co-Teaching Configurations. 124
   Suggested Resources 128

SECTION III: DIGGING OUT OF DISILLUSIONMENT 129

February 131
   Key Learning Goals 134
   Part I: Person-First Language and Disability Frameworks 134
   Part II: What Are Disability Studies? (Medical, Social, and
       Cultural Models) 136
   Suggested Resources 142

March 143
   Key Learning Goals 146
   Part I: Understanding Least Restrictive Environment (LRE) and
       Special Education Program Models 146
   Part II: Creating a Strength-Based Special Education Program. . . 150
   Suggested Resources 155

April 157
   Key Learning Goals 160
   Part I: We Work as Collaborative Professionals 160
   Part II: Build Up Your Team! How Can Special Education Teams
       Amplify the Support Paraprofessionals Can Provide? 162
   Suggested Resources 169

SECTION IV: REFLECTION, REVITALIZATION, REGROWTH 171

May 175
   Key Learning Goals 178
   Part I: Transition Planning. 178
   Part II: Transition Planning: Systems versus Person Planning . . . 184
   Suggested Resources 186

June **187**
  Key Learning Goals 190
  Part I: Early Intervention in Special Education 190
  Part II: Map Out a Curriculum Plan for Next Year 193
  Suggested Resources 196

July **197**
  Key Learning Goals 200
  Part I: Making a Plan for Year Two, Leadership, and Professional
    Organizations 200
  Part II: Learning Leaders 202
  Suggested Resources 205

SECTION V: RESOURCES **209**

Resource 1: Who Is Who 211

Resource 2: Intensive Lesson Plan Template 213

Resource 3: Annual IEP Calendar 217

Resource 4: IEP Sections Template 218

Resource 5: Case Law Review Template 220

Resource 6: Student One-Pager Template 221

Resource 7: AT Evaluation and Template 223

Resource 8: Bias Self-Reflection Guide 225

Resource 9: Coming Down the Ladder 226

Resource 10: Co-Teaching Modalities and Guide 227

Resource 11: Evaluation Template 228

Resource 12: Intensify Intervention Taxonomy 230

Resource 13: Paraprofessional Schedule 232

Resource 14: Transition Plan Template 236

Resource 15: Curriculum Planning Template 240

Index 243
About the Author 253

Acknowledgments

This book is a tribute to my work as a special education professional for more than twenty years and the amazing mentors who have supported my learning journey. I am a proud member of the special education professional community. We are fierce, passionate advocates for student success, inclusion, and opportunity. We care deeply for students and are forever strategizing a student learning challenge. We are a diverse group coming together from an endless variety of backgrounds. Our common thread is our belief that students deserve equitable access to and support in their education.

I could not have been successful in my teaching career without the mentorship, wisdom, and support of the mentors who have supported me.

A few notable mentors that I would like to especially acknowledge are Dr. Rona Pogrund, Dr. Margaret Macintyre Latta, Dr. Jean Rice, Vicki Davidson, Lyn Roberston, and Pat Stephenson who have been important mentors on my special educator teaching journey. Thank you for believing in me.

I have had colleagues who pushed me to think deeper. I am incredibly grateful for the endless discussions about teaching, learning, and student problem-solving. Thank you for allowing me space to wonder aloud and lean on your wisdom. In particular, the special education teaching teams at St. Vrain Valley School District, Boulder Valley School District, the Texas School for the Blind and Visually Impaired (TSBVI), TSBVI Outreach, and the Perkins School for the Blind. My work at the university level teaming with colleagues at Western Colorado University, the Colorado CEEDAR leadership team (Collaboration for Effective Educator Development, Accountability, and Reform), and the University of California, Berkeley's Research, Teaching, and Learning (RTL) and Center for Teaching and Learning (CTL). Colleagues in these organizations have consistently been thought partners and guides that have supported the deep thinking and development that goes into mentoring, special education evidence-based practices, and supporting teacher and instructor learning. Thank you for partnering with me and broadening my perspective.

I have an amazing family. My family, Lenny, Levi, and Stella, have endlessly supported me. I know I am typing away at my computer a lot, and you are forever understanding, loving, and patient. Lenny, you have been incredibly supportive on this book journey, and I am forever grateful. Kids, I have learned the most from being your mom, and feel so lucky to have you in my life. Thank you for being you and loving me.

I appreciate my parents and extended family. My mom is forever encouraging, ready to problem-solve, and always willing to edit my writing! Dad, thank you for always supporting me through my schooling and professional goals. My sister, Kelsey, is a best friend that I am so incredibly lucky to have in my life! My brother, Guilford, is always happy to get into a deep discussion! Thank you for your love and support!

Finally, to the field of special education and the wisdom learned from the disability advocacy movement. The brightest and most incredible teachers for me have been all the students I have worked with and the teaching teams I have been a part of. No two days are the same, and no student learning roadblock is too great. When you need to think outside the box, just ask a special educator or ask your students. They will likely have a bunch of creative ideas to work toward solving the issue!

Introduction

Welcome to *Mentoring Partnerships: A Guidebook for Inclusive Special Education*! This Guidebook is organized as a month-by-month journey supporting your mentoring partnership through the first year of teaching as a new special education teacher. It is designed to be a broad overview of first-year teaching in the field of special education for any new-to-the-field professional. Whether you are a first-year special education teacher who has never taught before or a teacher adding a new license to teach special education with several years of general education teaching experience, this Guidebook will provide month-by-month guidance to support your professional development. This Guidebook will provide an overview of best instructional practices within special education environments, special education law, procedures, program delivery, inclusive best practices, and programs and practices that are part of the field of special education. This Guidebook draws from a wide research base of evidence-based practices with a comprehensive citation list in the "Suggested Resources" section at the end of each monthly chapter. Please note, in order to keep the monthly deep dives as quick reads, most of the text does not include citations, as you would see in academic writing, and instead a reference list is included for each month along with internet resources.

This Guidebook does not address every possible area of special education programs and teaching practices. It is instead designed to walk your mentoring partnership using broad areas of practice with guided activities around specific topics to be completed within each month. The contents of this Guidebook aim at a broad range of timely special education topics, concepts, and practices but it is inevitable that essential items are missed. This Guidebook is meant to be a "consumable" manual designed to be marked up, dogeared, and utilized heavily throughout the first year of your teaching. You will note an overarching focus on your well-being and mentoring partnership across each section. This focus is purposeful to encourage you to consider both your professional learning and well-being alongside one another as you embark on this learning journey. Ideally these goals go hand in hand in order to build a sustainable teaching practice and spark joy in your work as a special education professional. Another overarching goal of the Guidebook is to develop your understanding of Universal Design for Learning (UDL) and strengths-based programming within special education. These are recommended frameworks for developing your special education program.

Each section of this Guidebook will provide guidance for evidence-based practices in special education and mentoring. Sections I to IV follow the academic calendar year as a special education teacher with just-in-time guidance, resources, checklists, and activities to be completed collaboratively between mentor and mentee. This Guidebook is meant to be read together between mentor and mentee from the beginning of the year to the end. Each section is geared to align with typical happenings during that period of the year—for example, progress reporting at the end of the semester—while resources and checklist items may also be helpful to revisit at any time of the year. Each section will guide mentor partnerships through information related to special education professionals' three primary roles: collaborator, Individual Education Plan (IEP) caseload manager, and intensive intervention teacher.

The reflections in this Guidebook will return to two central themes: (1) How do we determine evidence-based practices? and (2) How do we maximize our efforts to facilitate inclusive special education programs? Within each of the activities you engage in each month, you are encouraged to think deeply about each of these questions collaboratively as you launch into the monthly deep topics and reflections. Throughout the text, case study vignettes and illustrative activities are provided to support the learning and engagement of mentor and mentee, encouraging interaction with resources and content to help you consider these questions from multiple perspectives.

The structure of each monthly chapter begins with a "Case Study" to begin the discussion for the month as well as a "Monthly Checklist" to guide you through the activities and suggested actions for you and your mentor.

Also, each month, you will have a "Plan for Well-Being" activity and goal. Near the end of each monthly chapter, you will have a "Collaborate On" mentoring activity, which may include guidance on how to gradually learn about IEPs, intensive intervention, relationship building, or collaborative special education activities. These activities will typically be completed outside of your weekly or bimonthly meetings, because they are application activities with students, teams, or curriculums.

Let's take a moment to overview the content for each month and the corresponding key ideas related to special education program implementation and intensive intervention. In Section V of this Guidebook, there are several resources related to content covered in monthly "Going Deeper" sections. These resources are also flagged in these monthly overviews to call your attention to them.

In **August,** you will be getting to know one another and learn best practices for mentoring partnerships. You will learn about active listening, discuss ways to support one another, and exchange ideas about your communication and work styles. You will also make a plan for gradually releasing mentor support across the school year. This month will be an opportunity for mentors to share what they know is essential for mentees to learn and also for mentees to think about what they want to be sure is included in the mentoring plan for the year. The second part of your learning in August is an overview into the three primary roles of special education professionals. See resource 1, "Who Is Who," to help you get started with your team.

During the month of **September,** this Guidebook digs into intensive intervention and evidence-based instructional practices of special education. You will complete a KWL chart outlining what you already know about special education intensive intervention and high-leverage teaching practices. Next, you will outline what you hope to learn about explicit instructional practices with your mentor. See resource 2, "Intensive Lesson Plan Template," for instructional guidance.

Launching into **October,** you will learn about the history of the field of special education and the Individuals with Disabilities Education Act (IDEA), which governs special education programs. During the deep dives in October, you will walk through the IEP step by step, unpacking each section with some examples of best practices for the diverse areas of law implemented within the IEP process. See resources 4 to 6, "IEP Sections Template," "Case Law Review Template," and "Student One-Pager Template," to support your IEP caseload management.

Section II starts in **November,** where you will incorporate what you have learned about intensive intervention and the IEP process in considering how to design a special education program that has been framed using Universal Design for Learning (UDL). UDL helps us consider learner variability—that is, the idea that we all learn and think differently and have unique strengths and challenges that require an individualized approach to support learning strategies and accessible environments. In addition to UDL, you will learn about assistive technology (AT) and how UDL and AT can work together by combining proactive learning and environmental supports that make learning accessible for a wide range of learners. The deep dive finishes up with information about AT to support unique student needs. See resource 7, "AT Evaluation and Template," to help outline an AT evaluation and report.

Wrapping up the fall semester, in **December**, we think about mirrors and windows in our thinking that can teach us about bias, disproportionality, and evaluation considerations in special education. Mirrors are meant to represent us looking inward and reflecting on our own biases and assumptions about students and learning. Windows are meant to represent us looking outward to better understand systems that continue to result in there being less opportunities to succeed for students served in our special education programs. Having a better understanding of our inward and outward thinking helps us intervene to support students and advocate for better programs and services when we discover they are needed. See resources 8 and 9, "Bias Self-Reflection Guide" and "Coming Down the Ladder," for bias reflection activities.

Starting the spring semester in **January**, we delve into learning all about our special education teams. Depending on our special education program focus, we can be working with either smaller or more comprehensive teaching teams. Having a stronger foundation in how to work collaboratively with our teams and co-teaching configurations when working with general education teachers helps us to promote more inclusive and collaborative special education programs. See resources 10 to 12, "Co-Teaching Modalities Guide," "Evaluation Template," and "Intensify Intervention Taxonomy" to consider ways to collaborate as co-teachers, conduct evaluations, and intensify interventions.

Full steam ahead, in **February** we discuss the current research in the special education field, promoting a wider awareness of the issues of K–12 school systems/districts being framed by ableism and the continued discrimination in our communities toward people with disabilities. It is estimated that one in six people in the United States identifies as a person with a disability. Having a foundation in understanding ableism can help you see how environmental factors and societal constraints can be barriers to people with disabilities and how these factors create a disabling condition for people with disabilities.

In the middle of the spring semester, **March** is primarily focused on special education program configurations related to least restrictive environments (LRE) and discussing how we can create strengths-based programs that use UDL to proactively work toward more accessibility and success for students. Using a UDL framework can reduce barriers and enhance student strengths when special education programs are planned and implemented in these ways.

Nearly finished with the year, we settle into **April** by discussing your paraprofessional team. Taking into consideration all that you have learned related to collaborating across your team to implement an inclusive program using a strengths-based approach, you will consider how to collaborate with paraprofessional teams to support student success and independence. See resource 13, "Paraprofessional Schedule," to collaborate with your mentor to plan a real or hypothetical paraprofessional schedule.

End-of-the-year activities are the focus of **May**, where we discuss transition planning. Transition planning is an important component of special education programs because we understand the importance of collaborating with families and helping them plan for the future with their students. We emphasize the critical importance of transition planning that is guided by the principle of "nothing about me without me." This phrase means that the students' dreams, goals, and hopes for the future are at the center of the planning process. It also acts to reject the persistent infantilization of individuals with disabilities, regardless of their age, by emphasizing transition supports that are specifically tailored for and centered around the needs and aspirations of the person with a disability. Considering high school transition to be a final support that students are entitled to in our K–12 free and appropriate public education (FAPE), we want to help provide a roadmap for postsecondary success in college, career, and personal independence. See resource 14, "Transition Plan Template" and "Summary of Performance," to learn about the common sections on these two IEP-related reports.

Summer months provide us ample opportunity to reflect and make a plan for the next year so we can capitalize on the hard work from this year. In **June**, we explore how to make a plan for next year. This month also includes an overview about early intervention. You may not work at the elementary or early childhood levels, but it can be valuable to have an overview of early intervention services in special education. You will learn about what is typically included and an overview of IEP procedures for early intervention. See resource 15, "Curriculum Planning Template," to use for curriculum planning for your next year.

Finally, in the month of **July**, we will learn about leadership opportunities and professional organizations in the fields of special education and disability studies. You will consider plans for your future professional learning goals and for next year. Also, there are lots of opportunities in the field of special education to continue to grow in your professional work and the leadership roles that special education professionals are uniquely qualified to fill. We will consider those areas as well and provide some time to reflect and set goals for the future.

Let's get started!
Welcome to your new role as a special education teacher!

Section I
Laying a Foundation

Within Section I, we discuss the roles and responsibilities of special education teachers, several mentor and mentee activities that can be completed regarding communication styles, and procedures for the gradual release of mentor guidance over the year. The August guidance centers on several getting-started activities that will lay a foundation for your work as a new special education teacher and mentor. The next two months in Section I are September and October. They will dig into intensive intervention and the IEP, including an overview of special education law systems within special education and communities, and how to work across special education teams and with parents.

An important part of laying a foundation as you launch into your new special education teaching position is to have a clear understanding of the Individuals with Disabilities Education Act (IDEA, 2004). Within IDEA, there are overarching procedural safeguards that guide special education program implementation, which are outlined below.

1. Schools must *provide procedural safeguard notices* to parents/guardians. It is critical to offer these to parents at the beginning of any Individualized Education Plan (IEP) or evaluation meeting and verify that they have received them. A helpful strategy to ensure you have these printed, at the ready, is to have an "IEP" folder where the procedural safeguards are printed in multiple languages so you can provide them to parents and teams.

2. It is critical that teams have *parent/guardian participation* in IEP actions. By law, you must have attempted at least three times to have parental participation in an IEP/evaluation meeting documented in the IEP or evaluation report.

3. Parents always *have the right to access educational records*. These rights are protected by IDEA and the Family Educational Rights and Privacy Act (FERPA).

4. *Student confidentiality* of information is protected.

5. In order to proceed with evaluations, the evaluator/IEP team must have *informed consent* (or parental consent) in writing.

6. Any change made to a student's program that is linked to their IEP must provide *prior written notice*, which you will hear referred to as "PWNs." This includes when the school wants to add or deny services or change any aspect of the "least restrictive environment" (LRE) being provided to a student. This might, for example, include a change in which a student is served in a special education class for an additional part of the school day that had not been previously agreed upon in an IEP meeting.

7. Special education teams must ensure that evaluations, IEP reports, and any other information related to a student's IEP, uses understandable language and where something must be interpreted—for example, evaluation results—the team doing the evaluation must include someone who can explain and interpret those results. Additionally, this information must be provided in the native language of a parent/guardian if it is different from English.

8. Parents have a right to include an *Independent Educational Evaluation* (IEE) if they disagree with the school results, and parents always have the right to *request an evaluation* for their student; in that case, the school has sixty days to provide an evaluation after written consent has been received.

9. Parents have *"stay put" rights*, which means that they can disagree with proposed changes or a change to a student's least restrictive environment (LRE) that has resulted in a different school or program placement. If "stay put" is enacted, then schools must halt the process of undertaking the next steps in an IEP action until the dispute is resolved.

10. Further *dispute resolution options are available to parents, and they have a right to due process*, which starts with a written complaint and can end with a decision being made after a hearing if a resolution is not met before that time. Finally, parents can file a complaint with their state if the school is violating IDEA. And they can file a com-

plaint with the Office for Civil Rights for the US Department of Education if they believe their child has been discriminated against.

A key takeaway when thinking about procedural safeguards is that they don't spell out what should be included in an IEP but rather the ground rules of how parents/guardians interact with the school. To extend this point further, there is clear guidance from IDEA on what must be included within our IEP programs related to planning for each student. This guidance is commonly referred to as the Six Principles of IDEA (shown in figure 1).

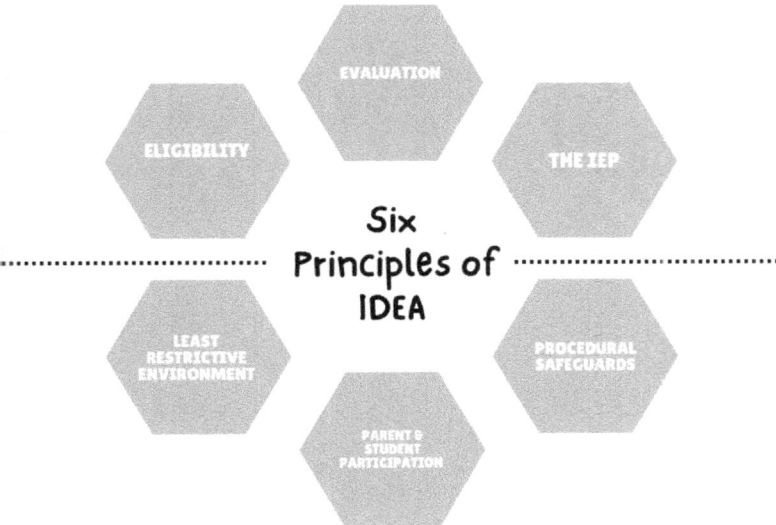

Figure 1. Six Principles of IDEA
This figure provides a visual overview of the six principles of IDEA.

Discuss these six principles with your mentor and jot down what you already know about each one. What are some questions you have about one or two that relate to your new special education teaching role and school building?

August

This case study is all about the enduring question of how special education professionals juggle it all. How can special educators do it all when we consider a day in the life of a mild-to-moderate special education professional?

CASE STUDIES

A Typical Day for a Special Education Teacher in a Mild-to-Moderate Middle School Resource Program

Sydney arrives at work at 7:25 a.m. on the dot every day. She has a student who has been struggling with coming to school on time because she takes care of her three younger siblings each morning; both of her parents are out of the house and working at their own jobs at 5:00 a.m.

Figure 2. Special Educators Do a Little Bit of Everything!
This figure depicts a teacher at her desk with a myriad of roles and responsibilities swirling around her head.

It is challenging for this student, but Sydney has set up a rewards system for her where she can eat free breakfast in Sydney's classroom every day that she arrives ten minutes before the bell. Sydney found that the breakfast invitation and the warm morning welcome were just what the student needed to get her younger siblings out the door to their elementary school, which is across the street from the middle school. Sydney has a wide range of check-ins like this that she does with students on her caseload in the morning before the first bell has even rung! She uses this time to catch up on email, while students file in and out of her room, grabbing their folders and checklists for their academic classes. Sydney has several students who store their academic materials in her room since it helps them to have a consistent place to charge their devices and keep their materials organized.

The first bell has rung, and Sydney's first intensive pull-out reading group arrives. In contrast to her breezy and warm social and emotional check-in before school began, this reading intervention time is highly structured. Students grab their bins and Sydney implements a highly organized, eight-step reading intervention that starts at the bell with a pre-assessment and ends like clockwork five minutes before the second-period bell with a post-assessment exit ticket. Sydney's students know this structure inside and out. Many of them have achieved two to three grade level gains in this reading program, and Sydney monitors their progress at least twice a week along with a quick review of their post-assessment exit ticket each day when they leave. This exit ticket helps her strategically plan for the next day's word-level review.

It is time for collaboration. Sydney visits two different math classes each day during second period, dividing the period into two halves and flip-flopping the push-in support each day so she is there at the beginning and end of each class multiple times per week. In this role, she adapts materials, provides one-on-one intensive support, and collaborates with the math team by providing parallel teaching of content at the beginning of the week. This team makes this co-teaching arrangement work well by sharing the lesson plans with one another each week on Wednesdays prior to discussing the next week's content as a teaching team. The team collaborates on the Google Docs, and each person selects a role from the list that they collaboratively create each week.

Later this morning, Sydney pulls out a couple of students at various times to go over issues that have come to her attention. These meetings are a chance for some collective problem-solving that needs to happen. She uses the rest of this planning time to schedule two IEP meetings by calling the parents of the students who have meetings coming up and checking in with the school psychologist to be sure she is able to be at the meeting planned for October, when they must go over evaluation data regarding a possible new eligibility area. One of the phone numbers is disconnected and Sydney does not have another contact number for that family, so she makes a note to speak with the front office administrator to see if there are updated contact numbers on file.

Oh my, where did the time go, it is time for lunch! Sydney has her lunch after the younger grades, and she likes to head down to the cafeteria to help facilitate the positive behavior support system games that are held at the end of first lunch for any student who chooses not to go outside. For her own lunch, she chooses a little well-being activity with a fellow colleague who loves to walk'n'talk about their favorite show after they grab a quick bite! Wow—what a beautiful day it is outside.

Afternoon comes in the blink of an eye. Three students needed some extra support on a big project that is coming up in social studies along with a handful of concerns from students from Ms. Richie's English language arts (ELA) class that are working on a group project. No problem! Sydney created a resource room "learning lab" that is open to any student—both those on her caseload and students from general education programs who self-select to come in when they need a little extra support. Sydney guides this support time with the help of a peer mentoring club that has five students participating this year. They are receiving course credit to support their peers who utilize the learning lab.

Sixth period is a combined intensive science and math co-taught class where Sydney has been partnering with her general education teaching teams for the last couple of years to create a differentiated curriculum that supports students served in the gifted and talented, special education, and culturally linguistically diverse programs. It is a lab format and provides enhanced instruction and additional peer mentor supports for students who are struggling—a particularly common need is content area literacy support.

It is nearing the end of the day, and Sydney has two final periods of pull-out resource groups where she provides individualized support and work toward executive functioning goals. During this time, she works on goal-related strategies that are individualized for each student and also has students make a "plan for the week" for their homework and to-do lists for the next day, which they keep in the folders that are stored in Sydney's room. As the end of the day grows near, her students are getting restless! She gets that, since she feels the same way at this point in the day. They typically play a literacy or math game to finish off the day before the students head off to the bus or afterschool activities. Sydney has a couple more IEP-related items to check off her list. She keeps a "daily log," which is a note catcher where she jots down any issues or to-do items that have bubbled up that day. She leaves her daily log at the center of her desk, so it is the first thing she sees in the a.m. A couple of student-specific notes are added to her daily log notes so she can follow up tomorrow and let them go for the evening. It was a great day; on to the next!

14   SECTION I

 STOP & JOT

- Reflect on Sydney's typical day with your mentor. What sounds familiar? What is different for you?
- What do you like about Sydney's day that you want to include in your "Plan for Well-Being" to incorporate into your own program and teaching practices?

As you consider Sydney's day in the life, map out your typical day in the hypothetical day that follows. You have time windows to help you, as well as a few other prompts to get you started. Circle your typical emotional state using the emoticon "mood meter" to identify how you might feel at each increment. If you cannot find an emoticon to describe your feelings, please add one of your own. Take about ten to fifteen minutes and then discuss with one another.

7–10 a.m. Mood meter? 😃 🙂 🤭 😴 😩 😙 🥴
Think of your first thing in the morning to-do's . . . What are students up to during this time?
10–2 p.m. Mood meter? 😃 🙂 🤭 😴 😩 😙 🥴
When do you eat lunch/take care of yourself? When do you chat with colleagues/collaborate/meet? What are students up to during this time?
2–5 p.m. Mood meter? 😃 🙂 🤭 😴 😩 😙 🥴
How does the school day wrap up? What are students up to during this time?
5–8 p.m. Mood meter? 😃 🙂 🤭 😴 😩 😙 🥴
What do you do after school, for example, engage in school activities or rush to support family needs? What are students up to during this time?

Special Education Mentoring
MONTHLY CHECKLIST: AUGUST

TO DO...	DONE	NOTES
Establish meeting schedule		
Assist with any IEP actions due in September		
Review selection & access to instructional materials		
Discuss lesson plannning, interventions, special education program planning		
Assist with classroom management procedures & first week of school plan		
Discuss medical, health, and school crisis procedures		
Review online learning tools, grading, and attendance procedures		
Complete *who is who* contact list		
Review the continuum of special education services in the building, i.e. mild to significant support needs		

OTHER CHECKLIST ITEMS UNIQUE TO YOUR SCHOOL DISTRICT

_____

_____

_____

ALSO FOR THIS MONTH

☐ Well-Being Goal _____

☐ Collaborate on Mentoring Activities

☐ Suggested Resources: follow up?

SPECIAL EDUCATION FOCUS

To support your goal setting, this section is meant for you to jot down one focus area/question in each of your primary roles.

☐ IEP: _____

☐ Intensive Intervention: _____

☐ Collaboration: _____

Note that anything italicized in the checklist is referring to a template in the back of this guidebook.

August Monthly Checklist

This checklist provides a roadmap for mentor discussions and timely special education roles and responsibilities typically occurring around this time of the year. There are spaces to add your own checklist items and goals within the three primary roles and responsibilities of special education professionals related to IEP caseload management, collaboration, and teaching specifically designed instruction also referred to as intensive interventions.

Key Learning Goals

1. Learn about mentoring supports including how to plan, develop, and adapt materials that reflect the learning needs of the new special education teacher—that is, the "mentee"—with attention to school context and potential caseload challenges.

2. Build an understanding of the three primary roles of special education teachers: caseload manager, collaborator, and intensive intervention teacher.

Part I: Getting Started in Your Mentoring Partnership?

The educational field has long appreciated the vital role of mentoring for beginning teachers. A strong, mutually beneficial, and productive relationship between mentor and mentee is the foundation of a successful first year as a special educator. Mentoring is a collaborative learning relationship that proceeds through purposeful stages over time and aims to promote future special educators' success in the roles and responsibilities that are included in their jobs. Mentors primarily use a combination of their own teaching experiences and best practices in the special education field to guide their work with their mentee.

Mentoring relationships can offer many types of support on this journey. Review the list below and rank them in order of importance from each of your perspectives. There may be priority supports missing from this list as well. Feel free to annotate or add an additional option. This will be a great way to get to know one another and also consider your own priorities.

The most important quality in a mentoring relationship for me is . . .

— emotional availability and understanding (e.g., supporting by listening, sharing experiences, providing encouragement) of the challenging aspects of teaching.

— support with school and district procedures, collaboration across teams, and assistance with IEP paperwork, progress monitoring, and procedures.

— support with curriculum, materials, behavior management, and other strategies.

— help with addressing professional areas such as cultural competence and diversity, supporting families, and integrating IEP goals into the general curriculum.

— encouragement of reflection through open-ended questions about data and implementation efforts to allow novice special education teachers to reflect on their practice.

Consider actions listed below that contribute to impactful and meaningful mentorship (Meyer, 2021).

- Active listening is a huge part of communication in a relationship. Active listeners listen to learn, and good mentors learn from listening.
- Intervening when the workload may seem overwhelming. Recognizing that new teachers have the same expectations put on them as do veteran teachers. In addition, helping with support on different levels and advocating when needed to lessen the strain for new teachers is a critical mentor role.
- Connecting with community circles within the teaching community. Find people to connect with that help, support, share stories, build relationships, gain knowledge, and share the same passions.

Meyer (2021) points to a particularly beneficial mentoring configuration worth noting here. A "shelter and develop" model (Rosenberg & Anderson, 2021) provides guidance for collaboration within mentoring partnerships and recommends a lightened workload in the first year to support teacher retention and well-being. In this model, "shelter" refers to strategies that lessen and simplify the teaching job, specifically in special education, that could be a lighter student caseload, gradual release in IEP caseload management in the fall, less unique lesson preparations for intensive intervention, and more time for support from the mentor within the workday. The "development" refers to the strategies that will create space for professional development tied to increasing teacher effectiveness such as classroom observations, co-teaching, coaching from instructional experts, and teaming up on challenging student caseload activities (i.e., in special education this might be working together on initial evaluations or functional behavior assessments throughout the first year). This model emphasizes that no matter what, school systems and districts must plan for new teachers to have opportunities for both shelter and development.

Communication Styles and Mentor Getting-to-Know-Each-Other Activity

At its best, mentoring can be a life-altering relationship that inspires mutual growth, learning, and development. Its effects can be remarkable, profound, and enduring; mentoring relationships have the capacity to transform individuals, groups, organizations, and communities. Even in the absence of more formal systems for "shelter and development" in your school district/system, mentoring a new teacher can have an exponential positive impact on well-being, growth, and retention for new teachers. Thank you for taking the time to partner with one another!

Establishing Your Mentoring Relationship Norms and Communication Preferences

Creating and developing a work relationship is an important step in mentoring. Use the activity below, which is tied to mentoring evidence-based practices, to determine the mentoring model that will work best for your partnership.

First, identify your communication style. It is important to remember that no communication style is right or wrong, good or bad, or better or worse than any other style. All people use elements of each style to varying degrees and/or in different situations. Some reflection questions will be included here to help you share your style and consider how your communication style might change when you are under stress, which can commonly occur in school settings.

What Is Your Communication Style?

The categories mentioned in table 1.1 are common communication types. Please circle the one that best describes your communication style. If you want to go deeper on this point, find any free communication style survey online to help you define which of these is your primary style.

Table 1.1.

Analytical/ Thinker	Direct/Driven	Expressive/ Passionate	Amiable/ Non-Direct

Now consider when you are *stressed or under pressure*. Does your communication style change? If so, which style do you typically gravitate toward? Please circle your style in table 1.2.

Table 1.2.

Analytical/ Thinker	Direct/Driven	Expressive/ Passionate	Amiable/ Non-Direct

Share with each other. Knowing and valuing each other's style will help you to navigate both the positive and negative situations in your mentoring relationship this year.

Useful Mentoring Advice

Consider advice that mentors have passed down from mentor to mentee as you embark on this journey with one another. Some musts to consider as you launch into the year:

1. **Love what you do**—find what you love about your job, love about your students, love about your life . . . and nurture those things since they will help you persevere when challenges arise.

2. **Plan and execute**—make a plan and do it! This advice is all about seeing things through. It will be challenging to always feel like, "I wish I would have. . ." Within this Guidebook, you will find practice advice on how to prioritize and juggle the never-ending responsibilities of being a special education teacher, which oftentimes means knowing when to put a pin in it for the day and pick it up tomorrow!

3. **Overdeliver**—find where you want to shine and do it! Play to your strengths, and don't be afraid to ask for feedback *and* praise when you have done a great job getting something accomplished with excellence!

4. **Find your people**—you will find there will be colleagues in your school who help you problem-solve, stay positive when something is challenging, and, overall, feel joyful. Find those people. They are your "marigolds"; seek them out for advice and support. Be wary of the "walnut trees" who may make a bad situation even worse (Gonzalez, 2013).

5. **Let it go**—an incredibly important piece of wisdom that we will come back to over and over within this Guidebook. Things will happen this year that will upset you in many ways, finding a way to compartmentalize those frustrations and move forward is a critical skill to protect your well-being.

6. **Keep yourself honest; you are a human, not a superhero**—you will make mistakes in your new role and don't forget to, first, give yourself grace and, second, take time to clean it up when you need to. Students will learn the most from your humanity and kindness. If you make a mistake with a student or colleague, which happens to all of us, find a way to clean it up and recommit to what you value.

An important consideration in mentoring, particularly as it relates to special education teachers, is both teacher well-being and effective coaching that is sensitive to the unique features of the field of special education.

Mentors can provide a roadmap in the first year for a new teacher that can help them to create stronger relationships in their school buildings and feel supported. Teacher well-being is crucial for ensuring a positive and effective learning environment for students (Darling-Hammond & Sykes, 2003). Special educators who are mentally, physically, and emotionally healthy are better equipped to provide quality education to their students. In contrast, teacher stress and unhappiness have been linked to negative impacts on teachers' physical health and emotional well-being. Teacher well-being can also lead to improved teacher retention rates and decreased absenteeism (Fotiadis et al., 2019; Shimer, 2018).

Take a moment to consider your well-being. Reflect on your past, present, and future well-being goals and experiences and discuss with one another.

Looking at table 1.3, consider your previous workplace experiences, list two or three next to the table, and consider how you felt in those workplaces. Did you typically feel joy? Camaraderie with your colleagues? Were there specific activities that were included in these workplace experiences that supported you in feeling connected, happy, and taken care of?

Finish reflecting on these questions (shown in table 1.3) and discuss with one another.

Table 1.3.

Previous work experience(s):	Current work experience(s):	Future work experience(s):
How did you typically feel in these workplaces? Why do you think you felt that way? Any specific experiences that stand out?	How have you felt so far? Why? Are there specific activities that are happening that make you feel good? Taken care of? Anything that is missing so far that you believe you need more of?	What would help you feel taken care of? What would help you to feel happy and fulfilled? What do you need when workplace experiences become challenging?

Learning about Mentoring Structures

Typical mentoring programs generally include these overall structures regarding work with new special education teachers:

1. *Mentors will establish clear expectations and communication plans*: Ensure that the expectations, goals, and communication practices of the mentoring relationship are clearly established and understood by both mentor and new special education mentee. This can include regular meetings, communication check-ins, and specific areas of focus that can be evaluated using a checklist of special education roles and responsibilities.

2. *Mentors will guide the professional development of their mentee by identifying strengths and challenges*: These must be related to the roles and responsibilities specific to special education teachers. This can involve goal setting, teaching observations, co-teaching, and more.

3. *Mentors provide constructive feedback*: Constructive feedback is essential for professional growth and setting goals. Providing specific and actionable feedback can help the special education teacher-in-training to develop their intensive intervention, caseload management, and collaborative techniques.

4. *Mentors are expected to share their own experiences and insights*: This can include strategies for classroom management, intensive intervention, case studies of their caseload students, teaching techniques and strategies for engagement, and professional development opportunities within the school, district, and professional organizations.

5. *Mentors encourage self-reflection and self-evaluation*: This can involve setting goals and regularly reviewing progress toward those goals.

6. *Mentors foster a supportive environment and build a caring relationship with their mentee*: Critically important is the creation of a supportive and collaborative environment that can help the teacher-in-training feel comfortable asking questions, sharing concerns, and seeking advice. This can also help to build trust and a sense of community within the school building and on the special education team. This final component can create positive well-being for new special education teachers by enveloping them in support, feedback, and collaboration.

Table 1.4 includes suggestions for how mentors might provide a "gradual release" for new special education teachers, which can be helpful as you consider the six areas of mentoring presented above. What do I mean by "gradual release"? Gradual release is defined as gradually providing less guidance as an individual feels more comfortable and confident. For example, when completing a specialized report as we do in special edu-

Table 1.4. Annual Guidance for Special Education Mentor and Mentee

Beginning of the Year: August to November	The mentor teacher demonstrates common IEP steps such as assessments interventions, co-teaching, collaborative teaming, and facilitating meetings. The mentor uses a shared demonstration model as the semester proceeds for the mentee to grow confidence.
Middle of the Year: November to February	Shared demonstration moves to guided and independent practice.
End of the Year: February to May	The mentee is independent in IEP actions, intervention, and collaborative teaming. The mentor reflects with the mentee and continues to provide support.

This table reviews overarching learning needs across the year for mentoring that are specific to special education and are related to the roles and responsibilities of new special education teachers.

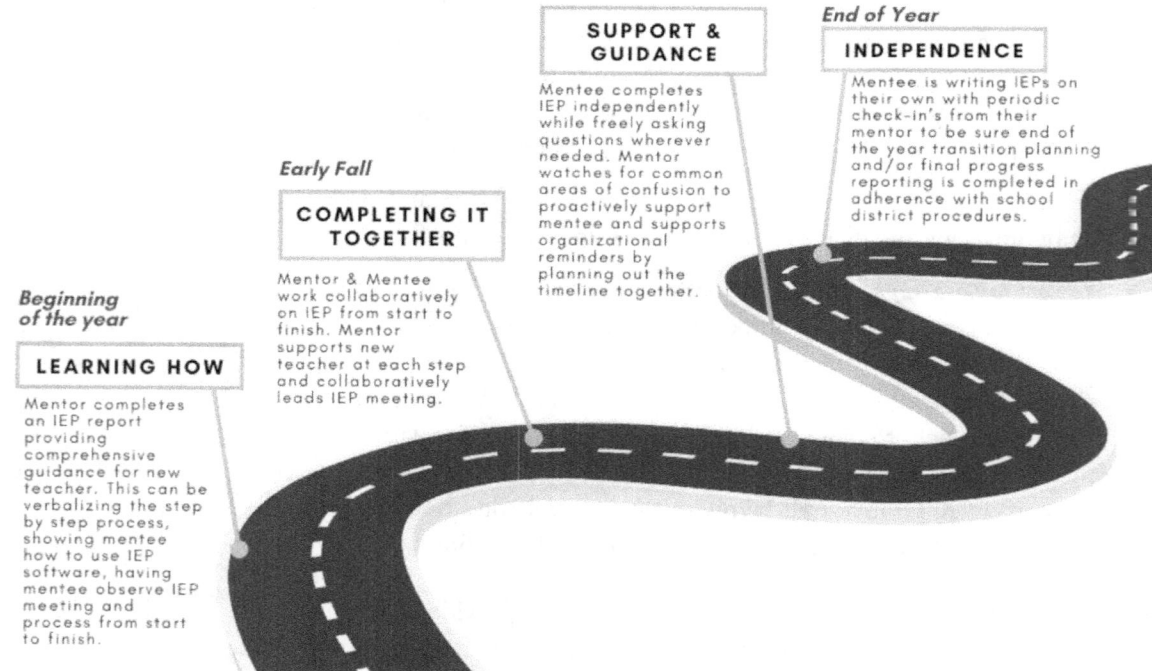

Figure 3. A Pathway for Gradual Release in Special Education Mentoring

This figure depicts a gradual release pathway for mentors and new special education teachers to proceed along as they collaborate on IEPS.

cation, such as an Individual Education Plan (IEP), gradual release from mentor to mentee may follow this timeline summarized in table 1.4.

Consider ways of providing gradual release across the year. Identify an action within IEP planning together such as conducting new evaluations, completing an IEP from start to finish, collaborating with parents, or some other action that is unique to your special education program. Use table 1.5 to map out how you can work together to gradually scale back support and guidance leading to independence by the end of the year.

 COLLABORATE ON

Table 1.5.

	Beginning of the Year	**Middle of the Year**	**End of the Year**
IEP Action			
Mentor Actions	More mentor actions:	Less mentor actions:	Least mentor actions:
Mentee Actions	More mentee observations:	More mentee actions:	Most/all mentee actions:

A final, important activity as you get started in your mentoring relationship is to find consistent times to meet. Another helpful tool discussed in this Guidebook is inviting each other into your classrooms. Mentees, it is valuable for you to observe intensive instruction, evaluations, positive behavior support systems (PBIS), co-teaching configurations, and so on. Mentors, it is valuable for you to step into your mentee's classroom to provide observational feedback, individualized support regarding caseload students, and more. Some suggestions are made in table 1.6 for you to discuss with one another and make a plan for the fall. At the end of the fall, consider how this plan worked and revise as needed for the spring semester.

 COLLABORATE ON

PART II: THE FIRST-YEAR SPECIAL EDUCATION TEACHER

Consider how this description of a typical first year of being a special education teacher relates to you and your work together this year. You may have seen this illustration previously depicting the phases of the first year of teaching. I would argue that this cycle repeats itself every year, and while the shifts may not be as drastic, the anticipation, survival (to some extent even for veteran teachers!), disillusionment, rejuvenation, reflection, and anticipation of the next year are stages that special education professionals will feel in big and small ways every year.

 GOING DEEPER

Table 1.6.

August	September	October	November	December
Meet weekly OR bimonthly? (*circle*) Time? _____	Meetings/times:	Meetings/times:	Meetings/times:	Meetings/times:
Any particular *instructional*, *behavioral*, or *evaluation* strategy being worked on? (*circle*) _____ What would be a good time to observe or collaborate? _____	Any particular *instructional*, *behavioral*, or *evaluation* strategy being worked on? _____ What would be a good time to observe or collaborate? _____	Any particular *instructional*, *behavioral*, or *evaluation* strategy being worked on? _____ What would be a good time to observe or collaborate? _____	Any particular *instructional*, *behavioral*, or *evaluation* strategy being worked on? _____ What would be a good time to observe or collaborate? _____	Any particular *instructional*, *behavioral*, or *evaluation* strategy being worked on? _____ What would be a good time to observe or collaborate? _____
No mentee observation this month.	Schedule a time to observe your mentee and provide feedback (1st one, sometime Sept./Oct.):		Schedule a time to observe your mentee and provide feedback:	Schedule a time to observe your mentee and provide feedback:

Please consider the cycle shown in figure 4 and discuss it with one another. When have you experienced one or more of these stages? How did you move through them?

How could we summarize the primary components for special education professionals? As special educators, we have three primary roles and responsibilities:

1. **IEP Caseload Manager**
2. **Collaborator**
3. **Intensive Intervention Teacher**

Working as a special education professional broadly consists of these three primary roles and responsibilities. For instance, your day may be

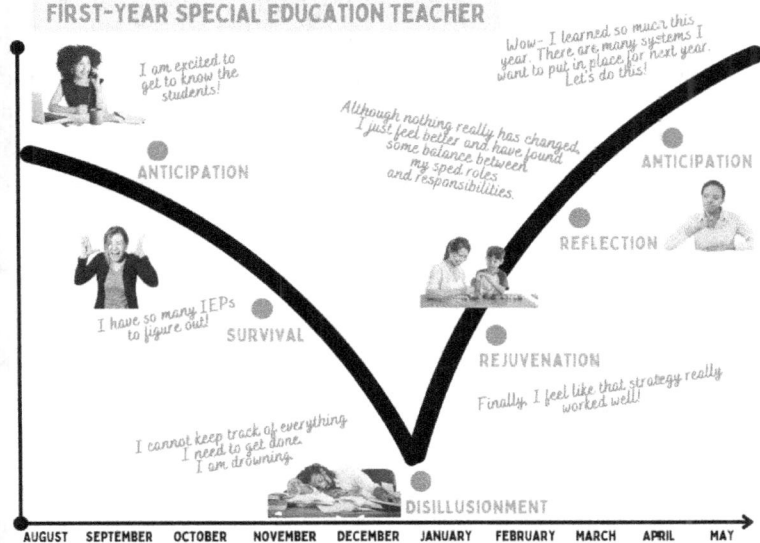

Figure 4. First-Year Special Education Teacher Timeline

This figure is adapted from Moir's Phases of the first-year teacher (adapted with permission from Ellen Moir, New Teacher Center, 1990, 1999, 2001). It depicts the cycle of anticipation, survival, disillusionment, rejuvenation, reflection, and anticipation that novice teachers (special education teachers) typically experience during their first year.

spent primarily working in co-teaching classrooms with your general education team members providing inclusive instruction and/or pulling small groups of students. In another program, you may work within a more restrictive learning environment with students who have complex learning needs. In this role, you may have other adults who are paraprofessionals in your classroom also working to support students. These more restrictive settings become even more distinctive as we consider the age and grade level of the students and the learning structures of the school building. With so many variations in program design and delivery, it is easy to see that special educators are flexible and problem-solving educational professionals who typically come into their workday with the expectation that it will most likely not be exactly the same as the day before. Let's take a close look at each of these three primary roles and responsibilities to learn what is typically included within each.

IEP Caseload Manager

Within this role, you are the lead facilitator of the Individual Educational Plan (IEP) for your caseload students. You are responsible for facilitating their IEP each year while completing tasks such as evaluating students for continued eligibility in special education, communicating with parents or guardians, progress monitoring IEP goals and academic progress. We can imagine this role as being "one-third" of our total roles and responsibilities, and you could potentially imagine your work week being divided into thirds, with this portion comprising around thirteen hours of your time within a forty-hour work week. As with many professional vocations, this role will sometimes take thirteen hours of your week while other weeks you will only spend five hours wearing your "IEP caseload manager" hat.

Let's take a moment to imagine this role and hypothesize some strategies that you think would help you be an effective caseload manager for your students. Several categories are listed below to help you brainstorm one strategy or strength you have in each area.

- Communication with others:
- Scheduling meetings:
- Facilitating meetings/agendas:
- Interpreting assessment results:
- Utilizing software to create reports:
- Collaborating with team members:
- Empathizing and understanding challenges experienced by others:
- Seeing patterns (think patterns in behaviors, learning, social skills):
- Managing multiple streams of information and synthesizing:

Collaborator

This portion of our roles and responsibilities extends across all areas of our work, but it is also important to consider this role and responsibility completely on its own. We collaborate within our job as a special education teacher across the school day and week, as well as from year to year. We collaborate with our teaching teams, with student families/guardians, and other community members, with administrators and district-level teams, and with all of the other members of our school building for a wide variety of reasons. These collaborative reasons include working with nurses who support healthcare plans for our students who require medical care while at school or when writing a collaborative report for an eligibility evaluation with members of the teaching team, and when working with general education teaching team members. This is a critical role in our profession, and it has exponential benefits for our students when we are willing to be collaborators. Simply, our students and programs need us to advocate for them. You will have many situations within each school year that require different kinds of collaboration, for example, discussions and collaborations that are hard, easy, complex, sensitive, or emotional.

What can we control in these collaborations that can look every which way? We can control our behavior, our communication, and how we choose to react. Why do I say this? Because it is inevitable that tough stuff will come up that requires careful collaboration, and how we choose to handle the situation will leave a lasting impression on all persons involved. Let's imagine your character strengths when it comes to collaborations in the past: think of all the things you have done in your life, family, work, when you were young, in the present day, and so on. Draw from those life experiences and remember your successes! What worked well for you when in tough situations? A couple of example situations are included here for you to jot down how you dealt with them.

- An argument about something you felt really passionate about:
- Someone was gossiping about you behind your back, and you dealt with it how?
- You have a great idea but no one else is on board with it, what did you do?
- An incident happened at work, and you feel partly responsible. How did you deal with the aftermath?
- You had a power struggle:
- You reacted to an injustice:
- You witnessed a crime or something done that was illegal, for example, shoplifting:

STOP & JOT

Intensive Intervention Teacher

We will dive deeper into intensive intervention within the section about evidence-based practices. Questions to help you consider this role are: How do we define "intensive intervention"? How do we know if we are actually providing evidence-based practices with our intensive interventions? These are important questions for special education teachers to consider. Let's break down this part of our role to make it more understandable.

If a student is found eligible for special education services, we will create an IEP collaboratively with the IEP team that outlines a comprehensive plan including our "service delivery" and the "intensive instruction" or "specifically/specially designed instruction" (SDI) needed by our students to support their academic progress. There are many other components of the IEP as well, but let's consider what is meant by intensive instruction.

KEY IDEAS

Intensive instruction is . . .

- specifically designed to be individualized to our students' learning needs.
- grounded in research that is designed to meet the needs of learners who share some or many of the same learner characteristics as our student.
- monitored using a consistent schedule to ensure that we know it is proving effective in helping our students to be more successful in the areas of eligibility outlined on their IEPs.

STOP & JOT

1. Consider an example student you or your mentor work with who is being provided intensive intervention to support their literacy learning needs. Is this intervention designed for learners who have similar learning needs to my learner?

2. Does my progress monitoring data show that my student is improving in their learning within the area being targeted by the intensive intervention I have implemented?

3. Am I implementing this intensive intervention with fidelity, that is, as I was trained to implement or follow the procedures outlined by the strategy, tool, or program?

CHARACTER STRENGTHS

Throughout this Guidebook, we will dig into well-being tips and strategies during each month. These are recommended focus areas that you can align with or use to create your own goal that is a better fit for what you need at the time. Many of these well-being strategies are synthesized from Yale University's The Science of Well-Being (MOOC). This is a free course that is designed to "rewire your brain" to grow your happiness and satisfaction. This Guidebook includes summaries of some of these great tools and resources, and I highly recommend you consider completing the free course found online: https://www.coursera.org/learn/the-science-of-well-being. This well-being activity encourages you to identify three or more character strengths that are true for you. Use the free survey found at viacharacter.org/character-strengths to identify your top three.

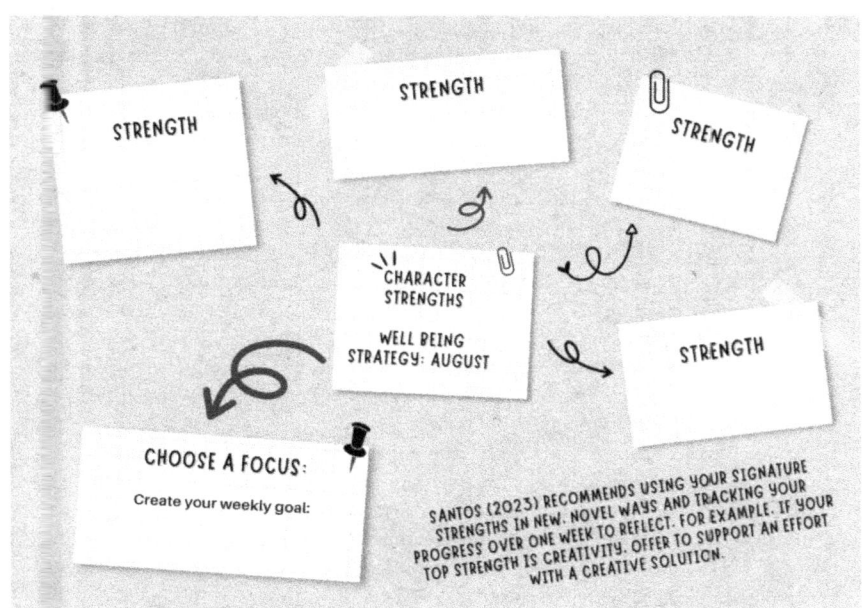

August Plan for Well-Being
Share your well-being goal each month with one another to support making it happen!

We will be discussing effective instruction and intervention in special education programs in the month of September. Consider reviewing resources in our resource list at the end of each monthly chapter to enhance your learning and build your professional library. On this month's list, in particular, consider adding *What Really Works with Exceptional Learners* (edited by W. W. Murawski and K. L. Scott) to your professional library to enhance your learning of best practices in special education across your roles and responsibilities as a new special education professional.

Archer, A. L., & Hughes, C. A. (2010). *Explicit instruction: Effective and efficient teaching*. Guilford Publications.

Basko, Aaron. The best advice my mentor gave me. *The Chronicle of Higher Education*. https://www.chronicle.com/article/the-best-career-advice-my-mentors-ever-gave-me?bc_nonce=ld09yjn70emxx9rlx9gmc&cid=reg_wall.

Berlinghoof, D., & McLaughlin, V. L. (Eds.). (2022). *Practice-based standards for the preparation of special educators*. Council of Exceptional Children.

Bogren, T. (2020). *180 days of self-care for busy educators*. Solution Tree Press.

Billingsley, B., Bettini, E., & Jones, N. D. (2019). Supporting special education teacher induction through high-leverage practices. *Remedial and Special Education, 40*(6), 365–379.

Claro, S., Paunesku, D., & Dweck, C. S. (2016). Growth mindset tempers the effects of poverty on academic achievement. *Proceedings of the National Academy of Sciences, 113*(31), 8664–8668.

Cornelius, K. E., Rosenberg, M. S., & Sandmel, K. N. (2020). Examining the impact of professional development and coaching on mentoring of novice special educators. *Action in Teacher Education*, *42*(3), 253–270.

Darling-Hammond, L., & Sykes, G. (2003). Wanted, a national teacher supply policy for education: The right way to meet the" highly qualified teacher" challenge. *Education policy analysis archives*, *11*, 33-33.

Duffy, M. L., & Forgan, J. W. (2005). *Mentoring new special education teachers: A guide for mentors and program developers*. Corwin Press.

Forgan, J., Weber, R. K., & Duffy, M. L. (2008, March). Special education teachers introduction to the field. In *Society for Information Technology and Teacher Education International Conference* (pp. 5060–5062). Association for the Advancement of Computing in Education (AACE).

Fotiadis, A., Abdulrahman, K., & Spyridou, A. (2019). The mediating roles of psychological autonomy, competence and relatedness on work-life balance and well-being. *Frontiers in psychology*, *10*, 460630.

Gonzalez, J. (2013). Find your marigold: The one essential rule for new teachers. *Cult of Pedagogy*. August 29, 2013. https://www.cultofpedagogy.com/marigolds/

Knight, J. (2021). *The definitive guide to instructional coaching: Seven factors for success*. Association for Supervision and Curriculum Development (ASCD).

Martin, C. C., & Hauth, C. (2015). *The survival guide for new special education teachers*. Council for Exceptional Children.

Mason, T. (2023). Mentoring Resilient Special Education Teachers: A Framework for a Supportive Mentoring Model. In Kutsyuruba, B.; Cochan, F. (Eds.), *Mentoring for Wellbeing in Schools*. Information Age Press (IAP).

Meyer, D. (2021). What makes a great teacher mentor? Elmhurt University (blog). https://www.elmhurst.edu/blog/teacher-mentor.

Murawski, W. W., & Scott, K. L. (Eds.). (2017). *What really works with exceptional learners*. Corwin Press.

Rosenberg, D., & Anderson, T. (2021). Teacher turnover before, during, and after COVID. In *Education resource strategies*. Education Resource Strategies.

Rutherford, P. (2005). *Twenty-first-century mentor's handbook: Creating a culture for learning*. Just Ask Publications.

Santos, L., Miguel, R. R., do Rosário Pinheiro, M., & Rijo, D. (2023). Fostering emotional and mental health in residential youth care facilities: A systematic review of programs targeted to care workers. *Children and Youth Services Review*, 106839.

Shimer, D. (2018). Yale's most popular class ever: Happiness. *The New York Times*, 26.

Stone, D., Patton, B., & Heen, S. (2010). *Difficult conversations: How to discuss what matters most*. Penguin.

Sweeney, D., & Harris, L. S. (2020). *The essential guide for student-centered coaching: What every K–12 coach and school leader needs to know*. Corwin Press.

Internet Resources

Office of Special Education and Rehabilitative Services Blog: https://sites.ed.gov/osers/.

That Special Educator YouTube channel: https://www.youtube.com/@thatspecialeducator1061.

The 40-Hour Teacher Workweek, by Angela Watson: https://join.40htw.com/.

Truth for Teachers, by Angela Watson: https://www.TruthforTeachers.com.

September

CREATING STRENGTH-BASED PROGRAMS

CASE STUDIES

This case study is all about the critical question of how special educators can create a strengths-based learning environment that promotes student agency, self-efficacy, and a positive growth mindset for students with disabilities.

Meet Jazmin, a high school junior with a passion for drawing. Jazmin enjoys drawing comic strip scenes depicting experiences she has in her own life being a creative teenager. Jazmin has Down syndrome and a diagnosed learning disability. She has consistently struggled to keep up with her classmates within her inclusive math class. She often feels discouraged and frustrated, leading to her having low self-esteem in social situations and a lack of self-confidence in her academics. Her teachers, however, recognize her potential and creative talent. They want to create a learning environment where Jazmin's strengths are nurtured and she can grow academically and socially.

Recently, Jazmin's art teacher introduced a new project that involves using math skills to create geometric art pieces. The teacher designed the project with the principles of Universal Design for Learning (UDL) in mind, incorporating ways for Jazmin to choose how she demonstrates her understanding through a project of her choice at the end. The project emphasizes Jazmin's strengths in art while also challenging and honing her math skills. It is particularly advantageous for Jazmin as well since she can be stubborn about how she wants to do something and using art is a great way to align her interests with an academic learning objective. Using art as a vehicle for learning, her special education teacher explains, is a way to provide multiple means of representation, action, and expression to ensure that all learners, including those with disabilities, have their learning needs met in a supportive and inclusive way. In addition, Jazmin's team and parents have been encouraging her to submit art pieces for the high school art show, which she can add to her application for a scholarship through the Ruby's Rainbow "Rockin' That Extra Chromosome" college scholarship competition. Ruby's Rainbow is an organization supporting students with Down syndrome to apply for scholarships to enroll in adapted college programs.

However, Jazmin's math teacher is uncomfortable with the project. He believes that students with disabilities need to be challenged and held to the same project standards as those without disabilities, which makes him resistant to providing Jazmin an alternative project. Consequently, he assigns the class additional math problems that Jazmin struggles to solve, leading to feelings of frustration and inadequacy. Jazmin's special education case manager and art teacher intervene on her behalf, advocating for her strengths and helping the math teacher understand how to align his teaching with the principles of UDL. Consider the case study questions below to imagine how Jazmin can be provided with a more strengths-based approach to her educational program.

Case questions:

- How can educators identify and build on the strengths of students with disabilities when creating effective learning strategies that promote student success and engagement? For example, should Jazmin's math teacher identify her strengths and use them as a starting point in creating math problems that align with her strengths, interests, and passions? What could that look like?
- How can educators understand the impact of negative stereotypes and attitudes on students with disabilities and their families?
- How can educators create an inclusive learning environment that promotes a growth mindset and a sense of positive self-efficacy for students with disabilities? For example, how can Jazmin's teachers collaborate to design a project that challenges but does not overwhelm her, allowing her to develop her math skills while building on her strengths in art? Another option is to provide more intensive support directly related to her math curriculum. What are the pros and cons of providing Jazmin with more math problems to practice math concepts she is struggling with?

Special Education Mentoring
MONTHLY CHECKLIST: SEPTEMBER

TO DO...	DONE	NOTES
Complete *Annual IEP Calendar*		
Review the *Intensive Lesson Plan* and plan out a lesson together utilizing it		
Discuss grading procedures, student data dashboards, & district graduation		
Review RTI/MTSS procedures for the school and district (including sped specific procedures for more restrictive placements)		
Access & plan ways to sign up for professional development opportunities		
Discuss mandatory reporting, FERPA, Manifestation Determination procedures		
Review Prior Written Notice (PWN) and demonstrate process		
Schedule first intensive intervention lesson shadow/observation		

OTHER CHECKLIST ITEMS UNIQUE TO YOUR SCHOOL DISTRICT

_____

_____

_____

ALSO FOR THIS MONTH

- [ ] Well-Being Goal
- [ ] Collaborate on Mentoring Activities
- [ ] Suggested Resources: follow up?

SPECIAL EDUCATION FOCUS

To support your goal setting, this section is meant for you to jot down one focus area/question in each of your primary roles.

- [ ] IEP: _____

- [ ] Intensive Intervention: _____

- [ ] Collaboration: _____

Note that anything italicized in the checklist is referring to a template in the back of this guidebook.

September Monthly Checklist

This checklist provides a roadmap for mentor discussions and timely special education roles and responsibilities typically occurring around this time of the year. There are spaces to add your own checklist items and goals within the three primary roles and responsibilities of special education professionals related to IEP caseload management, collaboration, and teaching specifically designed instruction also referred to as intensive interventions.

Key Learning Goals

1. Understand and utilize evidence-based practices in special education to support instruction.

2. Learn about and compare the components of explicit instruction (Archer & Hughes, 2010) and High-Leverage Practices (HLPs).

Part I: Evidence-Based Practices—
Why Align with Evidence-Based Instruction?

To implement explicit instruction, teachers need to break down complex skills or information into small, manageable steps and provide clear explanations, models, and guided practice. Special education programs are grounded in clearly outlined, explicit instruction tied to individualized student learning needs. Special education teachers should also provide frequent and immediate feedback, as well as multiple opportunities to practice and review. High-Leverage Practices (HLP) are effective and research-based approaches that can scaffold learning and support the academic and behavioral development of students. These practices are designed to give teachers the best strategies to help their students learn. An example of an HLP used to scaffold learning would be to offer students frequent and specific feedback, both during and after learning activities. Giving students feedback enhances student learning retention, leads students to produce better work, and can profoundly impact motivation. This month you will learn about evidence-based practices in special education programs, explicit instruction, and the High-Leverage Practices (HLPs). To get started, complete the KWL chart (figure 5) to review what you already know about high-leverage practices, explicit instruction, and intensifying interventions.

As you embark on planning your program, consider overarching best practices recommended for special education. Imagine that each component is simultaneously infused across the school day within your special education program in order to support student access, achievement, growth, and belonging. You may wonder how to do all of that! Take some time to discuss these overarching program implementation categories and think about how you might plan for the year. Use the framework below to discuss with one another each "best practice" and how it can be translated into everyday teaching practices.

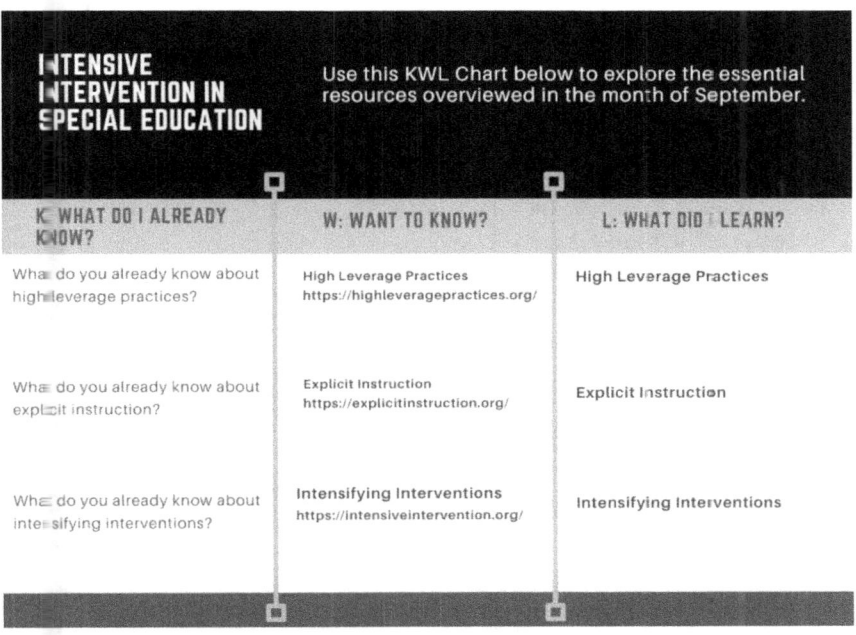

Figure 5. Intensive Intervention Activity Using KWL

This figure uses a "KWL" chart to help you explore what you already know, what you want to know, and reflect on what you learned regarding high-leverage practices. Also, keep in mind you will hear colleagues go back and forth about "research-based practices" (RBPs) and "evidence-based practices" (EBPs) related to both teaching curriculums and intervention curriculums. Consider what the differences are in how these two levels of research study validate their advice.

Complete the brainstorming table together.

Table 1.7.

Category	What to Consider?	Mentor Recommendations and Strategies
Management of both learning environment and student caseload	How do teams share teaching strategies and supports related to IEP goals (consider the classroom environment and team communication)?	
	How are teams collaborating on student IEP goals, accommodations, modifications, assistive technology (AT), behavior plans, etc. (consider the classroom environment and team communication)?	

Table 1.8.

Category	What to Consider?	Mentor Recommendations and Strategies
Student Engagement	Engaging students can be challenging, especially when differentiating for the individualized needs that may be present in a special education pull-out learning environment. Consider recommendations for creating and implementing classroom norms, rules, and routines. Also, how can teacher movement in the classroom and/or other technology tools support student engagement?	

Table 1.9.

Category	What to Consider?	Mentor Recommendations and Strategies
Student Assessment	School districts/systems will have numerous testing initiatives such as "benchmark" testing or other standardized testing systems. Discuss these systems and how they influence "data-driven" student support. Are the scores from these tests used for program placement? Also, what are the tools for IEP goal progress monitoring? What standardized evaluations are available to use and/or how can an educator be trained to use those evaluations to determine initial and reevaluation eligibility for special education programs?	

Table 1.10.

Category	What to Consider?	Mentor Recommendations and Strategies
Student Progress Monitoring	The Individuals with Disabilities in Education Act (IDEA) requires IEP goals be implemented and monitored to track progress or make adjustments to instruction when students are not making adequate progress. What are the methods for providing progress monitoring information to teams and parents? How are students included in progress monitoring? What are suggestions for how to provide positive feedback or redirect student attention to support motivation, positive behavior, and engagement? What are some suggestions for explicit feedback related to lack of progress? Other intensive instruction recommendations?	

Table 1.11.

Category	What to Consider?	Mentor Recommendations and Strategies
Teacher Collaboration and Co-Teaching	Depending on the special education program configuration, you will spend time co-teaching, providing inclusion support, and engaging in several other program delivery models. What are the recommendations for agreed-upon co-teaching configurations for inclusion in general education? What does inclusion look like in your school building? What has worked well and what could be better?	

Table 1.12.

Category	What to Consider?	Mentor Recommendations and Strategies
Implementation of Social-Emotional/ Behavior Supports	Providing a safe and respectful learning environment that proactively supports positive student behavior is likely a component of your special education program. What recommendations can help you create a respectful learning environment? What are the components of the Positive Behavior Support System (PBIS) in your school building/system? What are some recommendations to implement those components for a student who needs behavioral support? Finally, is there a continuum of support and collaboration with related services in your building or district/system? What does that look like, and do you have any recommendations for ways to navigate more "restrictive" supports for students?	

Table 1.13.

Category	What to Consider?	Mentor Recommendations and Strategies
Teacher Organization (instruction)	Organizing for instruction has unique elements in special education programs since many parts of the day may look different and/or your program may be primarily related to individualized student needs with little planning for content-based instruction. Discuss with your mentor the content instruction you are responsible for. How can you prepare for teaching? What accommodations and modifications may be needed? What teaching materials will be needed?	

Table 1.14.

Category	What to Consider?	Mentor Recommendations and Strategies
Teacher Procedures (daily, student supervision, attendance, etc.)	Another aspect of K–12 teaching is considering the many logistical components of our jobs, such as student supervision, emergency procedures, technology tools for student data and collaboration, etc. What are those procedures for your school building and what are tips, strategies, etc., that can be discussed?	

PART II: EVIDENCE-BASED PRACTICES—HOW CAN I IMPLEMENT EVIDENCE-BASED PRACTICES IN MY PROGRAM?

As you embark on teaching, maybe for the first time, a simple scaffolding model to support student learning in special education programs can be helpful to guide your thinking. Recall, scaffolding is a process of breaking down instruction to support students who need more individualized learning environments. This can take shape in different ways, such as instruction being delivered at a slower pace or breaking down concepts into small chunks in order to teach one part at a time with the goal of adding them all together (e.g., think of the word "together": it could be broken down into "to–get–her," with each letter combination sound being taught before putting the entire word "together"). Rapp and Arndt (2012) propose that scaffolding instruction can follow this format:

1. Modeling (I Do) (also described as Direct/Explicit Instruction [Archer & Hughes, 2016])
2. Guided practice (We Do)
3. Independent practice (You Do) (Rapp & Arndt, 2018)

Discuss this simple instructional and scaffolding process. Does your mentor use this method in some form? If so, how?

As we consider best practices in special education, Rapp and Arndt (2018) also recommend we frame our special education programs through an inclusive, person-first lens. There are some key ways to frame your thinking to align with these best practices of inclusive special education. Additionally, research related to UDL and anti-ableism frameworks has further developed the thinking in the field of special education to continue to be more inclusive and build on models of neurodiversity versus deficit-based programs. These approaches could all be categorized as "assets-based" in that they take a holistic, collaborative, strengths-based approach to implementing special education programs. Take a moment to consider these advancements, terms, and working definitions used within special education.

- **Presumed competence**—a strengths-based approach that believes students have the ability to learn, think, understand, and communicate (Rapp & Arndt, 2012).
- **Least dangerous assumption**—in the absence of conclusive data, educational decisions should be based on assumptions that, if incorrect, will be the least harmful to the student (Rapp & Arndt, 2012).
- **Person-first language**—identify the person first instead of the disability, for example, refer to a "student with a visual impairment" rather than a "blind student."
- **Acceptance of diversity being the norm**—instead of believing there is an "average" learner, recognize that we are all diverse and have different ways of learning (i.e., multiple intelligences, preference-based, strengths-based) (Rose, 2016; UDL, Cast.org, 2023).
- **Disability is part of the human experience**—to segregate students is arbitrary and leads them to have a "disenfranchised educational experience" (Jung et al., 2019, p. 4). Consider the recommended components of inclusive programs: (1) a universally welcoming environment; (2) less reliance on labels and more focus on supporting all students in the ways they need to be successful; (3) greater collaboration and leveraging of all educators in the building to support student learning; and (4) honoring student identity, strength, and abilities (Jung et al., 2019).
- **Growth mindset, resilience, and grit**—these frameworks are grounded in the science that the brain is always growing, and people can be developed through strategies, dedication, and hard work (Duckworth, 2016; Dweck, 2017).
- **Equity**—interrupt inequitable practices, examine one's own biases, and create inclusive multicultural school environments for all adults and students; through that, we then discover and cultivate the unique gifts, talents, and interests that every human possesses (Duncan-Andrade, 2022).

- **Neurodiversity**—challenge the assumption that students need "fixing" and are "broken." Instead, shift from a disability perspective to a diversity perspective and use strengths-based strategies to help students with disabilities be successful in life, school, and career/college (Armstrong, 2012; Hughes, 2016).
- **Ableism**—is a set of beliefs or practices that devalue and discriminate against people with physical, intellectual, or mental/psychiatric disabilities. It perpetuates the assumption that people with disabilities need to be "fixed" while anti-ableism advocates for continued efforts to eliminate societal barriers to full inclusion for people with disabilities, such as universal access to community spaces (Timberlake, 2020; Parekh, 2023).
- **Anti-racism**—consider adopting a policy and practice of actively opposing racism and promoting racial equality and equity in your special education programs through addressing issues of bias, disproportionality, and systemic inequalities in schools, programs, and communities negatively impacting students of color with disabilities (Hernandez et al., 2023; Connor & Annamma, 2016).

STRENGTH-BASED PROGRAMS

This approach recommends teams identify student strengths by recognizing the students' talents, interests, prior knowledge and experiences, attributes, and more. Students are seen as resourceful and resilient in the face of challenges, and approaches to crafting IEPs should be multidisciplinary, collaborative, and focus on a strengths-based review of prior academic, social, and behavioral performance. The IEP is ideally characterized by student abilities, strengths, and goals to assist students in continuing to make progress toward achieving the grade-level goals of their peers.

Consider these advancements, terms, and ideas. Discuss them with one another. What do you notice? What stands out to you?

PART III: EVIDENCE-BASED PRACTICES—WHAT TO INCLUDE WHEN IMPLEMENTING EVIDENCE-BASED PRACTICES

This next section will provide a list of Anita Archer's Evidence-Based Practices (table 1.15) and the High-Leverage Practices (HLP) previously investigated this month using the KWL chart. These are provided here for your reference.

Table 1.15. Evidence-Based Practices

1. Focus instruction on critical elements: Teach skills, strategies, vocabulary terms, concepts, and rules that will empower students in the future and match students' instructional needs.

2. Sequence skills logically: Consider several curricular variables, such as teaching easier skills before harder skills, teaching high-frequency skills before skills that are less frequently used, and ensuring mastery of prerequisites to a skill before teaching the skill itself.

3. Break down complex skills and strategies into smaller instructional units: Teach in small steps.

4. Design organized and focused lessons: Make optimized use of instructional time. Make sure your lessons are organized, sequenced, and focused.

5. Begin lessons with a clear statement of the lesson's goal and your expectations for what is to be learned and why it is important.

6. Review prior skills and knowledge before beginning instruction: Tell learners clearly what is being recalled from previous learning and provide a review of relevant information. Verify that students have the prerequisite skills and knowledge to learn the skill being taught in the lesson. This element also provides an opportunity to link the new skill with other related skills.

7. Provide step-by-step demonstrations: Model the skill and clarify the decision-making processes needed to complete a task or procedure by thinking aloud as you perform the skill.

8. Use clear and concise language: Use consistent, unambiguous wording and terminology.

9. Provide an adequate range of examples and non-examples: In order to establish the boundaries of when and when not to apply a skill, strategy, concept, or rule, provide a wide range of examples and non-examples.

10. Provide guided and supported practice: In order to promote initial success and build confidence, regulate the difficulty of practice opportunities during the lesson and provide students with guidance in skill performance.

11. Require frequent responses: Provide a high level of student-teacher interaction via questioning. Having the students respond frequently (i.e., by providing an oral, written, or action response) helps them focus on the lesson content.

12. Monitor student performance closely: Carefully watch and listen to students' responses so you can verify student mastery as well as make timely adjustments in instruction if students are making errors.
13. Provide immediate affirmative and corrective feedback: Follow up on students' responses as quickly as you can. Immediate feedback helps ensure high rates of success and reduces the likelihood of students practicing flawed or incorrect approaches to what is being learned.
14. Deliver the lesson at a brisk pace: Deliver the instruction at an appropriate pace to optimize instructional time, the amount of content that can be presented, and on-task behavior.
15. Help students organize their knowledge: Because many students have difficulty seeing how some skills and concepts fit together, it is important to use teaching techniques that make these connections more apparent or explicit.
16. Provide distributed and cumulative practice: Distributed practice refers to multiple opportunities to practice a skill over time. Cumulative practice is a method for providing distributed practice by including practice opportunities that address both previously and newly acquired skills.

Source: Archer and Hughes (2016).

In partnership with the Collaboration for Effective Educator Development, Accountability, and Reform (CEEDAR), the Council for Exceptional Children (CEC) developed and published a set of High-Leverage Practices (HLPs, 2017) for special educators, teacher candidates, and general education teachers to utilize as recommended best practices for supporting student learning. These HLPs are divided into four overarching categories:

1. Collaboration (HLPs 1–3)

2. Assessment (HLPs 4–6)

3. Social/Emotional/Behavioral (HLPs 7–10)

4. Instruction (HLPs 11–22)

For more guidance, HLP updates, research-based evidence, and resources for each HLP, visit https://highleveragepractices.org/.

HLP 1: Collaborate with professionals to increase student success.

HLP 2: Lead effective meetings with professionals and families.

HLP 3: Collaborate with families to support student learning and secure needed services.

HLP 4: Use multiple sources of information to develop a comprehensive understanding of a student's strengths and needs.

HLP 5: Interpret and communicate assessment information with stakeholders to collaboratively design and implement educational programs.

HLP 6: Use student assessment data, analyze instructional practices, and make necessary adjustments that improve student outcomes.

HLP 7: Establish a consistent, organized, and respectful learning environment.

HLP 8: Provide positive and constructive feedback to guide students' learning and behavior.

HLP 9: Teach social behaviors.

HLP 10: Conduct functional behavioral assessments (FBA) to develop individual student behavior support plans.

HLP 11: Identify and prioritize long- and short-term goals.

HLP 12: Systematically design instruction toward learning goals.

HLP 13: Make adaptations.

HLP 14: Use cognitive and metacognitive strategies.

HLP 15: Provide scaffolded supports.

HLP 16: Use explicit instruction.

HLP 17: Use flexible grouping.

HLP 18: Use strategies to promote active student engagement.

HLP 19: Use assistive and instructional technologies.

HLP 20: Provide intensive instruction.

HLP 21: Teach students to maintain and generalize new learning across time and settings.

HLP 22: Provide positive and constructive feedback to guide students' learning and behavior. (Note, this HLP is included in both social/emotional and learning categories).

Choose two HLPs for the month of September to focus on. You may have many more that interest you but use this opportunity to select two HLPs that you want to learn more about and implement in your program. Continue investigating HLPs in future months by adding them to your monthly checklists within the blank spaces for intensive intervention.

HLP:

HLP:

Create a learning goal for each HLP and identify one way you hope to implement it (this is only meant to capture your thinking and does not need to be formulated into a single comprehensive goal).

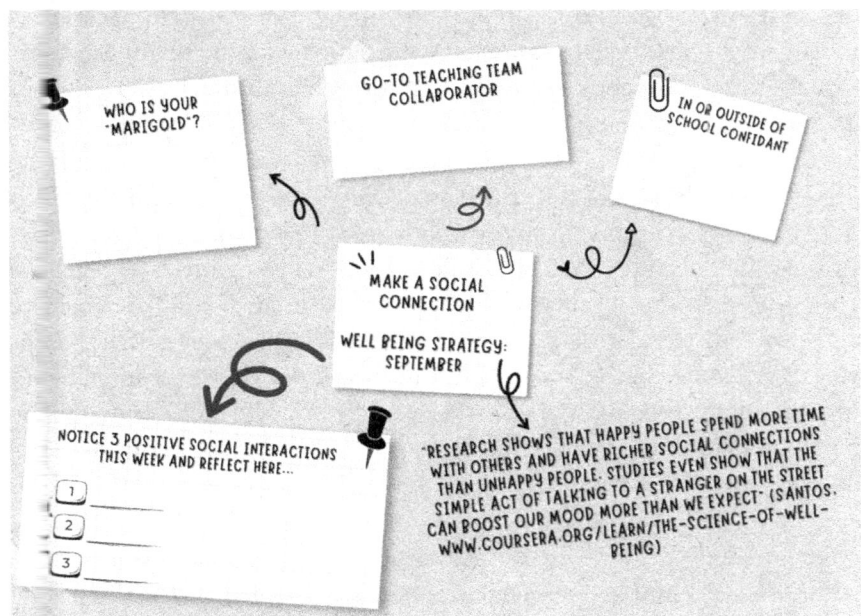

September Plan for Well-Being

For September, you are encouraged to cultivate your social connections. Find your people. You have some suggested activities around this in the well-being exercise included for this month. The first box suggests you find your "marigold," which is a reference to Jennifer Gonzalez's article from the *Cult of Pedagogy*, titled, "Find Your Marigold: The One Essential Rule for New Teachers" (2013). It is a great read and helps us think of how to find social connections in our school buildings that will be emotionally fulfilling (and also cautions us to stay away from those social connections that are not fulfilling). Other social connections that are critical are your "go-to" team members who are at the ready to answer your questions with no judgment. Don't forget the critical importance of having a connection that is outside of your team, potentially a confidant who comes from outside of your school building. This person *might* need to be someone other than a spouse, partner, or even family member. It can be helpful to have a confidant who you can share your frustrations with and hopefully help you to laugh about them! Sometimes it is too much for a family member to carry that load, so a confidant can sometimes be a "judgment-free" thought partner who will just let you get it out!

Share your well-being goal each month with one another to support making it happen!

46   Section I

COLLABORATE ON

Confirm Observations

The month of September is the launch of teaching observations and/or micro-teaching demonstrations. Let's take a moment to discuss these further. The first, teaching observations, can be conducted by mentors through observing their mentee teaching. These are incredibly impactful to use as a launchpad to grow and enhance your teaching practice. During this first year as a new special education teacher, professional learning research recommends that you have a minimum of four teacher observations, if possible, to support your growth in instruction, caseload management, and collaboration as a special education teaching professional. This Guidebook recommends you schedule these observations and debrief with one another within a day of the observation. It can have an even greater impact if mentees self-reflect on their own teaching by rewatching video recordings of these classes, though that may not be feasible. If possible, jot down ideas for next time and wonderings you have about individualized student needs as you watch the teaching clips. These are not evaluative and should be used to inform proactive and problem-solving discussions. The monthly checklists will prompt you to schedule these observations and hopefully they can be included in your mentoring partnership this year. If you did not complete the previous planning calendar for observations in the template provided in August, take a moment to do so now.

SUGGESTED RESOURCES

Anita Archer's *Explicit Instruction* website is comprehensively organized, with lesson exemplars for each component of explicit instruction. Similarly, the *High-Leverage Practices (HLP)* website contains a comprehensive video library with exemplars for all twenty-two HLPs divided into the four overarching HLP categories. Additionally, the books by Downing (2010) and Rapp and Arndt (2012) are both excellent references to support working with students with moderate to significant learning need areas and include invaluable resources to support your roles and responsibilities as a new special education teacher professional. See the website links and textbooks provided here to support growing your special education pedagogical knowledge for the month of September

Archer, A. L., & Hughes, C. A. (2010). *Explicit instruction: Effective and efficient teaching*. Guilford Publications.

Armstrong, T. (2012). *Neurodiversity in the classroom: Strength-based strategies to help students with special needs succeed in school and life*. Alexandria, VA: ASCD.

CAST. (2023). *UDL: The universal design for learning guidelines*. https://udlguidelines.cast.org/.

Connor, D., Ferri, B., & Annamma, S. (2016). (Eds.). *DisCrit: Disability studies and critical race theory in education*. Teachers College Press.

Downing, J. (2010). *Academic instruction for students with moderate and severe intellectual disabilities in inclusive classrooms.* Corwin Press.

Dweck, C. (2017). *Mindset-updated edition: Changing the way you think to fulfill your potential.* Random House.

Duckworth, A. (2016). *Grit: The power of passion and perseverance.* Scribner.

Duncan-Andrade, J. M. R. (2022). *Equality or equity: Toward a model of community-responsive education.* Harvard Education Press.

Harris, K. R., & Graham, S. (2017). Self-regulated strategy development: Theoretical bases, critical instructional elements, and future research. In R. Fidalgo, K. R. Harris, & M. Braaksma (Eds.), *Design principles for teaching effective writing* (pp. 119–151). Brill.

Hernandez, M., Lopez, D., & Swier, R. (2023). *Dismantling disproportionality: A culturally responsive and sustaining systems approach.* Teachers College Press.

Hochman, J. C., & Wexler, N. (2017). *The writing revolution: A guide to advancing thinking through writing in all subjects and grades.* John Wiley & Sons.

Hughes, J. M. (2016). *Increasing neurodiversity in disability and social justice advocacy groups [White paper].* Autistic Self Advocacy Network. Available online at: https://autisticadvocacy.org/wp-content/uploads/2016/06/whitepaper-Increasing-Neurodiversity-in-Disability-and-Social-Justice-Advocacy-Groups.pdf.

Jung, L. A., Frey, N., Fisher, D., & Kroener, J. (2019). *Your students, my students, our students: Rethinking equitable and inclusive classrooms.* ASCD.

Kauffman, J. M., Anastasiou, D., Badar, J., Travers, J. C., & Wiley, A. L. (2016). Inclusive education moving forward. In J. P. Bakken, F. E. Obiakor, & A. Rotatori (Eds.), *General and special education in an age of change: Roles of professionals involved* (*advances in special education*, vol. 32, pp. 153–178). Emerald Group.

McLeskey, J., & Council for Exceptional Children, and Collaboration for Effective Educator Development, Accountability, and Reform. (2017). *High-leverage practices in special education.* Council for Exceptional Children.

Pareth, G. (2023). *Ableism in education: Rethinking school practices and policies.* Routledge.

Rapp, W. H., & Arndt, K. L. (2012). *Teaching everyone: An introduction to inclusive education.* Brookes Publishing Company.

Rose, T. (2016). *The end of average: How to succeed in a world that values sameness.* Penguin UK.

Sheldon, E., & Erickson, K. (2020). Emergent literacy instruction for students with significant disabilities in the regular classroom. *Assistive Technology Outcomes and Benefits (ATOB), 14.*

Timberlake, M. (2020). Recognizing ableism in educational initiatives: Reading between the lines. *Research in Educational Policy and Management, 2*(1), 84–100. https://doi.org/10.46303/repam.02.01.5.

Internet Resources

Alice Keeler: https://www.youtube.com/user/mrsalicekeeler/featured.
Cult of Pedagogy: https://www.cultofpedagogy.com/.
Explicit Instruction: https://explicitinstruction.org/.
Swift Schools: https://swiftschools.org/.
Teaching Works, University of Michigan: https://tle.soe.umich.edu/HLP.
Teaching Like a Champion: https://teachlikeachampion.org/.
Council for Exceptional Children: https://highleveragepractices.org.

October

CASE STUDIES

The Whole Student

This case study is geared toward considering the ways we can individualize student learning and success by holistically considering a student's needs. As we think holistically about our students, ask yourself, how can educators recognize and address the impact of trauma and adverse experiences on the academic and social/emotional outcomes of students with disabilities?

Meet Isaac, a new student with autism, a visual impairment, multiple disabilities, and a challenging history of family trauma. Isaac has trouble adjusting at his new school because of the sensory overload and social anxiety that he experiences in the crowded hallways and noisy classrooms, which is related both to his visual impairment and sensory challenges due to autism. Teacher feedback in Isaac's previous school(s) noted that he often feels alone and isolated, leading to intense emotional outbursts and shutdowns where he refuses to complete academic activities. His new teachers are concerned about his well-being and want to create a supportive and inclusive learning environment that recognizes and addresses his social/emotional and accessibility needs.

Recently, Isaac's school started implementing a trauma-informed approach to teaching and learning for all students. The approach emphasizes understanding and addressing the underlying causes of behaviors rather than just focusing on the behaviors themselves. Using this approach, teachers work collaboratively to develop strategies and interventions that are compassionate, empowering, and culturally responsive. They also prioritize teacher and student self-care and stress reduction. This program will likely benefit Isaac, but the team has concerns on how accessible it will be for him related to his visual impairment and other disability areas.

Additionally, some teachers are resistant to the approach, believing that students with disabilities need stricter discipline and consequences for their behavior so they will learn boundaries and natural consequences.

They want to reinforce teacher-centered practices and more punitive measures that help students see the connection between natural consequences and misbehaving, even if there had been a trigger for the outburst. Another group of teachers in the building feel that this traditional approach will hurt emotional connectedness and a better approach is to focus on building relationships and understanding more aligned with the new trauma-informed program. Further, some teachers worry that Isaac, in particular, will struggle to make the emotional connections that are part of this program due to autism and feel uncertain on how to support his social/emotional needs. The school's administrator intervenes, making an argument based on research and best practices, emphasizing the importance of trauma-informed practice for creating an inclusive and positive learning environment for all learners. Consider some of the issues the teachers are grappling with and discuss with one another.

Case questions:

 STOP & JOT

- How can educators identify the underlying causes of behaviors in students with disabilities who have experienced trauma or adversity? For example, would it be helpful for all teachers at Isaac's school to engage in professional development and training to learn about the "four Rs" of trauma-informed practice: realizing the prevalence of trauma, recognizing symptoms of trauma, responding with compassion and sensitivity, and resisting re-traumatization? Or is it better to refer Isaac to his team anytime there are issues since he is greatly impacted by his disability areas—that is, teachers are worried they will not do the right thing with Isaac so he should spend more time in special education.

- How can educators incorporate culturally responsive teaching practices into a trauma-informed approach to support students with disabilities who have experienced trauma and adversity? For example, how can Isaac's teachers engage his family in the learning process and incorporate their cultural values and practices into the classroom to create a sense of belonging and support for Isaac? How important is it to involve Isaac's family in discussions about his ongoing progress at the new school?

- How can educators prioritize self-care and stress reduction for themselves and their students when taking a trauma-informed approach to teaching, learning, and caseload management? For example, how can Isaac's teachers incorporate relaxation techniques and provide positive affirmations when needed to one another when student situations escalate?

Special Education Mentoring
MONTHLY CHECKLIST: OCTOBER

TO DO...	DONE	NOTES
Discuss school culture and involvement		
Review & collaborate on the *IEP Sections Template*. Are any sections missing?		
Discuss types of student data collected utilizing common software systems		
Debrief IEP meetings observed or conducted reviewing completed IEP documents, addressing questions, and/or follow up actions needed.		
Review classroom management systems & make a plan to learn more.		
Review district templates for AT, Communication, and other special factor plans.		
Discuss the school district assessment schedule and make a plan for any unique accommodations needed.		
Schedule second intensive intervention lesson shadow/observation		

OTHER CHECKLIST ITEMS UNIQUE TO YOUR SCHOOL DISTRICT

_____

_____

SPECIAL EDUCATION FOCUS

To support your goal setting, this section is meant for you to jot down one focus area/question in each of your primary roles.

☐ IEP: _____

ALSO FOR THIS MONTH

☐ Well-Being Goal _____

☐ **Collaborate on Mentoring Activities**

☐ **Suggested Resources: follow up?**

☐ Intensive Intervention: _____

☐ Collaboration: _____

Note that anything italicized in the checklist is referring to a template in the back of this guidebook.

October Monthly Checklist

This checklist provides a roadmap for mentor discussions and timely special education roles and responsibilities typically occurring around this time of the year. There are spaces to add your own checklist items and goals within the three primary roles and responsibilities of special education professionals related to IEP caseload management, collaboration, and teaching specifically designed instruction also referred to as intensive interventions

Key Learning Goals

1. Understand the historical context of present-day special education programs and services.

2. Learn about how to use a strengths-based approach to Individualized Education Planning (IEP) to support caseload students and develop special education programs.

Part I: A Brief History of Special Education

GOING DEEPER

Students with disabilities have historically been shamefully underserved in our K–12 schools, if served at all. The disability movement and special education programs have only been truly in effect as federal law since the 1970s, but these special education laws did not extend to everyone until the early 1990s when the Individuals with Disabilities Education Act (IDEA) and Americans with Disabilities Act (ADA) were signed into law which included enforcement mandates. A previous law from 1975, the Education for All Handicapped Children Act (P.L. 94-142), framed IDEA. This Guidebook provides a general overview of this historical context and the summarized principles of IDEA. To get us started, a famous quote by Maya Angelou is a great frame for this "Going Deeper" discussion. She said, "Do the best you can until you know better. Then, when you know better, do better." So, knowing this historical context and current law helps us do the best we can, until it is time for us to do better.

Recall, IDEA has six principles that provide the mandates for special education services. These principles include:

KEY IDEAS

- free and appropriate public education (FAPE)
- appropriate education
- Individualized Education Plan (IEP)
- least restrictive environment (LRE)
- parent and student participation in decision-making
- procedural safeguards

In order to understand current special education programs, it is critical to examine where we have been. Prior to the 1970s, children with disabilities were unlikely to have attended school or, if they did attend school, there would have been considerable challenges and roadblocks to their success, for example, architecturally, school buildings were not required to be accessible, and teachers were not required to provide a "free and appropriate public education" (FAPE) until the 1990s. The first step toward easing the challenging road for students with disabilities was the landmark case decision, settled on May 17, 1954, in which the US Supreme Court decided in the *Brown v. Board of Education of Topeka* case that it was unconstitutional for educational institutions to segregate children by race. This landmark legal ruling would have far-reaching implications for the field of special education.

Early in the disability justice movement, the 1950s to 1970s is considered the "Professional Era," where people with disabilities were seen as broken, having deficits that could not be fixed, and/or they were considered "diseased." In fact, people with disabilities were commonly asked if they were sick and doctors recommended people with disabilities be institutionalized. Prior to the 1950s, people with disabilities were associated with negative stereotypes such as being a "menace to society," possessed, or infectious in a way that made them a danger to others and necessitated segregation, forced sterilization, and other inhumane acts prescribed by medical professionals.

Doctors were the primary informational resource, and their expert opinion was that people with disabilities were broken, diseased, pathological, atypical, and aberrant, and the common recommendation was to institutionalize them. Thus, disability was viewed as a characteristic of the person. Families were advised that this was not only best for the person with a disability but also best for their family, other children, and their communities.

What happened next? The disability rights movement shifted in part due to what is commonly called "The Parent Movement." This period coincided with the 1970s radicalism and civil rights movements related to other groups in society that were being treated unfairly and violently. The earlier stereotypes of disability were replaced with more humane, though still in many ways debilitating and deficit-based, views that perpetuated the belief that having a disability meant that someone was broken. People with disabilities were seen as objects to be fixed, cured, rehabilitated, and, at the same time, pitied as "victims" of their disabling condition and worthy of societal charity. This time brought about an increased emphasis on the "mental age" of a person with a disability—for example, the view that a student is functioning at the level of a three-year-old or a nonreader functions at the equivalent level of a toddler. Unfortunately, this language can still be heard in special education programs, and it should be noted that it does not align with best practices in special education programs today.

The parent movement also brought considerable attention to the emergence of "hidden disabilities," such as learning disabilities and other disability areas that cannot be visually detected. The language of "hidden disabilities" is still commonly used to foster sensitivity across teaching teams today. It should be noted that, during this time, the fundamental belief of a disability as a "problem residing within a person" did not change. This period also saw the beginning of the self-advocacy movement, where groups of disability rights advocates, composed primarily of people with disabilities, advocated for equal access to any building, community space, school, and so forth, that received federal funding. The 504 sit-in was a disability rights protest that began on April 5, 1977. At that protest, people with disabilities and the disability community occupied a federal building in San Francisco, California, in order to push for the issuance of long-delayed regulations regarding Section 504 of the Rehabilitation Act of 1973.

The next wave of reforms in the disability rights movement came in the 1990s to 2000s, when advocacy came from multiple perspectives—

Figure 6. Protestors Advocating for Progress for People with Disabilities
This figure depicts a picture of Judith Heumann and other disability rights advocates protesting at a government building. Her sign reads, "no more negotiation." *Source*: Hearst Newspapers via Getty Images.

that is, parents, educational professionals, and, most importantly, people with disabilities who were advocating for their own rights to access, achievement, and equitable opportunities in public education. Major components and milestones happened during this time. In particular, the Americans with Disabilities Act (ADA) and the Education for All Handicapped Children Act (Public Law 94-142) was comprehensively revised and reinstated as the Individuals with Disabilities in Education Act (IDEA). During this period, there was a notable normalization and acceptance of the principles and demands voiced by the disability movement. Efforts to support independent living and disability rights were intensified, and awareness of "person-first" needs with new thinking such as "nothing about me without me" became more common when planning was being implemented for adults with disabilities. New supports were instituted, such as supported employment and further efforts to allow for increased self-advocacy, community inclusion, and self-determination.

Take a moment to reflect with one another about the past and present of special education programs. Our new paradigms in special education are aligned with inclusive-based program implementation in school districts grounded in common language regarding students that emphasizes that all students means *all* students. This language refers to shifts in thinking such that any segregated special education program is not beneficial for students both in and outside of special education programs. The focus of inclusive education is to design learning experiences that are more inclusive and accessible for all students (UDL, Cast.org, 2023). Instead of seeing the individual as broken or needing to be "fixed," educators are encouraged to examine the learning environment, school building, curriculum, context, and so on. The emphasis in this approach is on support for individualized learning needs versus programs that students can "fit into."

Looking Ahead—The Evolutionary Trajectory of Special Education Laws

There are two noteworthy observations to consider regarding the evolution of special education. The evolution of special education laws in the United States, beginning from the Education for All Handicapped Children Act of 1975 to the Every Student Succeeds Act of 2015 greatly illuminate how various enactments have shaped today's special education landscape while reflecting society's changing attitudes and perspectives toward disabilities. This extends beyond just understanding the features of each law to analyzing how they collectively contribute to an ongoing mission of ensuring equal educational opportunities for students with disabilities. Consider these two observations below as you wonder about the future of laws protecting the rights of students with disabilities.

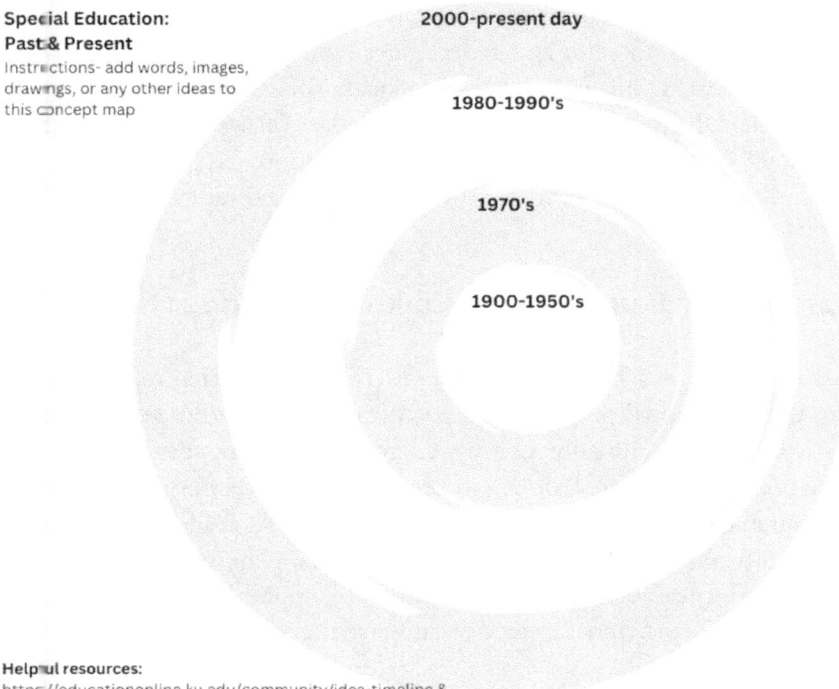

Figure 7. The Past and Present of Special Education
This figure depicts a concept map using circles to visualize our journey through special education laws and policies since the 1970s. Prior to that time, there was little in place safeguarding the educational rights of students with disabilities in the United States. See more special education history overview at Wrightslaw, https://www.wrightslaw.com/law/art/history.spec.ed.law.

- An in-depth analysis of the Education for All Handicapped Children Act of 1975 would reveal how it paved the way for the establishment of FAPE, IEP, and LRE, core components that are still fundamental to special education programs. This act is a landmark law that underscores the shift from exclusion and marginalization toward an inclusive approach.
- The reauthorization and renaming of this act as the Individuals with Disabilities Education Act in 1990 broadened the definition of disabilities and underscored several critical elements like transition services and parent involvement, thus reiterating the need to continually adapt and respond to emerging educational needs of students with disabilities.

The other observation to consider with one another is the role of states in shaping special education law. While federal laws set the foundation, state laws significantly shape special education policies and practices at a more local level, setting precedent with due process court cases that make their way to state and federal level courts. Understanding variations between state laws can help appreciate the geographical disparities within the US education system. States can vary on assessments accepted, timelines, services and program implementation, access to resources, under- or overrepresentation in disability areas, and more.

GOING DEEPER

PART II: THE INDIVIDUALIZED EDUCATION PROGRAM (IEP)

An Individualized Education Program (IEP) is a written report outlining the educational program that has been designed to meet a student's individual needs annually. Every student who receives special education services must have an IEP. The overarching goals of the IEP are to set measurable goals for the student and outline current academic and intensive intervention levels. The IEP must include a plan for intensive interventions, accommodations, modifications (if applicable to the student's educational plan), and services to support the student's access to their educational program.

Who Develops the IEP?

The IEP is developed by a team of individuals that includes the teaching and special education team, the student, and the student's parents/guardian(s). The team meets, reviews progress toward annual goals, assessment information, and present levels of performance available about the student, which they use to design an educational program to address the student's educational needs related to special education eligibility areas.

When Is an IEP Developed?

An IEP meeting must be held within thirty calendar days after it is determined, through a full and individual evaluation, that a student has educational eligibility in one or more of the disability areas listed in IDEA that necessitate special education services. A student's IEP must also be reviewed at least annually thereafter to determine whether the annual goals are being achieved, and the IEP must be revised in light of that information to ensure a student is making adequate progress toward their goals (see "Case Law Review Template" in Section V, "Resources," of this Guidebook). The IEP must include progress monitoring information related to annual goals.

What's in an IEP?

Each IEP must contain specific information, as described within IDEA. Additional resources are linked in the October section in the resources of this Guidebook related to current IEP best practices and implementation. The information that needs to be in an IEP includes (but is not limited to):

- The student's present levels of academic achievement and performance, describing how the student is currently doing in school and how the student's disability impacts their involvement and progress in the general curriculum.

- Annual goals for the student, meaning what parents and the school team think they can reasonably accomplish in a year. These goals are often formatted to be "SMART" goals, which stands for specific, measurable, attainable, realistic, and time-bound.

- The special education and related services to be provided to the student, including supplementary aids and services (such as communication devices or dual-language learner support from culturally and linguistically diverse student educational programs) and/or changes to the program or support for school personnel.

- The least restrictive environment (LRE) that best fits the educational needs of the student in order for them to be able to progress toward their IEP goals. This is simply defined as the amount of time learning in special education versus general education classrooms.

- Accommodations, modifications (if required), and supports necessary for the student to access the general education curriculum and instruction identified in the IEP. Accommodations are adaptations made to the general education curriculum to support student access, while modifications are changes to the target skills and standards being worked toward by general education student peers.

- How the student is to participate in state and district-wide assessments, including what modifications to tests the student needs.

- When services and modifications will begin, how often they will be provided, where they will be provided, and how long they will last.

- How school teaching teams will measure the student's progress toward the annual goals.

- Any other special factors related to students' educational impact and needed special education support.

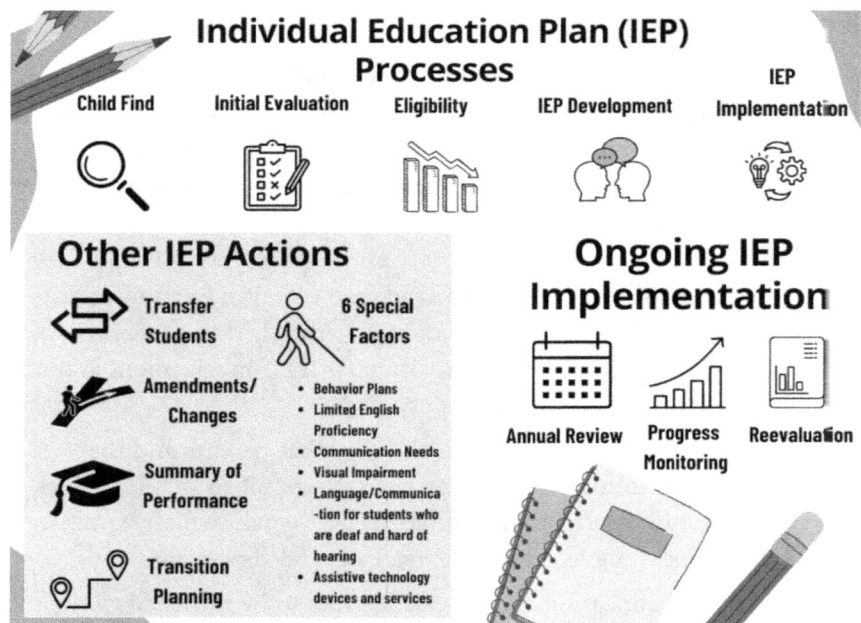

Figure 8. Individual Education Plan (IEP) Processes
This figure provides graphic representations and descriptions of IEP processes from the beginning of the IEP process, through reviews and ongoing implementation, and finally other IEP actions that will be included in your work as a special education professional.

Should Students Be Involved in Their IEPs?

Yes, they certainly can and should be involved in their IEP. IDEA requires that the student be invited to any IEP meeting where transition services will be discussed, and it is recommended that students be invited to their IEP team meetings at the earliest possible and appropriate time in order to be a part of the IEP team's decision-making.

There are some common issues that come up in the implementation of IEPs in special education programs in the United States. This Guidebook will present detailed IEP information to help mentoring partnerships to avoid these common IEP pitfalls, which can negatively impact student learning and lead to legal action being taken against a school district/system/school.

Regarding these issues, one is IEP goals not being aligned with *state standards*. Another issue is school districts/systems/schools being found to have "*cookie cutter IEPs*," which when examined closer, are found to be identical for all students. Another pitfall, it is critical to have *parent/ guardian input* in the creation of the IEP and there have been countless court cases where parents have needed to advocate for their involvement in the IEP process. *Determining the least restrictive environment (LRE)* can be an issue when not properly explained or not implemented as written in the IEP. Two other issues that come up with IEPs that are linked to one another are a *lack of robust progress monitoring and a lack of assessment data* to support educational team recommendations and parents/guardians not being made aware of their students' progress.

The overarching sections of the IEP are summarized in this Guidebook with "Stop and Jot" thinking questions to help guide the IEP discussion:

Introduction: The present levels section is an important component of the IEP. It must stay current every year with up-to-date information about the student. It starts with a short summary of the student, which is ideally strengths-based and highlights their talents, interests, family information, outside and inside school activities, and more. This first paragraph is an introduction to the student and should provide ways to get to know them and also showcase their strengths.

Write a three- to five-sentence introduction to yourself as if you were a student being supported on your caseload. Share with each other.

Present Levels Section: The present levels performance summary should include (1) academic information (current); (2) a review of disability and achievement records; (3) an evaluation or previous evaluation summary (one paragraph, when possible); (4) attendance and behavior history; (5) grades; (6) standardized testing; (7) teacher feedback; (8) progress monitoring, both summary and data linked to current academic performance; (9) information related to intensive interventions that are being implemented; (10) current accommodations, modifications, and so on; and (11) any parent feedback that has already been communicated.

Let's practice writing a present level section about an outside-of-school interest. Imagine you are interested in playing a new sport or taking on a new hobby. Write a present levels section for yourself regarding this new activity you hope to do. Keep it limited to two or three paragraphs and be sure to incorporate items 1 to 11 of the information mentioned above.

Parent and Student Input: There is typically a standalone section for student and parent input. It is critical to obtain parent/guardian/student input and consider soliciting feedback prior to the IEP meeting. Some efficient ways to obtain feedback beforehand are sending home a parent survey at the beginning of the year with a welcome letter and/or pre-meeting with parents/students and other teaching team members to discuss progress, goals for the year, and the like. Many school districts/

systems will require a student interview regarding transition services be done by the time the student is of a certain age. The student interview can be started as early as upper elementary school and is a great way to cultivate goal-directed students who are increasingly becoming more empowered through the support they are receiving in special education.

What are the requirements around student IEP interviews in your district/system/building? Where are the resources for student interviews and parent/guardian IEP surveys? Are there any further requirements specific to transition (student programs and supports for students who are eighteen and up) that can be captured here?

Adverse Educational Impact of Disability: Within the IEP report, special education professionals typically need to explain the adverse educational impacts of the disability-related areas of eligibility for students served in special education. Most school districts/systems have specific ways they want these sections written.

Please discuss that now and outline a template of the way this will be done on IEP reports. Is there a school district/system template or wording recommendation for documenting these adverse educational impacts on disability?

Transition Planning and Postsecondary Experiences: This Guidebook will devote some later resources to transition planning. For now, skip to that section and review it if you have an upcoming student transition (see May "Going Deeper" for information about transition planning if needed now). If there are no urgent IEP considerations related to a transition, then use the framework below to jot down any student on your caseload who will need a transition plan and any questions you have regarding transition planning you would like to discuss. Also, for earlier grade levels, consider transition planning and meetings that are common between early childhood and elementary school, elementary school and middle school, and middle school to high school.

Table 1.16.

Students Requiring a Transition IEP (fourteen-plus)	Students Requiring a Transition Meeting (younger grades transitioning to a new school next fall)	Transition Questions

Special Factors: Special factors refers to specialized educational plans associated with IEPs; often these extended plans are directly linked to legislation. Each state/district/system will have different procedures that are drafted and implemented within the IEP. Broadly speaking, students must have eligibility areas in their educational needs in order to meet the need for a special factor IEP action. Some broad categories are suggested in table 1.17, and each state/district/system will have differences.

Table 1.17.

Special Factor	Disability eligibility area that may include this special factor
Communication Plan	Sensory impairments, multiple disabilities
Learning Media Assessment	Visual impairment
Behavior Plan	Serious emotional disorder (SED), autism, multiple disabilities
Health Care Plan	Any disability area
Limited English Proficiency	Students who are dual language learners, served in culturally and linguistically diverse (CLD) or English language learner (ELL) programs
Assistive Technology	Any disability area (see more about AT in November's "Going Deeper")
Special Transit	Any disability area

The Communication Plan: The communication plan is for students who are deaf or hard of hearing. The plan must include a statement identifying the child's primary communication mode as one or more of the following: aural, oral, speech-based, English-Based Manual or Sign System, or American Sign Language. The IEP team cannot deny instructional opportunities based on the amount of the child's residual hearing, the ability of the parent(s) to communicate, or the child's experience with other communication modes.

Learning Media Assessment: The Learning Media Assessment is for students with visual impairments and students who are deafblind. The assessment will be completed by a Teacher of Students with Visual Impairments (TSVI). Depending on the student's primary learning needs—that is, their dominant area of special education eligibility—the TSVI will be considered the student case manager if the visual impairment is determined to be the most impactful area of disability. Oftentimes, if a student has multiple disabilities, the TSVI will be a member of the IEP team and not the case manager. The special education teacher needs to ensure partnership with the TSVI and certified orientation and mobility specialist (COMS) to fill out these plans if they are not already carried over in the IEP (from the previous year). These plans should be reviewed at the annual IEP meeting, updated, and implemented including related accommodations, goals, and so forth.

The Learning Media Assessment (LMA) offers a framework for selecting appropriate literacy media for a student who is visually impaired. A Functional Vision Assessment (FVA) should be done first in order to determine information about the student's vision. The COMS will also complete an orientation and mobility assessment in conjunction with the FVA. One related service professional may be licensed as both a COMS and TSVI, or there may be two team members supporting the student in these two learning domains.

Behavior Intervention Plan (BIP) or Positive Behavior Support Plan (PBSP): A Behavioral Intervention Plan is based on the results of a Functional Behavioral Assessment (FBA); at a minimum, it includes a description of the problem behavior, global and specific hypotheses as to why the problem behavior occurs, and intervention strategies that include positive behavioral supports and services to address the behavior.

Health Care Plan: This is a full list of the accommodations and interventions that the student needs in the course of the day from a doctor, a nurse at school, or that can be reasonably provided in the classroom, which are put together in the form of a medical management plan or health care plan. This plan is the basis of how to provide support for the student at school. These plans should be created in partnership with the school nurse or a district nurse. Questions or concerns around items on the health care plan may come up if working in an intensive learning needs classroom. These plans can be comprehensive, and teams may need to institute several medical support procedures with students who are served in more intensive multiple-disability special education programs. Be sure to ask questions if a procedure makes a team member uncomfortable or if you are unsure what would need to be done in an emergency situation. Some suggestions to consider if medical needs are extensive and the team is working to ensure FAPE that the student and family need to consider: (1) a shortened school day due to extreme fatigue, medical issues or procedures, and so on; (2) access to trained nursing support when needed and a plan for how this can be collaborated on, if needed/applicable (for some specialized supports); and/or (3) a plan for how the parent/guardian can come to the school to provide a procedure if something is needed but the school is not trained to provide it.

Limited English Proficiency (LEP): This plan would also be done in collaboration with the CLD or EL teacher. What needs to be included? For all LEP/ELL students with disabilities, the team must consider how the student's language needs relate to the IEP. Schools are guided to provide students with LEP with alternative language services to enable them to acquire proficiency in English and to provide them with meaningful access to the content of the educational curriculum that is available to all students, including special education and related services. The committee should consider the following questions:

- Has the student been assessed in English as well as their native language?
- Did the evaluation of the student with LEP measure the extent to which the student has a disability and needs special education rather than measure the student's English language skills?
- Does the disability impact the student's involvement and progress in the bilingual education or English as a second language (ESL) program of the general curriculum?
- What language will be used for this student's instruction?
- What language or mode of communication will be used to address parents or family members of the student?

- What accommodations are necessary for instruction and testing?
- What other language services (e.g., ESL, bilingual education) must be provided to ensure meaningful access to general and special education and related services?
- How is dual-language instruction or other assets-based approaches to students' dual-language skill being included in special education services and supports?

Examples of special education services needed to address the student's needs might include but are not limited to interpreters, bilingual speech and language therapy, bilingual counseling, and bilingual special education classes. Additionally, in the LEP statement on the IEP, it should be explained what language-related services are being implemented and explicit language-related interventions are being provided within the school day. This information should be created in partnership with the CLD teacher.

Assistive Technology (AT): This section of the IEP needs to spell out the assistive technology (AT) and augmentative alternative communication (AAC) device use implemented for the student. Assistive technology is included in the IEP in a manner that provides a clear and complete description of the devices and services to be provided and used to address student needs and achieve expected results.

A helpful resource to refer to is the OCALI Guide of Assistive Technology: https://www.ocali.org/up_doc/AT_Resource_Guide_6.pdf.

What Constitutes Assistive Technology?

According to ATIA (https://www.atia.org/), assistive technology (AT) is any item, piece of equipment, software program, or product system that is used to increase, maintain, or improve the functional capabilities of persons with disabilities.

- AT can be low-tech, such as communication boards made of cardboard or fuzzy felt.
- AT can be high-tech, such as special-purpose computers.
- AT can be hardware, such as prosthetics, mounting systems, and positioning devices.
- AT can be computer hardware, such as special switches, keyboards, and pointing devices.

- AT can be computer software, such as screen readers and communication programs.
- AT can be inclusive or specialized learning materials and curriculum aids.
- AT can be specialized curricular software.
- AT can be much more—electronic devices, wheelchairs, walkers, braces, educational software, power lifts, pencil holders, eye-gaze and head trackers, and much more.

Assistive technology helps students/adults who have difficulty speaking, typing, writing, remembering, pointing, seeing, hearing, learning, walking, and many other things. Different disabilities require different assistive technologies.

Special Transit: Transportation from school is an important part of the IEP. There is legislative precedent related to this, and it is also an important component of FAPE. For example, to illustrate what has been determined through case law precedent, if a student is best served in an autism-focused program at another school or some other site-based program that is both (1) a more restrictive LRE and (2) the best individualized educational plan for the student's academic program needs, then the team needs to provide every possible support required by law to accommodate the student and family. This is where special transportation comes in since it is both (1) accommodating an LRE IEP decision and (2) ensuring students have safe, accessible, and free transport to and from school that meets their unique travel needs. In summary, as part of the mandate of free and appropriate public education (FAPE), related services are required when determined necessary to assist a child with a disability to benefit from special education. As defined in the Individuals with Disabilities Education Improvement Act (IDEIA), transportation includes (1) travel to and from school and between schools, (2) travel in and around school buildings, and (3) specialized equipment (such as special or adaptive buses, lifts, and ramps), if required to provide special education for a child with a disability.

Much was covered in the sections on special factors (depicted in figure 9). Consider each one and discuss any questions that have emerged from reviewing them.

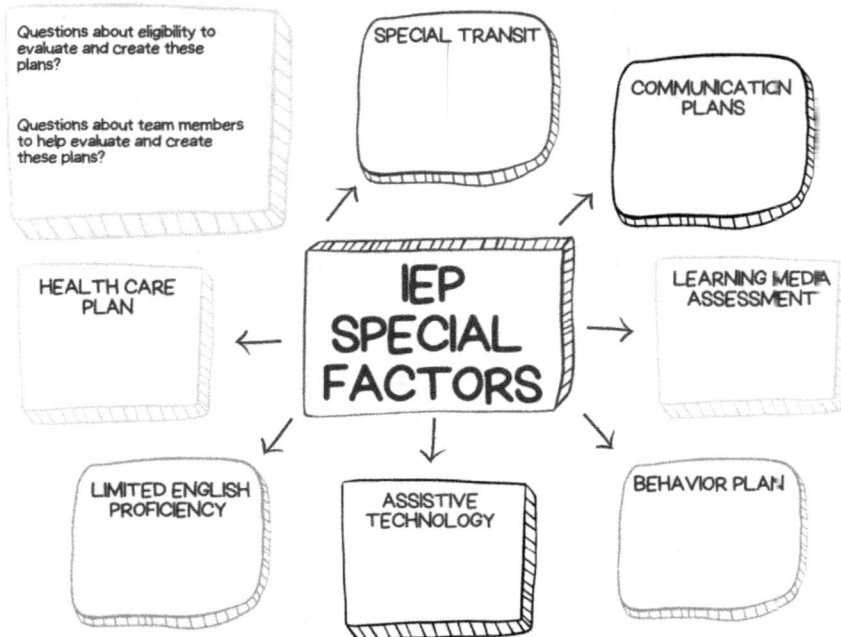

Figure 9. IEP Special Factors
This figure shows a concept map with IEP Special Factors in the middle with arrows to special transit, communication plans, learning media assessment, assistive technology, limited English proficiency, health care plans, and so on. These special factors plans include some of the types of reports that may be created related to IEP special factor areas.

Goals: Goals are typically linked to IEP eligibility/disability areas, state content standards, and are often written using a SMART goal format. Typically, special education teachers will report progress when report cards are given out.

Recall the present levels statement you created related to the new sport or hobby you wanted to try. Create a SMART goal for your new activity:

    S (specific)

    M (measurable)

    A (attainable)

    R (realistic)

    T (time-bound)

Each IEP will include templated sections that provide information about how services will be delivered for students supported in special education. These three sections are focused on the student's least restrictive environment. Remember, the ultimate goal of special education is to provide services, intensive interventions, and accommodations to support student achievement and successful inclusion in the academic program. It is critical that each of these sections be revisited each year with an IEP team where clear planning is detailed.

Service Delivery Statement: A narrative statement is typically included in this section. After the statement, you will choose the service and amount of service time per each category and provider that will be granted to the student. When asked about service delivery, you will notice "inside general education" or "outside of general education." These categories are not always indicated but if you see them in your school district then note that the one you choose is factored into the LRE percentage being planned on the IEP.

Least Restrictive Environment: The IEP report will include a discussion of the advantages and disadvantages of providing more specialized support both outside and inside the general education classroom. Some examples of language that might be included in the LRE section are provided here:

> Nikki is doing well in many areas of her program and has been working well in small groups in math and science. Ultimately, Nikki needs increased support to make adequate progress toward achieving her goals of self-regulating through her school day using her behavior support system and successfully completing academic work with prompting support. For this reason, we have added a supported morning small group class that is held in the middle school community center. This class is co-taught by a special and general education teacher.

Participation in Assessment: This section typically includes drop-down choices for accommodations or modifications needed on standardized assessments. Many school districts/systems will have an alternative diploma or some other indication on transcripts that explains if students have worked toward a different set of standards, which can include modified learning targets—that is, these standards are only appropriate for students identified by the IEP team as needing alternative academic standards and learning outcomes.

 **STOP & JOT** Review and discuss the three scenarios below related to each of these IEP components. Ask yourself: *Would this be okay to include in an IEP?*

Scenario #1: Sam is a third-grade student, and he has his good and bad days, having behavioral outbursts and leaving class when escalated on bad days. The special education team is supporting him with intermittent paraprofessional support within the general education classroom 60 percent of the time, and he has pull-out support services with a small group 40 percent of the school day in the special education classroom. If Sam has had too many outbursts on any given week, he is pulled into the special education classroom 100 percent of the time the next week as a consequence.

Would this be using evidence-based practices to support Sam?

Scenario #2: Reecy is not a great test taker. They will sometimes become upset, slam books down, and start crying when told there will be a big test coming up. For this reason, the team has decided to move them to the alternative state test, which can be skipped if a team decides to do so. Reecy does not receive other alternative testing support and there are concerns with this plan both related to unintended consequences and supporting Reecy's educational program.

What should the team do?

Scenario #3: Jack receives speech-language services on his IEP, but the speech-language pathologist (SLP) has been overloaded at another school and has not seen Jack for over a month. Jack's caseload manager is concerned that this lack of service will be a violation of his IEP, which stipulates that he receives thirty minutes of direct speech services every week and one hour of indirect speech services monthly. These direct and indirect supports can be met by collaborating with the teaching team, meeting one on one with Jack, and/or supporting small groups in Jack's general education classroom.

Is this a violation of the IEP? What should the special education caseload manager do?

Note: See "Suggested Resources" section at the end of this month for explanations for how each of these scenarios impacts the IEP.

Extended School Year (ESY): ESY refers to special education and/or related services provided beyond the normal school year for the purpose of providing FAPE to a student with a disability. ESY planning is part of the IEP process. ESY must be considered for all students with disabilities but is guided by state/district/system guidelines for eligibility for these services. ESY can be a contested issue in IEP meetings, and it is important to be informed regarding your district's "general" ESY policies, so you are ready to discuss them in an IEP meeting. The basic standard: ESY services are only necessary to provide FAPE when the benefits gained during the school year will be significantly jeopardized without ESY. This is why many special education teachers may dismiss ESY for students in mild-to-moderate special education programs since typical "regression" and "recoupment" is to be expected during the summer break—meaning that students will have some loss of skills (regression) and take time to relearn concepts (recoupment) in the beginning of the year, but it is not considered a significant loss of learning. Keep in mind that ESY is not (1) summer school, (2) compensatory services, (3) or some other extension of the school year. It must be found that ESY is needed in order to be provided as part of FAPE. Note that showing actual regression may not be required, but a case regarding regression must be made. IEP teams may be asked to review outside evaluations brought in by families supporting the possible need for ESY.

Accommodations and Modifications: As is described in the IDEA reauthorization, individuals with disabilities are to receive a free and appropriate public education (FAPE). This education must occur in the least restrictive environment (LRE), with supplementary aids and support when necessary. Additionally, Section 504 of the Rehabilitation Act of 1973 provides some clarification as to how these aids and supports are to be provided within the most appropriate LRE for individuals with disabilities:

> Aids, benefits, and services must afford an eligible student equal opportunity to obtain the same result, to gain the same benefit, or to reach the same level of achievement in the most integrated setting appropriate to the student's needs. These aids, benefits, and services are not required to produce the identical result or level of achievement for both students with disabilities and students without disabilities. (Section 504)

For the purposes of clarification, the following definitions are suggested to differentiate how individuals with disabilities receive "equal opportunity to obtain results and benefits" but may not necessarily "produce identical results or levels of achievement" as compared to students without disabilities. Students will participate in LRE environments and can be held accountable for performance in those environments through curricular adaptations.

Curricular Adaptation: Curricular adaptations are changes permissible in educational environments that allow the student equal opportunity to achieve comparable levels of access, results, benefits, and achievement to that of their peers. These adaptations consist of both accommodations and modifications. Some curricular adaptations do not fundamentally alter or lower standards or expectations in either the instructional or assessment phases of a course of study, and they can be designated as "accommodations." These accommodations provide access to the LRE and an opportunity to demonstrate mastery of performance standards or learning objectives.

Accommodations: Accommodations are changes in course content, teaching strategies, standards, test presentation, location, timing, scheduling, expectations, student responses, environmental structuring, and/or other attributes that provide access for a student with a disability to participate in a course/standard/test while they *do not* fundamentally alter or lower the standard or expectations of the course/standard/test.

Modifications: Modifications are changes in course content, teaching strategies, standards, test presentation, location, timing, scheduling, expectations, student responses, environmental structuring, and/or other attributes that provide the opportunity for a student with a disability to participate in a course/standard/test and that *do* fundamentally alter or lower the standard, target skill, or expectations of the course/standard/test.

COMMON ACCOMMODATION AND MODIFICATION CATEGORIES

Timing: changes in the length of testing, extra or extended time for learning activities, and so on. Possible accommodations:

- Provides extra time to read written text.
- Provides extra time to write responses.
- Provides extra time to use certain equipment.
- Helps students with short attention spans stay on task.

Scheduling: changes in when testing occurs. Possible accommodations:

- Coordinate the assessment with the effects of medication.
- Help students who have low frustration tolerance with scheduling accommodations.

Setting: changes in the place where an assessment is given. Possible accommodation:

- Out of classroom proctoring to support students who have difficulty focusing in a group setting.

Presentation: changes in how an assessment is given to a student. Possible accommodations:

- Students with sensory needs have assessments presented in different formats.
- Students needing differentiated literacy levels have assessment read aloud or use text-to-speech in order to hear assessment questions.

Response: changes in how a student responds to an assessment. Possible accommodations:

- Students with physical or sensory disabilities respond using speech to text or other assistive technology support.
- Students with executive functioning challenges related to memory, sequencing, directionality, alignment, organization, and other problems that may interfere with a successful performance on tests are able to use resources to support response accommodations.

There are many ways to think about accommodations and modifications. Additional strategies are Differentiation and UDL, which both recommend proactive support to accommodate a wide continuum of learners.

Differentiation is considered a teaching strategy, and, in contrast, accommodations and modifications are considered curricular and instructional adaptations that individualize for students who need academic, social/emotional, and behavioral support. Many educators argue that all students benefit from differentiated classrooms, which can be a way for increased universal support that builds more inclusive classrooms where all students thrive. One way to think about differentiation is to use the UDL framework, where educators plan backward for learning diversity and create more inclusive classroom environments. These classrooms are both inclusive and proactively designed, providing support and opportunities to accommodate differences and student variability. Planning for diversity is an approach of proactive learning design that can be accomplished at the same time as implementing accommodations and modifications that reactively support individualized student learning needs. Consider accommodations and modifications further by distinguishing whether a common support in Table 1.18 is an accommodation or a modification.

STOP & JOT

Table 1.18. Accommodations versus Modifications Game!

		Accommodation (A) or Modification (M)
1	Text-to-speech with no change to content or target skill	
2	Final exam with changed questions and fewer answer choices to pick from	
3	An altered vocabulary list of words that are linked to a different learning unit in social studies class	
4	Extended time to complete a test	
5	Using a technology device to complete a test instead of paper/pencil	
6	Adapted text from a fourth-grade to a second-grade Lexile level with no change to target skill	
7	A different project in a science classroom at a lower academic level about different content	
8	Fewer math problems for homework	
9	Allowing a student to write three paragraphs instead of five paragraphs on a final essay with no other changes to the target skills	
10	Using technology to complete a class presentation to record a video to be played for the class instead of presenting	

*See suggested accommodations or modifications answers in "Suggested Resources."

Reviewing the IEP from Start to Finish

Would it be helpful to review an IEP from start to finish now that you have learned more details about each section and component of the IEP? There are several helpful IEP resources listed in the resource section for October within this Guidebook. Using those resources, review all or part of an IEP to see how sections are written in your school/district/system.

What questions do you have about writing IEPs in your school/district/system?

Next, be sure to review the IEP software used in your school building. See the helpful checklist below to help you organize mentoring sessions around the question of "How do I do that in the IEP software?"

- Logging in and creating a new IEP.
- Finding caseload students and creating a "group" if possible.
- Creating IEP actions in the system—PWN, consent forms, and so on.
- Adding other team members.
- Efficiency suggestions and any other technology tips for using the system.
- Help desk contact for system issues.
- Add your questions:
- Add your questions:
- Add your questions:

 WELL-BEING

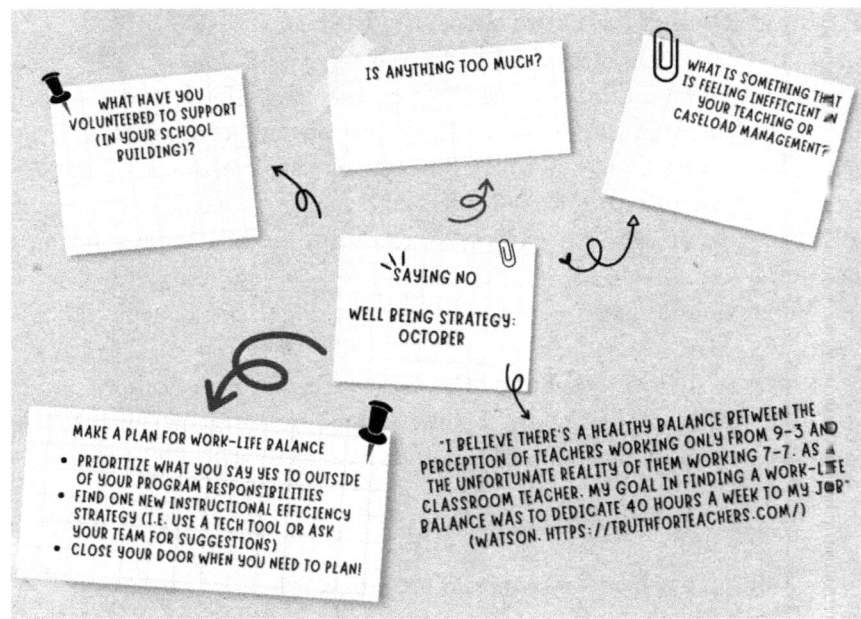

October Plan for Well-Being

For October, you are focusing on saying no. It is very challenging to say no to helping others in school buildings, whether it be teachers, administrators, or even students. Consider ways you can protect your time and well-being by saying no where you can and, also, using organizational systems to help say no when a student needs something but you cannot attend to it at that moment. For example, "Please add your question to our classroom parking lot or see me during study hall."

Share your well-being goal each month with one another to support making it happen!

 SUGGESTED RESOURCES

Agran, M., Brown, F., Hughs, C., Quirk, C., & Ryndak, D. (2014). *Equity and full participation for individuals with severe disabilities: A vision for the future.* Paul H. Brookes.

Agran, M., Jackson, L., Kurth, J. A., Ryndak, D., Burnette, K., Jameson, M., & Wehmeyer, M. (2020). Why aren't students with severe disabilities being placed in general education classrooms: Examining the relations among classroom placement, learner outcomes, and other factors. *Research and Practice for Persons with Severe Disabilities, 45*(1), 4–13.

Bateman, D. F., & Bateman, C. F. (2014). *A principal's guide to special education.* Council for Exceptional Children.

Bateman, D. F., & Yell, M. L. (Eds.). (2019). *Current trends and legal issues in special education.* Corwin Press.

CAST. (2023). *UDL: The universal design for learning guidelines.* https://udlguidelines.cast.org/.

Endrew F. V. Douglas County School District Re-1, 137 S. Ct. 988 (March 22, 2017).

Fowler, S. A., Coleman, M. R. B., & Bogdan, W. K. (2019). The state of the special education profession survey report. *Teaching Exceptional Children, 52*(1), 8–29.

Hoover, J. J., & Patton, J. R. (2017). *IEPs for ELs: And other diverse learners*. Corwin Press.

Rupar, A., & Kurth, J. (2023). *Equitable and inclusive IEPs for students with complex support needs*. Brookes.

Sage, J. (2018). *Happy student: The practical guide to functional behavior assessment and behavior intervention planning*. Rowman & Littlefield.

Watson, A. P. (2019). *Fewer things, better: The courage to focus on what matters most*. Due Season Press and Educational Services.

Wright, P. W., Wright, P. D., & O'Connor, S. W. (2010). *Wrightslaw: All about IEPs: Answers to frequently asked questions about IEPs*. Harbor House Law Press.

US Department of Education. (2018, December). *40th annual report to Congress on the implementation of the Individuals with Disabilities Education Act*. https://www2.ed.gov/about/reports/annual/osep/2018/parts-b-c/40th-arc-for-idea.pdf.

Internet Resources

Some invaluable IEP resources for both caseload management and sharing with parents:

Council of Exceptional Children: https://exceptionalchildren.org/topics.
IEPs Developing High Quality Individualized Educational Plans, Vanderbilt IRIS Center: https://iris.peabody.vanderbilt.edu/module/iep01/.
Ruby's Rainbow: https://rubysrainbow.org/.
TASH: Advancing Inclusion, https://tash.org/publications/research-and-practice-for-persons-with-severe-disabilities/.
Understood.org: Anatomy of the IEP, https://www.understood.org/en/articles/at-a-glance-anatomy-of-an-iep.
Wrights Law: https://www.wrightslaw.com/.

Suggested answers for "Accommodations versus Modifications": 1. A; 2. M; 3. M; 4. A; 5. A; 6. A; 7. M; 8. A; 9. A; 10. A

Suggested recommendations for IEP Scenarios #1 to #3:

1. This IEP scenario has a negative impact on the student due to a change in LRE for an entire week. Further, positive behavior strategies would not recommend that students receive a consequence in this way since the behavior outbursts are a manifestation of their disability and are better supported through positive behavior management strategies.

2. This IEP scenario is problematic since the student is being moved to an alternative testing plan without IEP team discussion and decision-making.

3. This IEP scenario is concerning since the student is not receiving speech and language services as outlined on the IEP and parents could sue the school district for compensatory services to make up the speech and language service time.

Section II
Getting into It

Welcome to November! You have likely felt that time has been flying by. The first three months of the school year bring so much anticipation and busyness that you may have not even noticed how tired you were feeling . . . until now. November may be bringing with it some feelings of "survival" and "overwhelm" as depicted on the "First-Year Special Education Teacher Timeline" (see figure 4 in the August chapter to revisit this timeline). At this time, you may want solutions to the overwhelming workload you may be immersed in, for example, *How can I be more efficient writing these IEPs?* Or, *Why is this behavior system not working for student Y?*— thinking to yourself, *Ugh, what am I missing here?* Solutions will emerge, maybe not right now, but they will come to you during the journey of the year. This is the time when your mentor, teacher, or others around you, having been through a period of "starting out" on their own teaching journeys, may be trying to comfort you and reassure you that it will get better—which it will. Unfortunately, during this period it is going to feel overwhelming whether you want it to or not. You may even feel that you have hit a wall at some point in the next few months and/or as you start the spring semester, too, and know that this is a very common feeling at this time of year. Some concrete suggestions for this time are the following:

1. Consider why you are feeling overwhelmed and jot down some of the solutions you are trying and how those have helped or not helped.

2. Plan for smaller increments—you may have already had some across-the-year planning done (i.e., the "Annual IEP Calendar," template in resource 3), so stick to the checklists in this book to help you plan

smaller during this time. Take your tasks one day or step at a time, which will help you feel less overwhelmed.

Discuss what you might be feeling: overwhelmed, uncertainty, questioning a student issue, or struggling with an issue on a teaching team. Use table 2.1 to discuss with each other as you launch into November.

Table 2.1.

Issue	What have you tried?	How did that go?	Jot down next-step suggestions:

Let's Jump into Section II

In the month of November, we will dig into proactively planning to support student variability using Universal Design for Learning (UDL) as a way to backward plan for incorporating diversity, inclusion, collaboration, teaming, and technology into our work. We have already discussed UDL in previous months and this month will provide more context into the brain, trauma-informed instruction, and neurodiversity. In December, we will learn about bias in special education. These are important issues to discuss with one another and also to reflect on privately in a safe, non-judgmental space. There are deeply rooted systems of inequity in our educational systems, and during December you will have an opportunity to learn more about theories and evidence-based practices of maximizing inclusion and minimizing bias. Finally, in January, we will delve into collaboration with related service team members and co-teaching models that can be used in special education across your teaching teams.

November

STUDENTS THAT ARE EXPERT LEARNERS

This case study digs into how special education teachers can design backward for diversity using Universal Design for Learning (UDL) and also be learning leaders in their school buildings. How can special education teachers utilize the UDL framework to provide inclusive and equitable instruction to students with learning disabilities?

Joshua is a special education teacher who has a diverse group of learners in his class who range from third to fifth grade, both with and without learning disabilities. Determined to provide a more inclusive and equitable learning environment for all of his students, he plans to use UDL as his framework for devising his weekly curriculum and instruction. He knows that applying this framework to teaching and his curricular design will provide a broad range of learning options that can be accessed by all students despite different backgrounds and abilities. It also enables students to learn about how they learn best—that is, to learn about their brains, strengths, and abilities. Joshua believes this can help him cultivate a learning community where students are working toward becoming "expert learners."

With high concern for ensuring accessibility and equity, Joshua learns from colleagues about various UDL principles he can apply in his classrooms, which range across all aspects of his lessons, focusing on representation, expression, and engagement. Joshua is very enthusiastic about using assistive technology (AT) to support students with their writing and reading of informational text. In particular, he hopes to highlight digital text as informational articles are read aloud using text-to-speech and teach students to follow along. In conjunction with this strategy, Joshua wants to teach students to annotate text using the comment feature in online technology tools they are using for the nonfiction text sets. He wants to offer various feedback alternatives such as peer review and engage students in mixed media sources such as videos, charts, audio tools, and tactile materials.

Joshua begins using the UDL framework in his class and quickly discovers challenges. Some students struggle to stay engaged with the materials despite relevant and high-interest content. He must assess how to provide assistance to students who need additional instruction or guidance with features of the tool or activity that are not accessible or comfortable for them. Another challenge that has emerged is that some students need refinements to their accommodations that had previously worked but are not working as well anymore. Using a variety of UDL-informed instructional approaches, he plans to gauge student progress, provide additional support where student progress needs improvement, and ensure all students have equal opportunities for success. Despite Joshua's enthusiasm, issues will inevitably crop up as he works to frame teaching and learning using UDL each week. Consider some of the specific challenges and suggestions for next steps.

Case questions:

- How can Joshua create a weekly curriculum plan that meets all the diverse learning needs of students with learning disabilities while ensuring that all students get individualized instruction based on their needs, preferences, and learning connections? What more can Joshua do to create expert learners in his inclusive third- through fifth-grade multilevel classroom?

- Joshua has a student with a hearing impairment. What is the best way for Joshua to ensure that his classroom is accessible to a student with a hearing impairment? Should he provide closed captioning, an ASL interpreter, or a combination of both? What are some ways to ensure that this student is making progress each week?

- How can Joshua provide all learners with equal access to age-appropriate and engaging resources and materials?

- Joshua has recently learned the term access friction, which explains the issue of some accommodations working at one point and then not working as well any longer. Look up this term and consider your own experiences with student accommodations that have needed adjustments over time.

Special Education Mentoring
MONTHLY CHECKLIST: NOVEMBER

TO DO...	DONE	NOTES
Discuss progress monitoring procedures		
Review *Student One-Pagers* and look at examples of these for your school district/system		
Review *Caselaw review template* and discuss any due process issues relevant to your school district/system		
Connect intervention curriculums to individualized student learning needs and special education programs, i.e. are there specific interventions related to programs		
Discuss parent communication plans and any challenges thus far with connecting with families		
Discuss what is working well, what needs support or adjustments in mentoring?		
Review district/system level assistive technology tools, resources, and statewide supports including any AT lending libraries		
Schedule third intensive intervention lesson shadow/observation		

OTHER CHECKLIST ITEMS UNIQUE TO YOUR SCHOOL DISTRICT

_____

_____

_____

SPECIAL EDUCATION FOCUS
To support your goal setting, this section is meant for you to jot down one focus area/question in each of your primary roles.

☐ IEP: _____

☐ Intensive Intervention: _____

ALSO FOR THIS MONTH

☐ **Well-Being Goal**

☐ **Collaborate on Mentoring Activities**

☐ **Suggested Resources: follow up?**

☐ Collaboration: _____

Note that anything italicized in the checklist is referring to a template in the back of this guidebook.

November Monthly Checklist

This checklist provides a roadmap for mentor discussions and timely special education roles and responsibilities typically occurring around this time of the year. There are spaces to add your own checklist items and goals within the three primary roles and responsibilities of special education professionals related to IEP caseload management, collaboration, and teaching specifically designed instruction also referred to as intensive interventions.

Key Learning Goals

1. Learn about Universal Design for Learning (UDL) approaches to curriculum design and teaching and consider ways they can be incorporated into your pedagogy along with assistive technology (AT) tools that can support UDL teaching and learning practices.

2. Analyze the research base in UDL and consider how the brain learns best and ways to cultivate brain-based learning into your intensive intervention and collaborative work with your teaching team colleagues.

3. Understanding how UDL and AT work in tandem to support student learning needs proactively and responsively.

Part I: Universal Design for Learning (UDL)

The Average Brain

Does the average student exist? Neuroscience suggests that the average student does not exist, and you may have seen evidence of this in your own teaching as well. Students share similarities with one another and instructional strategies that are effective for promoting engagement or understanding across a wide range of students, but does that mean that we can count on that always being the case? The short answer is no. All of your students will prove to be unique in their thinking. Despite this research explaining student variability (Cast.org; Rose, 2016), our school systems continue to gravitate toward teaching to an average student.

Using the framework of UDL, we can think about how to plan for diversity and collaboratively work with our teaching teams to better support student learning. At the same time, this approach to teaching has an added benefit for students who need specialized support and accommodations by creating a more accessible learning environment. These universal supports may give students what they need to access a learning activity and eliminate a barrier. Conversely, universal supports can enhance their learning by responsively providing them with other supports that enhance their learning.

In Todd Rose's book *The End of Average* (2016) he dispels the myth of an "average person" in various fields, including education, work, and sports. He suggests that there is no such thing as an "average" person because human characteristics, traits, and abilities are unique, complex, and multidimensional. The concept of the "average person" oversimplifies this complexity. Some selected areas of neuroscience that connect with his theories are detailed here.

Neuroplasticity: Neuroscience research has shown that the brain is highly adaptable and constantly changing—that is, we are constantly making connections and growing dendrites in our brain. Our brains respond to experiences, learning, and challenges in unique ways related to our individual strengths, experiences, and abilities. This highlights the variability in how different people's brains adapt and develop. Within special education, the ability of the brain to continue developing and growing its capacity to learn or understand is always on display. This can be seen when a student gets something for the first time and experiences a "eureka" or "aha!" moment. It is also seen when students make connections in their brain to something they know from their background knowledge making the new learning more memorable and understandable.

Individual Differences: Another area of neuroscience suggests that humans have significant variations in brain structure and function. This means that no two brains are exactly alike, and people may have different cognitive strengths and weaknesses, and their strengths can be built on to help them overcome challenges, for example, a student may say to themselves, "I know I learn best when I see a visual example of the pattern, so I better draw a description of the concept I am learning about."

Related to Individual Differences, UDL Emphasizes That Learner Variability Is the Norm, Not the Exception: A primary goal of UDL in K–12 programs is to develop expert learners who are empowered by their own agency and self-awareness. These are the attributes of expert learners that correspond to the three UDL principles (Meyer et al., 2014):

1. *Learners who are purposeful and motivated* (which is related to the UDL principle of engagement). This principle primarily refers to learners' abilities to be goal-directed, sustain their effort (especially within challenging tasks), and self-regulate using executive functioning skills as they learn—that is, checklists, planning schedules for larger projects.

2. *Learners who are resourceful and knowledgeable* (which is related to the UDL principle of representation). This principle refers to learners' abilities to activate and connect to prior/background knowledge, recognize strategies for remembering information and to structure and retain knowledge within content areas (i.e., science processes

that need to be recalled or understanding how to memorize social studies facts and timelines when needing to build upon this information in their general education classroom), and explicitly transfer and generalize what they learn across their school day (for this area, special educators are responsible for explicitly teaching students how to transfer their knowledge to other areas of learning).

3. *Learners who are strategic and goal-directed* (which is related to the UDL principle of action and expression). This principle refers to learners' abilities to plan and organize how they learn best by understanding how to capitalize on their strengths in order to be strategic learners and learn and implement self-monitoring strategies as they learn.

These foundational UDL concepts of addressing learner variability, reducing learning barriers, and developing expert learners are the basis of intentional and inclusive K–12 inclusive programs that will better support all students. Special education professionals can play a leadership role in using UDL to design instruction, support wider accommodation implementations (i.e., lead differentiation efforts on teaching teams), and support teaching team discussions on ways to consider how to provide flexible and engaging learning environments, using strategies and tools that address the varied needs and profiles of all learners in any given K–12 classroom. UDL recommends that we get away from planning for the "average learner," who does not exist, and instead use UDL-based design, broadening access to a wider range of learners. Additionally, UDL encourages us to expand our understanding of what is "normal" in learning. It suggests we expand what we include as normal variations in learning and as this awareness expands, we consider rejecting the concept of normal learning all together.

Some other factors to consider in addition to student variability and inclusive practices using UDL are highlighted below.

Complexity of Learning: Learning processes are intricate and can be influenced by various factors, such as genetics (which can predispose someone to have an aptitude for something but does not preclude someone from learning/doing something they are interested in), environment, background experiences, motivation, and interest. This complexity makes it challenging to predict how any one person will learn or perform in a specific context. There are many connections in special education related to the complexity of learning as well. Oftentimes, there is a misinterpretation of how this area of brain research connects to learning insofar as educators will feel that "motivation" or "interest" will only be present if the content is something the student cares about; for example, a student who likes cars will only want to learn about cars, so let's relate everything to cars! Sometimes students can have an extremely narrow interest tolerance (i.e., they really only care about cars!), but most of the time, motivation and interest can be found related to any content as long as students feel that they can be successful when they try to learn about it. Said another way, motivation shuts down when students are afraid they will fail. So, knowing that students must be motivated to learn about something can be helped by students identifying what motivates and/or does not motivate them, which will help teachers to create the conditions necessary for them to be successful.

Dynamic Brain Development: Brain development is an ongoing and dynamic process that can continue throughout a person's life. Different regions of the brain can develop at different rates, contributing to individual variation in abilities and preferences. Dynamic brain development is particularly important to consider in special education since it is necessary for students to make connections between information they already know and what they are learning. Oftentimes (potentially most of the time), we need to explicitly guide students to make these connections. Metacognition is a common strategy that teachers can use to support continuous dynamic brain development where we help students think about their own thinking. A strategy teachers can use to grow students' metacognition is to teach using "think-alouds" where they verbalize their thinking so students can hear an example of metacognitive processing.

Contextual Influences: The brain's responses can be highly context dependent. People may excel in one situation but struggle in another, which can be influenced by factors like trauma, stress, environment, feelings of belonging or mattering, and social interactions. Contextual influence is a complex issue that is uniquely relevant to special education since we can be observant of context and make adaptations where possible so students can experience more success. There are a myriad of factors contributing to student success in school. Students of color and students who live in poverty are overrepresented in special education and contextual factors are a critical component of this issue. Research has shown that certain racial and ethnic minority groups, particularly Black and Latino/Hispanic students, are more likely to be overrepresented in special education programs, particularly in categories like emotional or behavioral disorders, with an overall higher rate of Black and Latino/Hispanic students being identified as requiring special education services relative to White students (Department of Education, 2023). This overrepresentation has raised concerns about potential biases in assessment and referral processes, which our Guidebook will discuss more in

December's "Going Deeper." It is crucial to consider promoting a heightened awareness of any racial or socioeconomic factors that may hinder a student's academic success within educational settings. For instance, the absence of representation of people of color in the materials being taught or studied can be discouraging for students of color. Similarly, activities that require students to pay fees may not be accessible to students from low-income families, creating a disproportionate disadvantage. Additionally, students from diverse racial and cultural backgrounds with communication challenges, for example, language barriers or students with multiple disabilities who are emergent communicators, experience overwhelming challenges. We will discuss trauma-informed instruction at a deeper level to help guide special education program supports in the hopes of helping students to rise above these challenging contextual influences that affect their brain development.

Let's focus a bit deeper on trauma-related brain context since these social and emotional impacts are widely manifested in K–12 special education programs. This is due to the higher occurrence of trauma-related risk factors resulting in students being identified as eligible for special education services—that is, students impacted by issues related to poverty may have had less educational opportunities, which result in less success in school. Consider student case study excerpts related to trauma-impacted experiences and how these social/emotional impacts affect their learning.

> **Belonging in school**: "Fear and shame are common emotions I experience when things happen. I have such a negative view of myself, others, and the world. Every mistake I make or risk I take, such as making new friends or learning something new, can trigger my shame. It makes me feel like hiding, lashing out, or blaming others because I don't know how to deal with the overwhelming feeling that I'm a bad kid. I need you to understand what this is like for me." (Alexander, 2023, p. 152)

Consider this student's story. Are there any students on your current caseload who might feel this way? How do their behaviors communicate how they are feeling?

> **Relationships and beliefs students have about themselves**: "It may feel like I'm trying to make you upset on purpose when I do the opposite of what you ask me to do. Other grown-ups I've trusted have hurt me when they have gotten angry with me. I'm testing you to see if you will abuse me too." (Alexander, 2023, p. 153)

Discuss how teachers cultivate trust with their students. How can you cultivate trust with your students? Are there things that are happening or have happened that might threaten that trust?

> **Life in school**: "I may work hard to always do the right thing at school, never wanting to let anyone see my insecurities. Inside, I am drowning in anxiety, though. Just because you can't see it doesn't mean it's not there. Help me learn that it is okay to be a kid who makes mistakes and that I will be accepted for being myself—faults and all." (Alexander, 2023, p. 152)

Do you have any students who focus on mistakes and shut down when they happen? Do you have students who will not try at all? Could that be because they are afraid of making a mistake?

In the frame below, draw a picture of a "supported student." This is a simple mindfulness activity related to our thinking about trauma-informed instruction. Take a minute to sketch a student (it can be a stick figure) and include words, images, and so on, that can be included for your student so they have the support they need to be successful in school each day. Don't forget the sensory, emotional, learning, and social support that you think would be critical to have on board. Please title your drawing.

 STOP & JOT

Understanding trauma is an important step to providing trauma-informed instruction in your special education program. It is highly probable that you will encounter students impacted by trauma in your work as a special education teacher. First, research related to trauma to consider is that the impacts of trauma are real and can affect brain development. These negative impacts can be made better by implementing trauma-informed instruction. Also, consider that trauma is prevalent. In fact, it is more common than we care to admit. It is estimated that 60 percent or more of K–12 students have experienced one or more major traumatic experiences in their lives (Alexander, 2019). This estimate may have risen since the pandemic, during which time research has documented that collective trauma issues were experienced by most students in unique ways, for example, students might still be afraid to have a mask off in a public setting or may have lost a loved one. Trauma is considered toxic to the brain and can affect development and learning in a multitude of ways. In our schools, we need to be prepared to support students who have experienced trauma, even if we don't know exactly who they are. While trauma has negative impacts, children are incredibly resilient, and in positive learning environments, they can grow, learn, and succeed.

Learning about the brain helps special educators contextualize trauma-impacted behaviors and challenges that are emerging for students. Additionally, this information regarding trauma and the brain can be helpful to share within our school buildings and across teaching teams in order to devise teaching strategies to support students suffering from trauma-related impacts.

The *prefrontal cortex* is our *problem-solving hub*. Within this part of the brain, our consciousness frees us to respond instead of reacting to life events. In this area, we make choices so we can intentionally create new options for ourselves and others. The freedom of choice is an evolutionary change in perspective from feeling victimized to feeling empowered. This part of our brain is actually not fully developed until we are twenty-five years old.

Next, our *limbic system* (located in the middle under the prefrontal cortex) is our *connections and relationships hub*. Our relationships directly shape the structure and function of this part of the brain. Our human connections create and strengthen neural connections in the brain. This system thrives on and needs emotional connections. When the limbic system is being threatened, students may exhibit the behaviors shown in table 2.2:

Table 2.2.

Blame	Verbal Aggression	Social Issues
"He made me do it!" "She made me sad." "You have to make it better." "He did it first!"	Name-calling: "Fat, stupid, ugly . . ." "I hate you!" "If you don't _____, you can't be my friend!"	Attention seeking (connection avoidance) Approval seeking ("Can I be on green if . . .") Relationship resistant or reluctant

Table adapted from the Conscious Discipline Program (n.d.)

Finally, our *brain stem* is our *safety net*. This part of the brain functions optimally when it feels safe, and yes, you have got it, this part of the brain alerts our fight, flight, or freeze reactions when it feels threatened. This system needs to feel safe and when we are out of our "choice-making" prefrontal cortex, or our relationship-hub limbic system has been betrayed, our brain stem will jump into action. Some behaviors are listed in table 2.3 that can appear when students feel this system is being "threatened."

Table 2.3.

Fight	Flight	Freeze
hit, kick, punch, spit, push, bite, physical aggression	withdraw, run, hide, elope, scream, crawl	cry, whine, give up, give in

Table adapted from the Conscious Discipline Program (n.d.)

In combination with the brain systems and their chemical reactions to environmental triggers, students will also have compounded impacts to their behavior related to stress and ongoing stress. Whether stress is related to the classroom context or not, it can impact their behavior and success. Let's learn about the three primary categories of stress and then discuss some scenarios.

Positive. This stress might include a brief increase in heart rate and mild elevation in stress hormones. This keeps us positive about life and energized. It is beneficial and essential for us to have an overall sense of well-being.

Tolerable. Serious, temporary stress responses, buffered by supportive relationships. This is related to daily things in life that cause us stress and potentially some upset, frustration, and so forth.

90 Section II

Toxic. Prolonged activation of stress response systems in the absence of protective relationships. This excessive, prolonged stress response in the body and brain is considered "toxic stress," and it can have damaging effects on our learning, behavior, and health across our lifespan (adapted from Center on the Developing Child, n.d.).

Let's consider some cause-and-effect scenarios related to the brain, trauma-informed instruction, and stress shown in figure 10. What are some strategies that could be used in these situations?

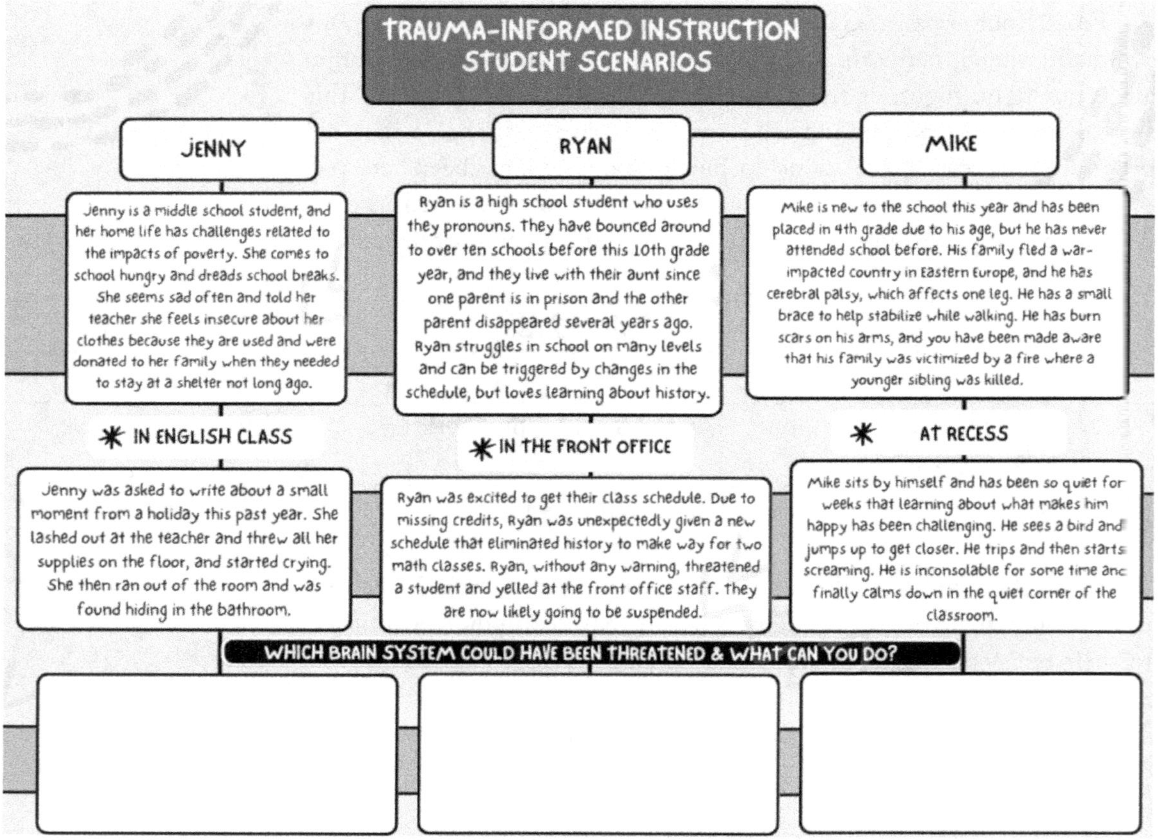

TRAUMA-INFORMED INSTRUCTION STUDENT SCENARIOS

JENNY
Jenny is a middle school student, and her home life has challenges related to the impacts of poverty. She comes to school hungry and dreads school breaks. She seems sad often and told her teacher she feels insecure about her clothes because they are used and were donated to her family when they needed to stay at a shelter not long ago.

RYAN
Ryan is a high school student who uses they pronouns. They have bounced around to over ten schools before this 10th grade year, and they live with their aunt since one parent is in prison and the other parent disappeared several years ago. Ryan struggles in school on many levels and can be triggered by changes in the schedule, but loves learning about history.

MIKE
Mike is new to the school this year and has been placed in 4th grade due to his age, but he has never attended school before. His family fled a war-impacted country in Eastern Europe, and he has cerebral palsy, which affects one leg. He has a small brace to help stabilize while walking. He has burn scars on his arms, and you have been made aware that his family was victimized by a fire where a younger sibling was killed.

✳ IN ENGLISH CLASS
Jenny was asked to write about a small moment from a holiday this past year. She lashed out at the teacher and threw all her supplies on the floor, and started crying. She then ran out of the room and was found hiding in the bathroom.

✳ IN THE FRONT OFFICE
Ryan was excited to get their class schedule. Due to missing credits, Ryan was unexpectedly given a new schedule that eliminated history to make way for two math classes. Ryan, without any warning, threatened a student and yelled at the front office staff. They are now likely going to be suspended.

✳ AT RECESS
Mike sits by himself and has been so quiet for weeks that learning about what makes him happy has been challenging. He sees a bird and jumps up to get closer. He trips and then starts screaming. He is inconsolable for some time and finally calms down in the quiet corner of the classroom.

WHICH BRAIN SYSTEM COULD HAVE BEEN THREATENED & WHAT CAN YOU DO?

Figure 10. Trauma-Informed Instruction Student Scenarios
This figure provides three student scenarios to discuss with each other. Students Jenny, Ryan, and Mike have various trauma-related scenarios in specific settings within the school building for you to consider and problem-solve.

Universal Design for Learning

Providing trauma-informed instruction and other specialized supports that are unique and needed in special education is made easier by framing programs using UDL. Recall, UDL is an educational framework and set of principles aimed at creating inclusive and accessible learning environments that accommodate the diverse learning needs of all students, including those with disabilities. The core goal of UDL is to design instruction and curriculum that is proactively flexible, adaptable, and accessible to a wide range of learners, reducing the barriers to learning. Students may still need accommodations beyond the universal supports of UDL, and those can be implemented in addition to UDL. The key principles of UDL are (1) providing multiple means of representation, which means students are provided content and information in various formats (e.g., text, audio, video, graphics) to cater to different learning preferences and abilities. This ensures that students can access information in the ways that work best for them. Next, (2) multiple means of engagement that offer diverse options for engaging students' interests, motivation, and attention. This might involve varying the ways in which content is presented, options for group work, allowing for choice in assignments, and incorporating real-world scenarios into lessons. Finally, (3) multiple means of expression that allow students to demonstrate their understanding and knowledge through various means, such as written assignments, oral presentations, multimedia projects, or hands-on exploration activities. UDL is based on the belief that educational barriers can be reduced or eliminated through proactive design and that inclusive teaching benefits all students, not just those with disabilities. By providing multiple pathways for learning and expression, UDL helps create more equitable and effective educational experiences for everyone. Cast.org has comprehensive resources to support curricular and instructional design approaches that are aligned with UDL.

PART II: ASSISTIVE TECHNOLOGY (AT) AND CURRICULUM PLANNING

What Is Assistive Technology (AT)?

Assistive technology (AT) is comprised of products, equipment, and systems that enhance learning, working, and daily living for persons with disabilities. Please note, objects can be designed to function as AT "off the shelf," like an iPad, or something can be created, adapted, or modified to be AT such as an augmentative alternative communication (AAC) device that has been modified to work in a particular way for an individual (Assistive Technology Industry Association, ATIA). What does AT do? It helps students/people who have difficulty speaking, typing, writing, remembering, pointing, seeing, hearing, learning, walking, and many other things. Different disabilities may require different AT. What is not included in AT? Typically, hearing aids are not included, nor is anything that is surgically implanted.

According to IDEA (2004), AT is considered low- or high-tech tools, as well as the training and maintenance required for tools to function. In addition to AT "tools," IDEA requires the implementation of AT services. Thus, these services are worth noting and discussing here.

The term "assistive technology service" means any service that directly assists a student with a disability in the selection, acquisition, or use of an AT device. This term includes the following categories:

A. the evaluation of the needs of such child, including a functional evaluation of the child in the child's customary environment;

B. purchasing, leasing, or otherwise providing for the acquisition of assistive technology devices by such child;

C. selecting, designing, fitting, customizing, adapting, applying, maintaining, repairing, or replacing assistive technology devices;

D. coordinating and using other therapies, interventions, or services with assistive technology devices, such as those associated with existing education and rehabilitation plans and programs;

E. training or technical assistance for such child, or, where appropriate, the family of such child; and

F. training or technical assistance for professionals (including individuals providing education and rehabilitation services), employers, or other individuals who provide services to, employ, or are otherwise substantially involved in the major life functions of such a child. (IDEA, 2004)

How do you choose the right AT? From ATIA, most often, the choice is a team decision composed of professionals and consultants trained to match particular AT to specific needs. An AT team may include family doctors, general and special education teachers, speech-language pathologists, rehabilitation specialists and engineers, occupational therapists, and other specialists, including consulting representatives from companies that manufacture AT.

Who pays for AT? The answer depends on the technology, the use, and the user. Many kinds of AT may cost you little or nothing, even for some very expensive items. Some examples:

- *School systems* pay for general special education learning materials as well as technology specified in an IEP.
- *Government programs* (Social Security, veteran's benefits, or state Medicaid agencies) pay for certain AT if a doctor prescribes it as a necessary medical device.
- *Private health insurance* pays for certain AT if a doctor prescribes it as a necessary medical or rehabilitative device.
- *Rehabilitation and job training programs*, whether funded by government or private agencies, may pay for AT and training to help support individuals with disabilities having accommodations needed for work- or life-related activities.
- *Employers* may pay for AT that is seen as a reasonable accommodation to enable an employee to perform essential job tasks.

Please note, an IEP team is required to consider AT, and lack of funding cannot be a reason AT was not considered. There are AT evaluation processes, and many states have state-wide organizations that can support your students needing a specific device by loaning a device for "trialing" in order for you to collect data on its effectiveness in supporting the IEP goals and program it is being recommended for.

Who uses AT? Most students who are served in special education programs will benefit from AT, and there are low- to high-technology solutions available. A unique group of AT users are students with multiple disabilities who benefit in multiple ways from AT supports that can provide access to academic learning, for example, text-to-speech with some additional support such as a switch or an AAC device. Keep in mind, in most of our educational systems and school districts, students are provided a technology tool as part of their learning environment such as a Chromebook or iPad. When considering AT solutions to support learning, evaluate the effective uses of the current technology device to support learning needs. For example, if a student with literacy-based disability areas is attending a school district using Chromebooks, work with them to utilize the Read and Write Google toolbar to activate text-to-speech, annotation tools, speech-to-text, and so on.

There is a wide range of AT evaluations and inventories to help IEP teams work collaboratively to determine tools, services, and supports that could benefit and accommodate a student. Two summarized student scenarios are provided below as a collaborative activity to practice using these AT evaluation tools together.

AT AND UDL

By proactively planning with UDL to support student variability in their learning and diversity in their backgrounds and abilities, we can infuse support early on and throughout the learning process. In addition to UDL, we can be responsive to learners' unique needs using reactive AT interventions to support accessibility and achievement.

Scenario #1: Recall the case study from the beginning of November regarding Joshua implementing a UDL approach to the teaching and learning in his special education program. He wanted students to write and read informational text using text-to-speech and follow along with the text being highlighted as it was read aloud. He wants to offer various feedback alternatives such as peer review and engage students in mixed media sources such as videos, charts, audio tools, and tactile materials. Consider a unique student situation related to Joshua's classroom for a student named Rosaria. Joshua already has instructional activities designed so that students can access informational text using text-to-speech on their school-issued Chromebooks. He is enhancing this plan for one of his fourth-grade students who needs differentiated informational text at the first-grade level that she can read alongside her peers (see how to do this using Newsela.com). At the time of day that Joshua sees this student, it is particularly loud in the room. His student also needs writing support to summarize the text she reads, including some sort of graphic organizer, support getting started with her writing, and an AT tool to be used for writing since she has limited access to the keyboard. Consider this scenario together first using the "SETT" (Zabala, 2005) and next brainstorm some ideas using one or more of the Wisconsin Assistive Technology Inventory (WATI) checklists (https://www.wati.org/). Use figure 10.5 below to brainstorm collaboratively.

Scenario #2: One of Joshua's teaching colleagues, Aleisha, works with students served in an intensive learning needs program. She has been collaborating with the SLP regarding a new student who is ready to transition to a new AAC (augmentative alternative communication) system. Joshua will be facilitating a co-taught literacy block with Aleisha and wants to imagine how he can incorporate a new student who uses an AAC system. What are some of the best practices for including students who use AAC in literacy learning activities? With your mentor, learn collaboratively about AAC systems (see suggested resources below) and also how to engage emergent literacy learners by reviewing Karen Erickson's Center for Literacy and Disability Studies resources. Something to consider in this case study scenario are the four questions Erickson (2017) recommends special educators ask themselves when considering students' literacy and communication levels that are listed below. Discuss these with one another along with the suggested AAC systems to discover more about communication and emergent literacy learners. Reflect on the Scenario #2 questions after learning more.

Questions to determine if a student is an emergent or conventional literacy learner:

1. Does the student know most of the letters most of the time?
2. Does the student engage actively during shared reading?
3. Does the student have a symbolic means of communication and interaction?
4. Does the student understand that writing involves letters and words?

If the answer to one or more questions is "No," then an educator should use a comprehensive emergent literacy intervention.

Internet Resources for Scenario #2:

- Emergent Literacy: https://www.med.unc.edu/healthsciences/clds/
- Picture Exchange Communication System: https://pecsusa.com/pecs/ (Pyramid Educational Consultants)
- Examples of AAC devices at Enabling Devices: https://enablingdevices.com/
- American Speech-Language-Hearing Association: https://www.asha.org/

Reflection Questions

- What are methods for engaging emergent and/or conventional literacy learners using AAC systems in a literacy lesson?
- How could teams prepare AAC systems to support student vocabulary use and development within literacy lessons?
- What other key takeaways can be jotted here for Scenarios #1 and #2?

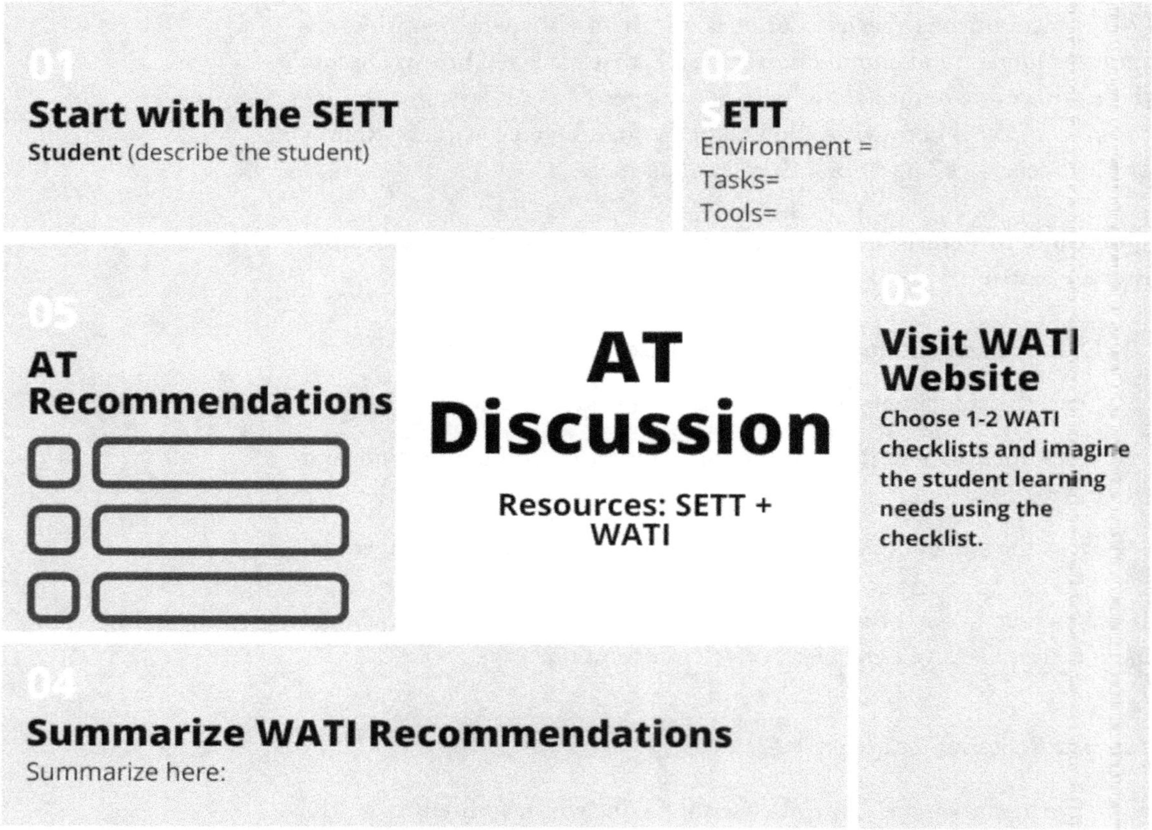

01
Start with the SETT
Student (describe the student)

02
SETT
Environment =
Tasks=
Tools=

05
AT Recommendations
☐ ▭
☐ ▭
☐ ▭

AT Discussion
Resources: SETT + WATI

03
Visit WATI Website
Choose 1-2 WATI checklists and imagine the student learning needs using the checklist.

04
Summarize WATI Recommendations
Summarize here:

Figure 10.5. AT Discussion Organizer
This graphic organizer provides space to consider AT planning for a student on your caseload.

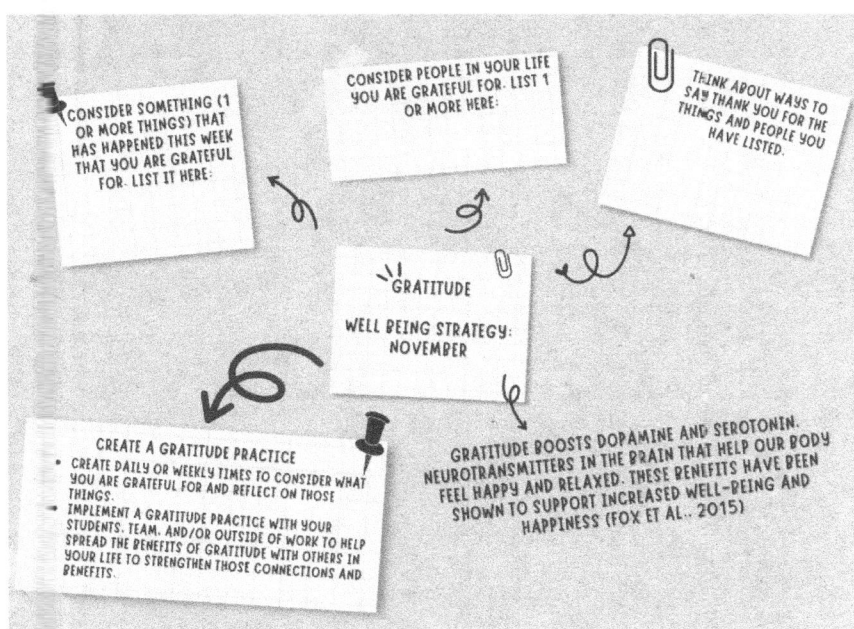

November Plan for Well-Being

For November, you are practicing gratitude, which can be challenging when you feel too busy to stop for a minute—*even to be grateful*. Surprisingly, gratefulness acts like an "express lane" on the freeway to happiness. It works to find what you are grateful for and practice daily gratitude because it shifts your negative thinking patterns to more positive, optimistic ones. Try it! A great place to start is to thank each other for taking the time to learn and collaborate in this mentoring partnership this year!

Share your well-being goal each month with one another to support making it happen!

Alexander, J. (2019). *Building trauma-sensitive schools*. Brookes Publishing

Alexander, J. (2023). *Building trauma sensitive schools: Your guide to creating safe, supportive learning*. Group, 1, 15.

Barnes, M. D., & Gonzalez, J. (2015). *Hacking education: 10 quick fixes for every school*. Times 10 Publications.

Busaj, C. (2022). *The new assistive tech: Make learning awesome for all!* International Society for Technology in Education.

Chardin, M., & Novak, K. (2020). *Equity by design: Delivering on the power and promise of UDL*. Corwin Press.

Dalton, E. (2022). Universal design for learning: UDL basics. In J. McKenzie, K. Nseibo, C. Samuels, & A. Karisa (Eds.), *Disability studies in inclusive education*. Advance preprint. DOI: 10.25375/uct.21701177.

Department of Education. (2023, May). *Students with disabilities*. https://nces.ed.gov/programs/coe/indicator/cgg/students-with-disabilities

Edyburn, D. L. (2023). Reimagining the future of special education technology. In D. Cockerham, R. Kaplan-Rakowski, W. Foshay, & M. Spector (Eds.), *Reimagining education: Studies and stories for effective learning in an evolving digital environment* (pp. 281–292). Springer International Publishing.

Erickson, K. A. (2017). Comprehensive literacy instruction, interprofessional collaborative practice, and students with severe disabilities. *American Journal of Speech-Language Pathology, 26*(2), 193–205.

Fox, G. R., Kaplan, J., Damasio, H., & Damasio, A. (2015). Neural correlates of gratitude. *Frontiers in Psychology, 6*, article 1491.

Gargiulo, R. M., & Metcalf, D. (2022). *Teaching in today's inclusive classrooms: A universal design for learning approach.* Cengage Learning.

Grant, K., & Pérez, L. (2022). *DIVE into UDL: Immersive practices to develop expert learners.* International Society for Technology in Education.

Hall, T. E., Meyer, A., & Rose, D. H. (Eds.). (2012). *Universal design for learning in the classroom: Practical applications.* Guilford Press.

Meyer, A., Rose, D., & Gordon, D. (2014). *Universal design for learning: Theory and practice.* CAST Professional Publishing. https://publishing.cast.org/catalog/books-products/universal-design-for-learning-meyer-rose-gordon.

Murawski, W. W., & Scott, K. L. (Eds.). (2019). *What really works with universal design for learning.* Corwin Press.

Novak, K., & Tucker, C. R. (2021). *UDL and blended learning: Thriving in flexible learning landscapes.* IMpress.

Rose, T. (2016). *The end of average: How to succeed in a world that values sameness.* Penguin UK.

Sacks, S. Z., & Silberman, R. K. (1998). *Educating students who have visual impairments with other disabilities.* Paul H. Brookes Publishing Co.

Siegel, D. J. (2015). *Brainstorm: The power and purpose of the teenage brain.* Penguin.

Silverman, S. K. (2010). What is diversity? An inquiry into preservice teacher beliefs. *American Educational Research Journal, 47*(1), 292–329.

Souers, K. V. M., & Hall, P. (2018). *Relationship, responsibility, and regulation: Trauma-invested practices for fostering resilient learners.* ASCD.

Ward, S., & Jacobsen, K. (2014). A clinical model for developing executive function skills. *Perspectives on Language Learning and Education, 21*(2), 72–84.

Zabala, J. (2005). Ready, SETT, go! Getting started with the SETT framework. *Closing the Gap: Computer Technology in Special Education and Rehabilitation, 23*(6), 1–3

Internet Resources

American Speech-Language-Hearing Association: https://www.asha.org/.
Angela Watson's Truth for Teachers podcast related to trauma-informed instruction: https://truthforteachers.com/truth-for-teachers-podcast/trauma-informed-teaching/.
Assistive Technology Industry Association: https://www.atia.org/.
Center on the Developing Child: https://developingchild.harvard.edu/.
Center for Literacy and Disability Studies: https://www.med.unc.edu/healthsciences/clds/.
Conscious Discipline: https://consciousdiscipline.com/.
Cult of Pedagogy: https://www.cultofpedagogy.com/.
Dive into UDL: https://www.diveintoudl.com/, UDL online companion to professional learning about UDL.
Enabling Devices: https://enablingdevices.com/.
Executive Functioning Practice: https://www.efpractice.com/about-5-1-.
Perkins: https://www.perkins.org/paths-to-technology/, Technology solutions for students with multiple disabilities and sensory impairments.
Pyramid Educational Consultants: Picture Exchange Communication Systems, https://pecsusa.com/pecs/.
Texthelp: https://www.texthelp.com/
Shake Up Learning/Google Suite: https://shakeuplearning.com/.
Universal Design for Learning: www.cast.org.
Wisconsin Assistive Technology Initiative: https://www.wati.org/.

December

PARTNERING WITH PARENTS

How can teachers create a program environment that welcomes and connects with students and families to support academic success, inclusion, and accessibility in the classroom and school building?

Maria, director and founder of Puerto Rican Parents of Students with Disabilities (PRPSD), is the parent of a child with a physical disability. She has been heavily involved in advocacy work, such as consulting with educators, school board leadership, and city- and state-level government leadership to improve access to, quality of, and inclusive practices in education for students with disabilities. Her research suggests that funding, power imbalances within school systems, and overarching negative attitudes impact students with disabilities' educational experiences.

Maria has researched how various policy and practice initiatives can align with UNESCO's vision of education for all (https://www.unesco.org/en). She has campaigned for the government to provide adequate funding and resources to meet students with disabilities' unique needs. Ways that are working to support these efforts are to ensure teachers have training and programs to support more inclusion and the development of classroom interventions that incorporate evidence-based practices in special education.

Maria and her team have uncovered many barriers for students with disabilities, such as lowered expectations in their academic programs, assumptions that students should be pulled from academic inclusion classes because they cannot keep up, and reduced resources within school programs. In addition, in the school building there are issues related to inaccessibility of physical spaces, and social and emotional challenges related to exclusionary special education programs. They have also uncovered unsettling information about higher rates of suspensions for young students of color who are served in special education and a higher rate of students of color being served in special education programs across the state particularly in more restrictive classroom environments. They must decide how to address these challenges, whether through partnering with community organizations, advocating for change, and/or using data-driven methods to provide feedback and recommendations for educators, policymakers, and administrators.

Case questions:

- What problem-solving strategies can Maria and her team employ to effectively address the identified barriers for students with disabilities, such as lowered expectations, assumptions leading to removal from academic inclusion classes, reduced resources, issues related to bias and discrimination, and/or physical inaccessibility?
- How can educators support the development of the personal agency, self-advocacy, and self-determination of students with disabilities and their families?
- How can educators create a curriculum that respects, reflects, and values the diversity of students with disabilities? For example, should they demonstrate inclusivity in the curriculum by providing examples of the contributions people with disabilities have made to society, innovation, history, and advocacy for change, for example, individuals such as Judith Heumann, Haben Girma, or Alice Wong?

Special Education Mentoring
MONTHLY CHECKLIST: DECEMBER

TO DO...	DONE	NOTES
Check in on sped classroom PBIS system		
Review formal and informal observation procedures by the administrative supervisors		
What IEP assistance is needed? Writing up a plan, crafting goals, PWN, evaluations?		
Discuss an overview of the district's programs (i.e. continuum of supports for students served in special education). What types of programs are available, (i.e. autism-specific, behavior, etc.)		
End of semester record keeping and how to complete/send progress monitoring notes		
If haven't already, discuss school CLD programs and translation supports for student families who speak a different home language		
Shadow a formal assessment for eligibility area you have not completed yet or is new to you		
If not already, schedule third intensive intervention lesson shadow/observation		

OTHER CHECKLIST ITEMS UNIQUE TO YOUR SCHOOL DISTRICT

_____

_____

_____

SPECIAL EDUCATION FOCUS

To support your goal setting, this section is meant for you to jot down one focus area/question in each of your primary roles.

☐ IEP: _____

☐ Intensive Intervention: _____

ALSO FOR THIS MONTH

☐ **Well-Being Goal**

☐ **Collaborate on Mentoring Activities**

☐ **Suggested Resources: follow up?**

☐ Collaboration: _____

Note that anything italicized in the checklist is referring to a template in the back of this guidebook.

December Monthly Checklist

This checklist provides a roadmap for mentor discussions and timely special education roles and responsibilities typically occurring around this time of the year. There are spaces to add your own checklist items and goals within the three primary roles and responsibilities of special education professionals related to IEP caseload management, collaboration, and teaching specifically designed instruction also referred to as intensive interventions.

Key Learning Goals

1. Assess the historical and cultural contexts in which special education systems are operating and examine the ways these systems and contexts influence the identification, placement, and programming of students who need specialized support services.

2. Recognize the role of implicit bias in special education, describing how it creates negative outcomes for students of color, students impacted by the negative effects of poverty, and students who are dual language learners.

3. Examine the influence of cultural diversity on instructional design in special education, focusing on how principles of equity and inclusion can be used to promote ideal pedagogical practices that uplift, honor, and value students' unique contributions and strengths.

PART I: UNDERSTANDING SPECIAL EDUCATION SYSTEMS

Using systems thinking can help us understand how our educational system perpetuates negative cycles that lead to more students of color and students from low socioeconomic backgrounds to be identified as needing special education services. It is important to note that discussions around bias and disproportionality issues do not lead us to conclude that we do not or should not serve students who need educational support within special education programs. They are instead focused on determining how we can proactively remove barriers, create more learning opportunities, and ensure more positive outcomes for students of color and students from high poverty backgrounds in our educational systems. How can our educational programs promote and elevate achievement for all students? That is the question we will be wondering about.

Albert Einstein said that problems cannot be solved with the same mindset that created them. This is thought to mean that in order to solve a problem, we must see it with a deeper awareness and more detailed thinking. Systems thinking is a way to embark on this process and to think about the world. It is not about reducing the world to small parts each examined individually but instead by embracing the complexity that emerges from the interconnection of its parts. Systems thinking has been used by fields such as public health, management, organizational behavior, and sustainable development. People don't become systems thinkers out of the box: to become systems thinkers, we often need to learn to think of *what else could be affecting a problem* because simple cause-and-effect scenarios might not be enough to explain what has happened. Linear thinking is cause-and-effect thinking: one cause has one effect. Even in this Guidebook, last month you attempted to assign a cause-and-effect explanation for trauma-informed student scenarios. You may have wondered how to choose just one possible "cause" since there seemed to be so many interconnected variables that had a high likelihood of impacting the students' behavior. Sometimes this type of explanation works well, such as when student A (cause) says something mean to student B (effect), which you saw with your own eyes, and so now you talk to both and help them sort through the problem. Easy, right? If it happens that way every time, with a simple cause and effect, then linear thinking is quite effective in solving this kind of human problem.

However, our K–12 world is made up of many complex relationships and interrelationships that have a myriad of causes and effects that create cycles like we see within special education. Systems thinking gives us a tool to use when attempting to deduce the issues, solutions, supports, and, potentially, other team members that need to be looped into a situation in order to understand a much more complex problem.

Systems thinking can be a powerful approach for special educators to see where successes and problems for students fit in the larger systems within school, community, and teaching teams, and how those factors are all connected. Instead of forcing different stakeholders (e.g., teams, parents, etc.) to work together, systems thinking provides a clear understanding of why we need to work together as well as some of the barriers that may be making it difficult for us to work together. We can then address those barriers and have a better understanding of each person's perspectives and the situation.

Using table 2.4, consider how you can shift your thinking to embrace a systems thinking approach to your new roles and responsibilities as a special education professional.

Special education has many systems that perpetuate themselves in negative ways, such as the practice of pulling students out of class for specialized services, which can have a negative impact on the student socially and also lead to problems related to the content they may be missing in the class they were pulled from. We have many students within our programs that have had negative experiences in their schooling, and their parents or other family members may have also had negative experiences in their previous K–12 schooling. We may have students who are impacted by the negative effects of poverty or have just recently relocated to our school or country. Further, we may have students who will be challenged by their ability to communicate, which creates frustration and isolation, or others who have physical disabilities that can be seen by

Table 2.4.

Linear Thinking	Systems Thinking	Real World Application in Special Education
Try to control chaos to create order.	Try to find patterns within the chaos.	Imagine all the strategies that may aid a student's learning wherever a barrier is emerging.
Try to fix symptoms.	Be concerned with the underlying dynamics.	There are many challenges related to students and families that we cannot fix. Instead of addressing the ways in which those dynamics impact students negatively, we acknowledge that there are aspects of the problem that are out of our control. We can work toward coming up with creative solutions to make the situation better, for example, keeping school supplies at school since supplies cannot go from home to school easily.
Believe students are predictable.	Believe that student behavior is unique and can be unpredictable.	I have never met the same student twice but oftentimes teachers will make assumptions about how a student will behave—that is, they assume that because a student is similar to student XYZ, they will behave just like XYZ. Sometimes this may be true; sometimes it will not. Instead, look at what is motivating these behaviors along with the other unique factors that are true for the student, and take those into consideration while keeping in mind that context can also affect the student.
Be concerned with assigning blame.	Try to identify patterns.	When things don't go as planned, which will often be the case, it is easy to gravitate to a linear way of thinking about the issue instead of identifying patterns, which would help to improve our outcomes. For example, when we create an instructional plan that fails many times, we will gravitate toward blaming something for the failure, for example, "A student was being disruptive," "I don't have enough resources to teach my lessons, so they are bound to fail," and so on. Instead, systems thinking would encourage us to identify possible causes that can help us make a positive change, so our lesson goes better next time.

others and therefore may have been the target of bullies or other forms of aggression and discrimination. These examples reflect how systems thinking can help us see actions, reactions, and happenings by using a lens that allows for multiple perspectives. Let's try it!

Thinking Scenario: Explore interconnected systems using an "unfolding" student story. An unfolding story simply means you are seeing what happens in stages that help to create a fuller picture of what is really going on. When we use linear thinking, this story is more straightforward and each instance is another "issue" that has come up in the student's day, whereas systems thinking encourages us to look at the fuller picture across the school day.

The school day begins, and it is ten minutes into class. Henry has come into the classroom with dirt on his face, dirt on his pant legs, and a ripped shirt. His hair is a mess, and he has been crying. He is angry. He throws his supplies down on the ground and sends a spray of pencils from a front pocket that was left unzipped. Another student yells at him for hitting her with a flying pencil, while a small group of students on the other side of the room are now completely off-task and looking at something on a student's cell phone (which is supposed to have been put away at the bell).

What can you see?

What do you think might have happened with Henry?

More background: Henry has a physical disability that affects one of his arms, and he has some facial effects on one side that cause his mouth to stay slightly open. Knowing this about Henry, do you think there are other factors in what could have happened?

A bit more background: In addition, Henry's dad has not been able to find a job since the pandemic caused him to go on medical leave due to COVID, and he still has many long-term effects related to COVID that affect his energy level and breathing. The family has just lost their home, and you have recently learned that they are staying with another family member, but the only space available is a basement room where the family needs to sleep on the floor.

Back to the classroom: Henry glances at the off-task group. The students in the small group are not paying attention. They used to be Henry's good friends, but they have become distant since Henry does not participate in the afterschool club with them anymore due to transportation issues affecting his family. Due to these changes in the family's finances, he has been forced to catch a ride with another student he does not know but who lives close to where his family is staying.

 **STOP & JOT** Using a circle, draw Henry's name in the middle along with the words "Henry came in late with dirt on pant legs/ripped shirt." Add the notes you jotted above in this way:

- Those that are directly related to the middle circle add to the first line from the circle with Henry's name.
- Create another level of circles around Henry and add factors within each that impact the first layer of circles.
- Draw lines from the secondary circles to the first circles to indicate if they may have impacted or have been the result of those secondary circles.
- Consider a third level of circles: What could we imagine the secondary circles were a result of? For example, "academic challenges" below could have a third layer of circles describing Henry's disability areas, the history of those challenges, and how they impact his learning (see the example in figure 11 of systems thinking related to Henry).

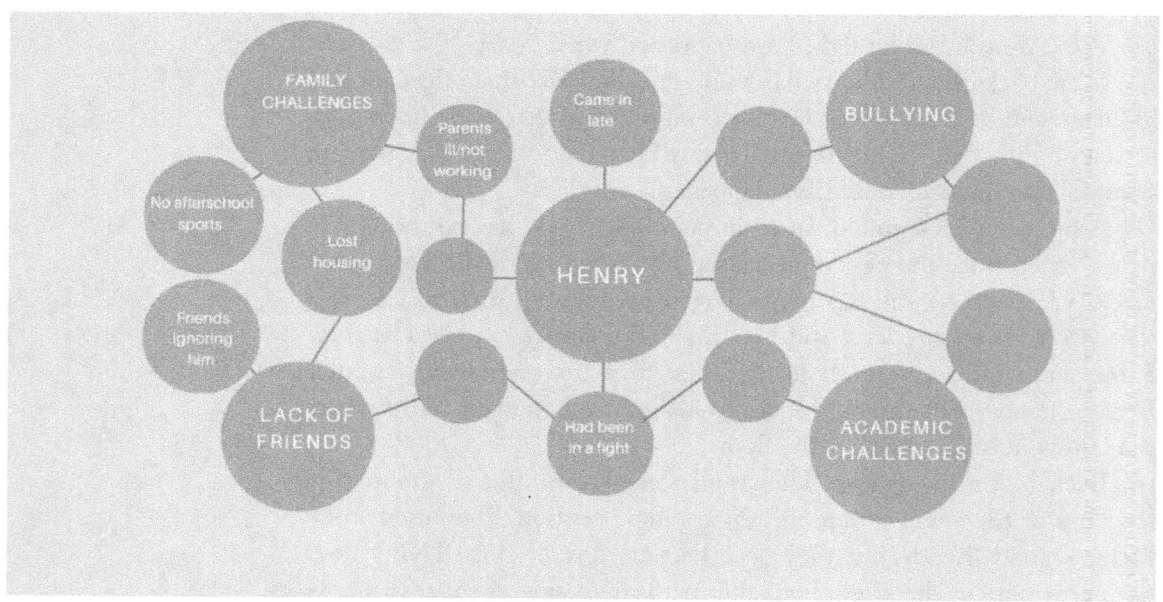

Figure 11. Henry: Student Mapping Exercise

This mind map image presents factors and results that are related to Henry, for example, his friends ignoring him, his inability to attend club anymore with friends, and so on.

Part II: Bias, Disproportionality, and Evaluation

Understanding Bias

GOING DEEPER

In order to develop deeper awareness, as we must do with systems thinking, it is critical to reflect on our bias that impacts the short- and long-term outcomes we set for our students. Each person has their own cultural history and lifetime of experiences that shape how they think and judge others—even if they are trying not to. Research demonstrates that most people hold unconscious and implicit assumptions that influence their judgments and perceptions of others in characteristic areas such as race, gender, age, ethnicity, sexual orientation, abilities, socioeconomic status, and more. Put simply, we all have biases, and reflecting on what those biases are will help us to effectively "talk back to them." When we talk back to our biases, we are able to interrupt our thinking and identify where we might have been swayed by our bias or mistakenly confirmed an incorrect assumption that was a result of our bias. Bias, whether implicit or confirmation, is usually considered to affect individual behaviors, but it can also influence institutional practices and structures, which is our reason for discussing it as it relates to special education accommodations, eligibility, and services (Hart & Lindsay, 2024). Another important consideration to remember is that becoming racially literate and culturally sensitive is a journey, not a destination, and it is important to give yourself time and space to learn more about these ideas and then keep learning! Recalling the famous Maya Angelou quote shared in Section I, "Do the best you can until you know better. Then, when you know better, do better."

Let's learn a bit more about bias and then try out a research-based strategy that can help us unpack bias in future situations whenever the need arises.

Some types of bias that can affect our teaching, interactions, and student success include:

- implicit
- confirmation
- racial
- gender
- grading

Bias is an inclination, prejudice, preference, or tendency toward or against a person, group, thing, idea, or belief. Biases are typically unfair or prejudicial and are often based on stereotypes rather than knowledge or experience. Bias is usually learned, although some biases may be deeply held from early experiences in life. Bias can develop at any time in an individual's life. It can have both a negative impact and a positive one, for example, believing that all students of a certain race are talented in a particular subject can lead us to be more persistent in our teaching and motivation with students that match that race. For example, there is a common bias that Asian students are more likely to achieve in math, which might lead us to continue to support their learning through our teaching and potentially be more persistent in our support if challenges arise.

Additionally, common biases that manifest in a variety of beliefs and ideas about students can be about these characteristics:

- race
- ability/disability/ableism
- ethnicity
- gender
- religion
- sexual orientation
- socioeconomic background
- educational background
- qualities and/or actions related to students' families

Within school systems, the attitudes of teachers and students toward a student with a disability, or student with a disability who is also a student of color, or a student with a disability and another identifying characteristic that is different than that of the larger group, can negatively impact student achievement (Starck et al., 2020). Unfortunately, bias continues to be an issue in school settings and our society because bias is a belief that favors or discriminates against one group over another (adapted from the National Center for Educational Statistics, n.d.). It can make us feel uncomfortable and defensive to talk about it.

One difficulty with bias is that people might not recognize it or be conscious of their biased attitude and therefore might not feel that bias affects the way they interact with others (Starck et al., 2020; Hart & Lindsay, 2024). This is one area of self-awareness that is needed. Another is understanding; systemic bias occurs when everyday practices that exclude students from opportunities can perpetuate the advancement of one group over another. As we consider race and culture, another issue that comes up for students negatively impacting their academic performance is "stereotype threat." Stereotype threat refers to the student feeling a risk of confirming the negative stereotypes associated with their race, ethnicity, gender, cultural group, and other categories as well. Recognizing all of these issues that are potentially being felt or experienced by students helps promote self-awareness in teachers so they can interrupt these negative cycles (adapted from Duncan-Andrade, 2022).

Teachers may hold bias, including unconscious bias, toward ethnic and racial groups, and this bias may be compounded if those students are also affected by negative impacts of poverty. Across a building, school-based systemic bias occurs when minority groups, such as Black or African American students, have less access to and become progressively less successful in their academic programs across their entire academic career in K–12. Yet, another illustrative example of systemic bias can be found in the curriculum when there is a lack of high quality, culturally relevant instructional materials for students who are second language learners or Black (Billingsley & Bettini, 2019; Starck et al., 2020; Muhammad, 2020).

Understanding Our Bias

How can we examine our own bias and larger systemic bias occurring in special education? One way is to use "mirrors and windows" in our thinking so these issues that are negatively impacting students can be uncovered. Mirrors are meant to represent us looking inward and reflecting on our own biases and assumptions about students and learning. Windows are meant to represent us looking outward to better understand systems that continue to result in there being less opportunity for success for students served in our special education programs. Continue to consider your "mirrors" and "windows" as you proceed in this "Going Deeper" reading.

Learning about Disproportionality

Consider that bias leads to disproportionality, or unequal representation, of ethnic or racial groups in special education. Disproportionality often is determined using a standard risk ratio that compares the risk of one group to the risk of all combined groups. At this time, in our country, Black students are nearly twice as likely as White students to be labeled with an intellectual disability or having a serious emotional disability. While other groups, such as Asian students, are underrepresented in special education (adapted from PEW Research, 2023). The results of biases in our schools affect whether a student is fully included, as well as their self-perception as a "bad student," "not smart," or "not valued or cared about." Many times, our students feel that they don't belong and that their teachers "don't like them." You might hear this described as othering, which means students are made to feel excluded and devalued.

The issue of disproportionality is important to unpack further, given its gravity in our K–12 special education systems—that is, the overrepresentation of students of color, students who are culturally and linguistically diverse (CLD), and students impacted by poverty are being served at higher rates in our special education programs, which is a pervasive issue across the United States (adapted from the National Center for Educational Statistics, n.d.). Disproportionality in special education refers to the overrepresentation or underrepresentation of certain racial, ethnic, or demographic groups among students who receive special education services when compared to their representation in the overall student population. This phenomenon is a significant concern within the field of education because it suggests that some groups of students may be more likely to be identified as having disabilities or placed in special education programs than others, which is often due to factors unrelated to their actual disabilities or educational needs (Cruz & Rodl, 2018; Williams & Elliott, 2023; Hart & Lindsay, 2024). Key points about disproportionality in special education include:

1. Overrepresentation occurs when a particular group is identified for special education services at a higher rate than would be expected based on their population size. For example, if a specific racial or ethnic group is identified as having a disability at a significantly higher rate than their peers, then this fact indicates the overrepresentation of that group in special education services.

2. Underrepresentation, conversely, occurs when a group is less likely to be identified for special education services than would be expected based on population size. This can result in students who genuinely need support not receiving appropriate services.

3. Underrepresentation due to exclusion relates to another important group of students that is underreported as learning within inclusive general education programs in our K–12 educational systems. This population of students is thought of as the "1 percent" of students with low-incidence disabilities, and they are most often segregated from their general education peers in restrictive special education settings.

4. Causes: disproportionality can result from various factors, including biases in assessment and referral processes, cultural misunderstandings, limited access to quality educational resources and opportuni-

ies creating a gap in learning and opportunity. For example, students who are impacted by the challenges inherent to living in poverty may not have attended preschool or had educational opportunities that would support their readiness for kindergarten, which can start a negative achievement cycle starting with eligibility for special education services in elementary school.

5. Legal implications: disproportionality raises legal and ethical concerns related to civil rights and equal educational opportunities. It may violate laws such as the Individuals with Disabilities Education Act (IDEA) and Title VI of the Civil Rights Act of 1964, which prohibit discrimination in education.

6. Multiple states have comprehensive efforts to address disproportionality underway. Within these efforts, schools and districts are encouraged to implement strategies and policies to identify and reverse the disproportionality of some student groups being overrepresented and underrepresented in school districts/systems. This includes revising assessment practices, providing culturally responsive education, promoting increased inclusion, and ensuring that students are evaluated for special education services in a fair and unbiased manner.

Bias, disproportionality, and fair/unbiased evaluation systems can feel like an overwhelming concept when thinking about all the issues we are currently facing in special education programs across the United States. In this Guidebook, I will propose two strategies to help you consider how you can reflect on your own bias, and then outline another strategy that can be used to support a teaching team when working toward school-wide issues of overrepresentation or underrepresentation in special education programs.

In Section V, "Resources," of this Guidebook, you will find a self-reflection guide that can support your journey in unpacking and "talking back" to your bias (see "Bias Self-Reflection Guide," resource 8). Try out this strategy and reflect with one another on how it went.

STOP & JOT

- Which implicit bias test did you complete? Why did you choose this one?
- How did you reflect on it using an arts-based approach? Please note, our reason for using arts-based exploration is because it encourages different ways of thinking and reflecting, which can be especially helpful when confronting emotionally charged ideas.

112　Section II

- Did you create any goals around an unconscious bias you recognized in your own thinking? What are your ideas for talking back to your bias so you support your students in different ways?

The Ladder of Inference (Argyris, 1982), represented in figure 12, can help support productive discussions related to student success and goal progress across school-based special education teams. The ladder metaphor can help teams consider the data being used to make eligibility determinations for special education. Discussions can branch into thinking about instruction, inclusion, student "mattering" or "othering" within the school culture, assessment, program access, and so on. See questions below to reflect upon individually or together in your mentoring partnership. An additional copy of this Ladder of Inference concept map is included in the "Resources" section of this Guidebook.

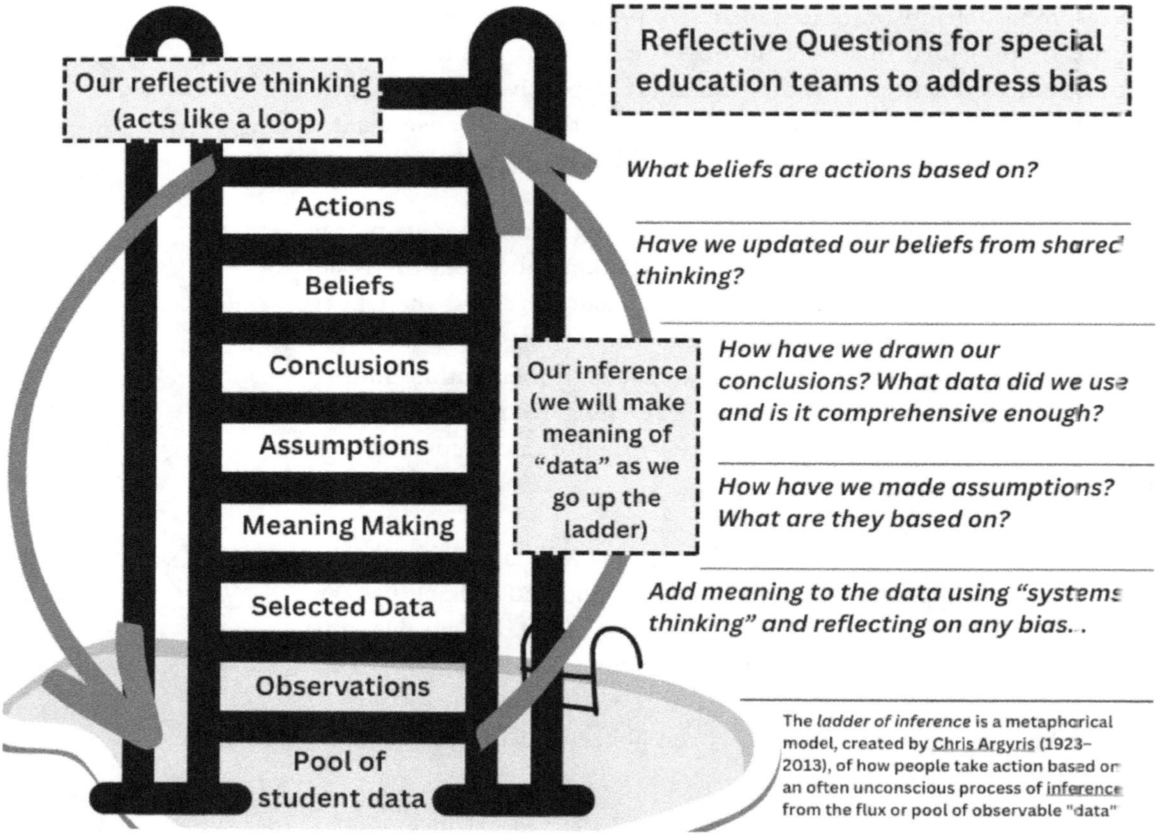

Figure 12. The Ladder of Inference

This figure depicts a visual of the Ladder of Inference, originally created by Argyris (1982) to help teams consider the assumptions that may be affecting their thinking and planning for students.

1. The *Ladder of Inference* suggests that when presented with a range of information/data/facts, we select what fits with a belief we already hold about that situation. Consider these suggestions as they relate to your students: What information/data/facts are "fitting" our belief? What information/data/facts are you wondering about?

2. The *Ladder of Inference* suggests that this dynamic can lead to instances where other information is being ignored. Could this be happening with a student(s) on your caseload? Are there other factors that might be contributing to the negative outcomes? In other words, are there outside factors leading to this outcome, or does your student not feel a sense of "belonging" or "mattering" in their classroom environment, which is contributing to lowered outcomes?

3. The *Ladder of Inference* warns us that our beliefs become stronger based on that good decision we have made (a feedback loop). Could there be instances where we have made a decision related to a student that could have been seen from another perspective or had other outcomes?

4. Consider your progress monitoring methods that are included in your evaluation procedures and how you implement interventions to support student learning and growth. What are they? How are they going? How can those methods be improved as you consider our beliefs becoming stronger based on the good decisions that have been made related to a student's educational program?

Using Systems Thinking to Interrupt Bias and Disproportionality in Special Education

KEY IDEAS

When we use a systems thinking approach, we can review student situations from a wider perspective to understand the challenges resulting in the lack of student success. This approach encourages us to consider bias, attitudes, and other system-related challenges that might impact student success. These could be a lack of resources or educational opportunities in and outside of school having a negative impact on student learning. We can then ask better questions, such as, how can the issue of lack of resources be addressed or what other services can be implemented to support the wider issues a student is experiencing in and outside of school?

WELL-BEING

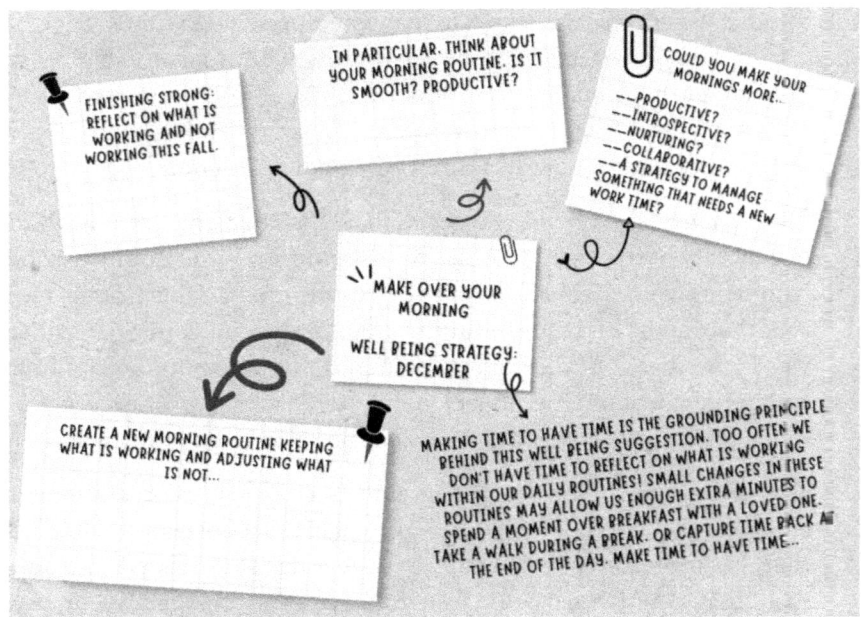

December Plan for Well-Being

For December, you are making over your morning! This tip to "make over your morning" is a great place to become "unstuck." Are you finding you don't have enough time to collect your thoughts? Do you need some peace in your day or an extra moment for self-care? Making over your morning could provide some time for you or could be a way to destress at a time of the day that has become unruly. I hope this recommendation works some magic for you!

Share your well-being goal each month with one another to support making it happen!

COLLABORATE ON

Using the templates provided for December, "Collaborate On" for a reflective discussion on ways that bias can impact our work as special education teachers and share any goals you created to support your growth in this area.

SUGGESTED RESOURCES

After reflecting on your unconscious bias, you may wonder what ways you can expand your thinking related to teaching and intervening that will create more "belonging" and "mattering" for the students most vulnerable to being overrepresented in special education—that is, how you can work toward reversing these negative loops of overrepresentation. Some resources are recommended below. This is by no means an exhaustive list, but it is a great way to start.

1. **Become active in cultivating Black voices in your teaching**: visit the achievethecore.org website and review the article "A Stroke of Genius," which digs into Gholdy Muhammad's, PhD, Cultivating Black Genius' Historically Responsive Literacy (HRL) framework.

2. **Advocate for disability social justice**: add Alice Wong's podcast of first-person stories from the twenty-first century, *Disability Visibility*, https://disabilityvisibilityproject.com/podcast-2/.

3. **Include best practices** by using the "Your Students, My Students, Our Students" guide on how you can *Rethink Equitable and Inclusive Classrooms* (Jung et al., 2019).

4. **Lead anti-racism and culturally responsive efforts** in your school district/system using *The Antiracist Roadmap to Educational Equity: A Systemwide Approach for All Stakeholders* (Williams & Elliott, 2023).[add one line to list]

5. ***Do the Work!*** Check out the *Antiracist Activity Book* written by W. Kamau Bell and Kate Schatz and take time to do the work so you can support, advocate, and lead anti-racism efforts in your program and school districts/systems.

Argyris, C. (1982). The executive mind and double-loop learning. *Organizational Dynamics, 11*(2), 5–22.

Bell, W. K., & Schatz, K. (2022). *Do the work!: An antiracist activity book.* Workman Publishing.

Billingsley, B., & Bettini, E. (2019). Special education teacher attrition and retention: A review of the literature. *Review of Educational Research, 89*(5), 697–744.

Birdsong, M. (2015). *The story we tell about poverty isn't true.* https://www.ted.com/talks/mia_birdsong.

Bruner, J. S. (1971). The process of education revisited. *The Phi Delta Kappan, 53*(1), 18–21.

Cruz, R. A., & Rodl, J. E. (2018). An integrative synthesis of literature on disproportionality in special education. *Journal of Special Education, 52*(1), 50–63.

Duncan-Andrade, J. M. R. (2022). *Equality or equity: Toward a model of community-responsive education.* Harvard Education Press.

Hart, C., & Lindsay, C. (2024). Teacher-student race match and identification for discretionary educational services. *American Educational Research Journal.* Prepublished March 6, 2024. https://doi.org/10.3102/00028312241229413.

Jung, L. A., Frey, N., Fisher, D., & Kroener, J. (2019). *Your students, my students, our students: Rethinking equitable and inclusive classrooms.* Association for Supervision and Curriculum Development (ASCD).

Muhammad, G. (2020). *Cultivating genius: An equity framework for culturally and historically responsive literacy.* Scholastic Incorporated.

Muhammad, G., Martinez, L., Baylis, L., Aguilar, E., & Eakins, S. L. (2023). *Unearthing joy: A guide to culturally and historically responsive curriculum and instruction.* Scholastic Inc.

National Center for Educational Statistics. (n.d.). Digest of educational statistics. https://nces.ed.gov/fastfacts/display.asp?id=64.

Parekh, G. (2023). *Ableism in education: Rethinking school practices and policies.* Routledge.
PEW Research. (2023, July 24). What federal education data shows about students with disabilities in the US. https://www.pewresearch.org/short-reads/2023/07/24/what-federal-education-data-shows-about-students-with-disabilities-in-the-us/.
Reynolds, C. R., Altmann, R. A., & Allen, D. N. (2021). The problem of bias in psychological assessment. In C. R. Reynolds, R. A. Altmann, & D. N. Allen, *Mastering modern psychological testing: Theory and methods* (pp. 573–613). Springer International Publishing.
Starck, J. G., Riddle, T., Sinclair, S., & Warikoo, N. (2020). Teachers are people too: Examining the racial bias of teachers compared to other American adults. *Educational Researcher*, 49(4), 273–284.
Tatum, B. D. (2003). *Why are all the Black kids sitting together in the cafeteria? The meaning of difference: American constructions of race, class, gender, social class and sexual orientation,* 213–223. Basic Books.
Timberlake, M. (2020). Recognizing ableism in educational initiatives: Reading between the lines. *Research in Educational Policy and Management*, 2(1), 84–100. https://doi.org/10.46303/repam.02.01.5.
Thorpe, H. (2017). *The newcomers: Finding refuge, friendship, and hope in an American classroom.* Simon & Schuster.
Williams, A., & Elliott, B. (2023). *The antiracist roadmap to educational equity: A system-wide approach for all stakeholders.* ASCD.

Internet Resources

Play Spent (poverty simulator): https://playspent.org/.
The Opportunity Atlas: https://opportunityatlas.org/.
Western Education Equity Assistance Center: https://weeac.wested.org/.

January

Teamwork Makes the Dream Work

How can special educators effectively communicate and collaborate with their teaching team, paraprofessionals, and related service professionals in a special education setting to ensure that students with disabilities receive the support they need to reach their full potential?

Meet Sophie, a special education teacher who has just started working at a middle school as the caseload manager for twenty-five students spanning sixth to eighth grades. She is excited to collaborate with her teaching team, paraprofessionals, and related service professionals since she knows that her students will be more successful if they work as a team. However, Sophie quickly realizes that effective communication and collaboration can be challenging due to differences in schedules, attitudes, workload, and expertise.

To enhance collaboration, Sophie decides to organize a bimonthly before-school meeting to discuss a plan for providing accommodations and modifications for her caseload students. She invites all teaching team members, related service professionals, and paraprofessionals to the meeting after ensuring the timing of the meeting is workable with team member schedules. During the meeting, some team members disagree on the best approach for providing support for the various students, and others voice concerns about their workload because they believe that some of the ideas that have been posed will lead to "extra work" for them. Also, they think particular students will not respond well to the new changes adding to their reluctance to get on board. Some team members are noticeably vocal about two students in particular that happen to be students of color and have significant behaviors that require a comprehensive set of behavior plan procedures—if this happens, then try this, or conversely, in this context, try this strategy. Related to these two students, the positive behavior redirections are only used by some team members while other team members don't see them as effective and instead insist that firm consequences such as missing out on a fun activity or being pulled from their elective class will work best because they will lead students to know that they will have a consequence for misbehavior. Another caseload student with Down syndrome requires executive functioning structures within general education inclusion classes to support grade level academic achievement. These structures are critical to support transitions and daily "checklists" that some teaching team members believe are not worth the effort because the student will sometimes refuse to check her tasks off the checklists. Sophie is troubled by these approaches to students' individualized learning needs since they seem to be grounded in philosophical disagreements between the adults as opposed to being in the best interest of the students. Sophie feels that the inconsistency in program support has led to an increase in behavioral incidents for the two students who require behavioral redirection. It has come to her attention that it is due to punitive discipline administered by two specific team members when incidents occur. Considering this decline in success for these two students, Sophie realizes that effective collaboration not only requires strong communication skills but also strong leadership skills aligned with student Individualized Education Plan (IEP) goals and accommodations.

To address the central conflict, Sophie needs to find a way to ensure that all team members have a voice and contribute to the decision-making process while still keeping the team moving forward in her caseload management leadership role. She decides to use a consensus-building process to come to agreement on how to support IEP accommodations, behavior supports, and, when needed, modification plans for her caseload students. The consensus-building process requires all team members to contribute information and ideas, listen actively to the views of others, and work together to reach agreement on IEP implementation ideas.

 STOP & JOT

Case questions:

- How can Sophie ensure that all teaching team members, paraprofessionals, and related service professionals have the opportunity to voice their concerns and contribute to the decision-making process in these meetings? Can Sophie create the type of team environment where all members feel comfortable and valued even when there are disagreements about an approach with a student?
- How can Sophie demonstrate strong leadership skills to guide the decision-making process while ensuring all team members feel

valued and heard? For example, should Sophie prioritize the use of collaborative tools like a shared online document or use visual aids to help make complex ideas related to IEP processes such as a positive behavior plan more accessible?

- How can Sophie manage conflicting viewpoints and ideas among her teaching team, paraprofessionals, and related service professionals to ensure that the team stays on track to meet student needs? For example, should Sophie confront issues of bias toward students? Should Sophie address these types of statements directly, such as the belief that there is no point in providing positive support to student XYZ because they will keep misbehaving in class no matter what is tried because that student is just a troublemaker?

Key Learning Goals

1. Identify the roles and responsibilities of teaching teams, paraprofessionals, and related service professionals in a collaborative team.

2. Summarize the characteristics of effective collaboration and co-teaching in a special education setting, including strong communication, trust, and respect among team members.

3. Create a collaborative team professional development plan that promotes the use of Universal Design for Learning (UDL) principles and effective co-planning strategies.

PART I: WORKING WITH YOUR RELATED SERVICE SPECIAL EDUCATION TEAMS

GOING DEEPER

Collaboration is the name of the game in special education. As discussed earlier in this Guidebook, collaborative work can be thought of as one-third of your job as a special education teacher. For this month's "Going Deeper," we will discuss ways to approach collaborative work—that is, best practices for working on a team and developing team norms, unique aspects of special education teams, and, finally, co-teaching configurations.

Developing core beliefs about students' learning and inclusion can be useful to frame the work of teaching teams. Some common core beliefs in special education teaming include a strong belief in the ability of students to be successful, valuing the contributions of all team members, shared leadership, the belief that collaboration is critical to student and team success, and a commitment to the idea that care for each other and students is important for team well-being.

Section II

Special Education Mentoring
MONTHLY CHECKLIST: JANUARY

TO DO...	DONE	NOTES
Observe another LRE or feeder school program		
Review assessment plans for spring and any accommodations needed for caseload students		
Review Annual IEP calendar, what is coming up for spring?		
Deep dive into paraprofessional support and working across special and general education teams. Teams have likely been discussed, but now address concerns and enhance these teams.		
Review collaboration with teaching teams and related service professionals		
Train on a new evaluation protocol and discuss learning from December's dive into bias related to evaluation procedures.		
Shadow another evaluation procedure that has not been reviewed yet, i.e. initial, reevaluation, student with multiple disabilities		
If not already, schedule a fourth/final intensive intervention lesson shadow/observation		

OTHER CHECKLIST ITEMS UNIQUE TO YOUR SCHOOL DISTRICT

_____

_____

_____

SPECIAL EDUCATION FOCUS

To support your goal setting, this section is meant for you to jot down one focus area/question in each of your primary roles.

☐ IEP: _____

ALSO FOR THIS MONTH

☐ Intensive Intervention: _____

☐ Well-Being Goal

☐ Collaborate on Mentoring Activities

☐ Collaboration: _____

☐ Suggested Resources: follow up?

Note that anything italicized in the checklist is referring to a template in the back of this guidebook.

January Monthly Checklist

This checklist provides a roadmap for mentor discussions and timely special education roles and responsibilities typically occurring around this time of the year. There are spaces to add your own checklist items and goals within the three primary roles and responsibilities of special education professionals related to IEP caseload management, collaboration, and teaching specifically designed instruction also referred to as intensive interventions.

The special education educator can act as a (1) coordinator, (2) organizer, (3) leader, (4) consensus builder, (5) advocate, (6) manager, (7) counselor, and more! This also might mean wearing lots of hats in meetings and collaboration. These hats could be:

- supportive roles—where special educators are "communicators and empathetic listeners";
- facilitative roles—where special educators are "leaders and empowerers";
- informative roles—where special educators are "sharers and collaborators"; or
- prescriptive roles—where special educators are "action planners."

When considering these roles and responsibilities, it is important to be aware of the roles of your related service team members. You have likely become familiar with related service team members already, and the "Going Deeper" reflections in this section will provide you with an opportunity to discuss how to collaborate more effectively with team members now that you are six months into your year. In special education, related service team members are professionals who provide specialized support services to students with disabilities to help them access and benefit from their educational program. These services are typically outlined in a student's IEP and are addressed by the team member with specific expertise. Descriptions of related services are included below.

1. **Speech-language pathologist (SLP)**: They work with students who have communication disorders, speech impediments, swallowing challenges or related medical considerations, or language delays to improve their speech and language skills. They can work in medical, school, and rehabilitation settings.

2. **Speech-language pathologist assistant (SLP-A)**: They work under the supervision of an SLP, see above.

3. **Occupational therapist (OT)**: OTs help students develop fine motor skills, sensory processing, and self-care abilities to participate more effectively in educational activities. OTs can oftentimes support areas of executive functioning as they relate to activities of daily living/life (ADLs).

4. **Physical therapist (PT)**: PTs assist students who have physical disabilities or mobility challenges in improving their physical abilities and access to the educational environment and ADLs.

5. **School psychologist**: They conduct assessments, provide counseling, and support students' social-emotional and behavioral needs, helping to create a positive learning environment.

6. **Educational diagnostician**: Ed diagnosticians are not licensed in all states, but many states employ Ed diagnosticians, and they conduct assessments and other eligibility procedures and paperwork.

7. **Specialized instructional support personnel or behavior specialist** (special education teachers or coaches sometimes called "TOSA" or "teacher on special contract"): These professionals may include behavior specialists, adaptive physical education teachers, or other specialists who provide individualized support based on students' unique needs; they can include applied behavior analysts (ABA specialists).

8. **Audiologist**: Audiologists work with students who have hearing impairments or hearing-related issues, ensuring that they have access to appropriate hearing devices and support.

9. **Certified orientation and mobility specialist (COMS)**: They work with students who are blind or visually impaired, teaching them skills for safe and independent mobility in their surroundings, which can include cane skills, working with guide dogs, human guides, and other environmental navigational supports.

10. **Certified teacher of students with visual impairments (TSVI)**: They work with students who are blind or visually impaired, teaching them skills related to academic learning, accommodations, braille, and the like. The field of visual impairment includes the Expanded Core Curriculum (ECC), which includes a comprehensive set of adaptive learning competencies related to needs unique to students with sensory impairments.

11. **Deafblind specialist**: Some states will have deafblind specialists who work with students who have dual sensory impairments of hearing and visual impairments or there will be multiple specialists working on the team who are TSVIs, COMS, and teachers who work with students who are deaf or hard of hearing.

12. **Sign language interpreters**: These professionals assist students who are deaf or hard of hearing by providing sign language interpretation services to facilitate communication.

13. **Counselors and social workers**: They provide emotional and behavioral support to students, helping them manage social challenges and emotional well-being.

14. **Assistive technology (AT) specialist**: These specialists assist students in using assistive technologies, both high and low tech,

and devices that aid in communication, access to curriculum, and achieving independence.

15. **Augmentative alternative communication (AAC) specialist**: These specialists are typically SLPs with added assistive technology professional background or have specialized skills in working with AAC.

16. **Transition specialist**: School districts with separate transition programs may employ transition specialists who provide supported work experiences, as well as comprehensive and coordinated programming for students in eighteen-plus programs.

17. **Nurse**: Dedicated nursing support is becoming more common on K–12 school-based teams to support the medical needs of students served in special education.

18. **Special education directors or special education coordinators**: These professionals typically lead at a district/system level and work with teams to support overarching goals, implementation, and due process issues that arise.

The composition of a related service team may vary depending on the individual needs of each student as outlined in their IEP. These professionals collaborate with special education teachers and other educators to ensure that students with disabilities receive a comprehensive and inclusive education tailored to their specific learning needs, disability areas, and accommodation requirements.

- Is there anyone missing from the related service team list that is on your school or district-based special education team?

- What questions do you have regarding special education case management/leadership? School districts/systems can have varying rules for student caseload team management—that is, depending on the disability that is considered a student's primary disability, a service team member with related experience will often be the lead of the team.

- What are the rules for student IEP team leadership? Have any issues around leadership for collaboration come up? Take a moment to discuss.

- What are the school/system/district systems for collaborating with related service professionals related to IEP actions and when student needs come up, for example, shared collaboration over email, IEP software systems, regular meetings, and so forth.

 **GOING DEEPER**

PART II: WORKING WITH YOUR GENERAL EDUCATION TEAMS AND CO-TEACHING CONFIGURATIONS

It is critical that special education teachers collaborate across their teaching teams to promote inclusion of students served in special education. An ideal configuration promoting collaborative inclusive models is co-teaching. Collaborating in this way takes time and can be challenging even for practiced teams, so rest assured, co-teaching is a long-term goal that ideally grows over time.

What is co-teaching? Co-teaching models are collaborative teaching approaches in which two or more educators work together to plan for and instruct a diverse group of students. These models foster inclusive and differentiated learning environments. They are an ideal way to provide special education services because two teachers, one specializing in content and the other supporting accommodations and differentiation of that content, provide a well-resourced learning environment for students. Figure 13 describes commonly used co-teaching models.

One Teach, One Support/Observe
One teacher has primary instructional responsibility, while the other gathers specific observational information on students or the instructing teacher. The key to this strategy is to focus on what is being observed.

One Teach, One Assist
One teacher has primary instructional responsibility, while the other assists students with work, monitors behaviors, or corrects assignments. The teacher's assistance can help support differentiation and scaffolding while circulating in the classroom.

Station Teaching
The co-teaching pair divides the instructional content into parts. Each teacher instructs one of the groups, and groups then rotate or spend a designated amount of time at each station. Often, an additional station where students can work independently will be used along with the teacher-led stations.

In visual representations:
Teacher= T & Student = S

Parallel Teaching
Each teacher instructs half of the students. The two teachers address the same instructional material using the same teaching strategies. A benefit of this approach is the reduction of the student-to-teacher ratio.

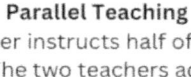

Supplemental Teaching
This strategy allows one teacher to work with students at the expected grade level while the other teacher works with students who need the information or materials re-taught, extended, or remediated in some way.

Team Teaching
Well-planned, team-taught lessons exhibit an invisible instructional flow with no prescribed division of authority. Using a team teaching strategy, both teachers are actively involved in the lesson. From the student's perspective, there is not a clearly defined leader as both teachers share the instruction, are free to interject information, and are available to assist students and answer questions.

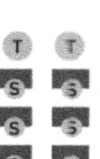

Figure 13. Co-Teaching Configurations

This figure shows the six primary co-teaching configurations and descriptions for each unique to inclusive special education programs.

Best Practices in Co-Teaching on Inclusive General Education Teaching Teams

Keep in mind that simply placing students within general education settings does not constitute *specialized instruction*, so it is critical to collaborate across our general education teaching teams to: (1) co-instruct, (2) co-plan, and (3) co-assess (Murawski, 2010). This Guidebook includes some broad suggestions in each category that only scratch the surface of best practices of co-teaching. To keep growing your learning of co-teaching, draw upon the selected resources shared this month. If we enlisted a metaphor when thinking of co-teaching it would be the "marathon" not the "sprint," when it comes to building that collaborative partnership. This means creating co-teaching configurations and strong relationships will take time and will be iterative as you revise and recharge those partnerships each year. Some dos and don'ts are outlined below to get you started!

Co-Teaching: Dos and Don'ts

- Do: Make time for planning and collaboration.
- Don't: Distinguish between students—that is, using the language of your students (or worse yet, "IEP students") and my students (general education students) negatively impacts the classroom culture and co-teaching relationship.

    1. *Co-Plan: Dos and Don'ts*
        - Do: Be consistent and find a weekly planning time that will work for both of you, even if you plan over digital communication each week in order to collaborate and keep open lines of communication.
        - Don't: Complain about the issues related to time for planning and collaboration, advocate for what you need to your administrator and present a plan that will work.

    2. *Co-Instruct: Dos and Don'ts*
        - Do: Support continuous improvement for students and your instructional planning using data-based decision-making and a scaffolded approach to instruction (i.e., break complex content into smaller sections).
        - Don't: Create a division between the two teaching professionals instead of consistently working collaboratively to instruct students.

3. *Co-Assess: Dos and Don'ts*
    - Do: Progress monitor students frequently and review data continuously to make adjustments to instruction—rule of thumb is progress monitoring a minimum of every ten days of instruction.
    - Don't: Rely on high-stakes or infrequent assessment to evaluate student progress. (*Dos and Don'ts* adapted from Murawski & Scott, 2017)

In your mentoring partnership, brainstorm some co-teaching ideas for the scenario presented below.

Rashad, a student with a hearing impairment, uses ASL (American Sign Language) and benefits from technology supports such as live closed captioning and other learning supports that provide guidance on assignments such as visual checklists, content broken down into smaller chunks, and other executive functioning supports. The special education team discussed that these supports could actually benefit the majority of the students in the English class with other learning needs, many of whom are also served in special education programs. Rashad's special education caseload manager, Lauren, is optimistic about these AT supports promoting an inclusive learning opportunity for all learners, regardless of disability or barrier. Lauren already pushes into the English class along with a sign language interpreter, but she primarily supports Rashad each day by paying attention to the lesson and differentiating where she can on the fly. In an effort to make this push-in support better, she proposes teaching the next unit using a co-teaching model and wants to make a plan with her mentor to pitch this to the English teacher. Create a three-sentence "elevator pitch" introducing the idea, and list two to three ways that Lauren can work collaboratively with the English teacher to plan for and implement co-teaching best practices.

TEAMWORK MAKES THE DREAM WORK!

We cannot work inside a vacuum as special education caseload managers. We must work collaboratively with our teaching and related service providers in order to cultivate student and program success. It is critical that beneficial strategies for students are widely shared across teams and progress monitored continuously by multiple team members broadening the feedback on what is working for a student. For instance, AT tools that are working well for a student must be shared with the teaching team and home, ideally, and any training needed to have that critical learning support implemented across the school day and beyond.

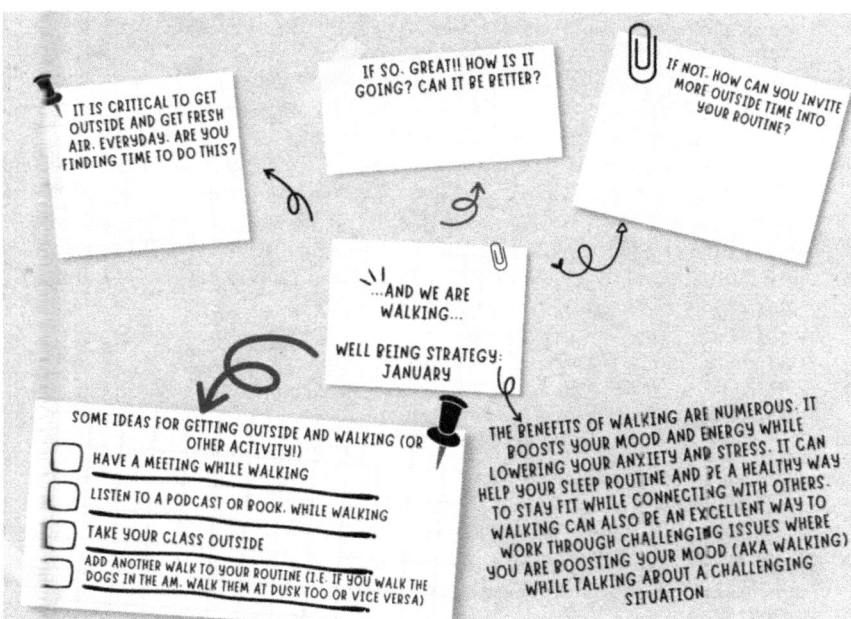

January Plan for Well-Being

For January, you are encouraged to get outside, weather permitting, and go for a walk. Consider meeting with teaching team members while walking during part of your lunch or during a collaborative planning session. The key is to invite more movement into your day, which will support both your well-being and physical health.

Share your well-being goal with one another each month to support making it happen!

Revisit Observations, Evaluation Shadowing, and Visiting Other LREs

In the monthly checklists, there are suggestions around observing one another as a way to grow your teaching. Ideally, three to four non-evaluative observations are beneficial for new special education teachers so mentors can brainstorm student-specific solutions, intensify interventions, and learn new instructional methods. These same benefits can be found when new special education teachers observe other programs, mentor teachers, and shadow evaluations. One resource in particular can provide a helpful collaborative activity related to these observation activities. Reviewing the National Center for Intensifying Interventions (NCII) taxonomy of intervention intensity tools and resources could be a great activity to determine where to add more intensity in a student intervention. Review the categories of intensifying interventions: strength, dosage, alignment, attention to transfer, comprehensiveness, behavior supports, and individualization. See resources here: https://intensiveintervention.org/.

SUGGESTED RESOURCES

Bateman, D., & Cline, J. L. (2016). *A teacher's guide to special education*. Association for Supervision and Curriculum Development (ASCD).

Causton, J., & Kluth, P. (2016). *Thirty days to the co-taught classroom: How to create an amazing, nearly miraculous and frankly earth-shattering partnership in one month or less*. CreateSpace Independent Publishing Platform.

Frank, C. L. (2020). Collaboration and co-teaching. Essentials of special education: What educators need to know. In C. Frank & S. Richards (Eds.), *Essentials of special education: What educators need to know* (pp. 124–139). Routledge.

Friend, M., Cook, L., Hurley-Chamberlain, D., & Shamberger, C. (2010). Co-teaching: An illustration of the complexity of collaboration in special education. *Journal of Educational and Psychological Consultation*, *20*(1), 9–27.

Friend, M. (n.d.) *Collaborating with colleagues and co-teaching like a pro (Webinar)*. Council of Exceptional Children.

Fuchs, L. S., Fuchs, D., & Malone A. S. (2017). The taxonomy of intervention intensity. *Teaching Exceptional Children*, *50*(1), 35–43.

Hentz, S. M., & Jones, P. M. (2011). *Collaborate smart: Practical strategies and tools for educators*. Council for Exceptional Children.

Murawski, W. W., & Kramer, A. (2017). Beyond just "playing nicely." In W. W. Murawski & K. Scott (Eds.), *What works with exceptional learners*. Corwin Press.

Murawski, W. W. (2010). *Collaborative teaching in elementary schools: Making the co-teaching marriage work!* Corwin Press.

Ntim, E. K., Vanderpuye, I., Kpodeo, I. A., Assie, R. A., & Derkye, C. (2021). Expanded core curriculum and academic achievement of students with visual impairment. *Advances in Social Sciences Research Journal*, *8*(6).

Scruggs, T. E., & Mastropieri, M. A. (2017). Making inclusion work with co-teaching. *Teaching Exceptional Children*, *49*(4), 284–293.

Internet Resources

Friend, M., Collaboration for Educators: https://coteach.com/.
National Center for Intensifying Intervention: https://intensiveintervention.org/.
California State University Northridge (CSUN) Center for Teaching and Learning: https://www.csun.edu/center-teaching-learning/about.

Section III
Digging out of Disillusionment

You may feel more confident in your three primary roles as a new special education teacher at this point of the year. Recall, the primary roles are collaborator, intensive intervention, and Individualized Education Plan (IEP) caseload manager, and as you settle into the spring semester, these may feel much more straightforward than they did in the fall. For instance, some IEP procedures may seem routine, while others may still seem new. Many individualized student interventions are starting to feel more fruitful as relationships feel more solid with your caseload students, and you know who to ask and where to go when issues arise that need a team effort. Finally, the collaborative relationships with your caseload student parents, teaching team members, and leadership may feel more familiar as you have gotten over the hump of constantly feeling "new to the building." Now, fellow teachers know you in the hallway, and you feel more comfortable bringing up issues that are a concern for the teaching team with possible strategies to share.

All in all, things are better! In many ways, you might be feeling better! But you might also be feeling a bit overwhelmed at the same time. Why does this happen? Possible reasons are both inside and outside of school. This time of year can bring weather-related slumps to our mood. Also, you may be facing stress related to activities after the holiday break that brought rest or a lack of rest; another factor could be uncertainty regarding workload and student challenges in the spring semester. I want to assure you that if you are feeling this way, it is a commonly shared sentiment, and this time of year can commonly bring feelings of disillusionment. If you are feeling particularly low, I recommend enlisting all the well-being strategies from the fall semester and taking a few moments to review the well-being strategies for this month to help ground you.

The next three months in Section III of this Guidebook will hopefully also feel grounding to you. They are all about "why" you may have chosen to work as a special education professional, which is different for each person who chooses a career in special education. While at the same time, there are likely commonalities across all of us regarding why we do what we do. Sometimes these are related to past experiences we may have had in our K–12 experience, where a particular teacher or program made a difference for us, or a family member has inspired us to follow this path, or a passion for social justice and equity for all students drives our passion to be a changemaker in special education.

Consider Your "Why?"

Why have you chosen to be a special education professional? In February, we will consider our "why" related to special education advocacy and develop an understanding of anti-ableism frameworks that encourage us to continue to advocate for more accessible learning environments; in March, we will learn about determining least restrictive environments (LRE) and special education program frameworks that can provide insights into your inclusive program planning; and in April, we will focus on paraprofessionals and revisit our collaborative focus as an essential feature of working as a special education professional.

Take a moment and reflect on your "why" with one another. What was the driving force behind you choosing to become a special education professional? What keeps you going when you experience challenges in your role? Jot down ideas below and add images, doodles, or drawings to explore your "why," if a creative approach to these questions speaks to you.

February

DISABILITY JUSTICE

CASE STUDIES

How can educators use strengths-based social justice approaches to better support students with disabilities in their academic and social-emotional learning?

Meet Latifa, a high school teacher with a social justice passion for teaching students with disabilities and working as a special education advocate. Latifa's experience has shown that too often students with disabilities are marginalized and excluded from the mainstream academic and social activities of their peers. While Latifa is committed to offering high-quality instruction and support, she recognizes the importance of utilizing positive and empowering approaches that focus on students' strengths and interests rather than their challenges. She has become interested in enlisting more Universal Design for Learning (UDL) practices throughout her inclusive program in order to plan backward for student variability. She has been inspired to imagine an educational environment that capitalizes on student diversity rather than seeing differences as deficits or things that need to be fixed. Latifa is also sensitive to the legal and ethical frameworks that have paved the way for more inclusive, person-first environments. She is particularly interested in better understanding how ableism is discriminatory and how she can infuse a social justice framework of anti-ableism into her special education program. She attended a conference last summer and learned that ableism includes both unconscious bias and overt discrimination against people with disabilities, seeing them as incapable of academic success. She wants to create an inclusive culture that is anti-ableist by identifying barriers, treating her students equitably, and advocating for better accessibility and opportunities for students served in her program and across the school.

As a result of her commitment to strengths-based approaches, Latifa has developed an inclusive and innovative program that promotes student success and engagement. Latifa understands that strengths-based approaches improve self-efficacy, a sense of belonging, and the ability to contribute to one's community. She ensures a variety of learning materials and activities are available that consider the needs of students with different learning abilities and other disabilities that require environmental accessibility and adaptations.

Latifa is also faced with supporting a new student, Jet, who has a diagnosis of autism and difficulties socializing. Jet has faced many challenges in the past and occasionally has severe outbursts in class requiring intensive positive behavior supports. Latifa must identify the best way to support Jet to promote his social and academic success. Latifa has learned that technology supports can make a difference for Jet, and when teachers follow a structure in their daily activities, he feels less anxious which results in a lower chance that he will have an outburst. She has to decide whether to focus on his strengths (such as his exceptional memory) or to develop remediation strategies to improve his areas of challenge (such as social interaction and problematic behavioral outbursts).

Case questions:

- Should Latifa focus on Jet's strengths or work on his challenges; for example, should she organize a pull-out social resource class where Jet practices social scenarios with Latifa? Or another example, should Latifa create opportunities for Jet to utilize his exceptional memory to support his learning, or should she focus on improving Jet's social interaction skills through specific interventions with peer mentors?

- How can Latifa create a collaborative environment on her teaching team that celebrates diversity and promotes inclusiveness?

- What can overarching school-based programs do to ensure that students with disabilities feel empowered and belonging in the general education classroom? How can school-based programs consider ableism issues in their buildings that feel discriminatory to students with disabilities?

Special Education Mentoring
MONTHLY CHECKLIST: FEBRUARY

	TO DO...	DONE	NOTES
	Observe another LRE or feeder school program		
	Review the curriculum adoption process for school district/system and how to make a request for new curriculum materials		
	Collaborate on conducting a behavior-related observation for a student in need of a behavior plan and supports		
	Discuss collaboration with teaching teams and review what is working well and what challenges have emerged around differentiation and accommodations for caseload students		
	Depending on grade level, discuss transition meeting procedures for students served in your program		
	Using the *Co-Teaching Modalities & Guide* collaborate on planning for or coteaching a lesson		
	Shadow another evaluation procedure that has not been reviewed yet, i.e. initial, reevaluation, evaluation for a student with multiple disabilities		
	If not already, schedule a fourth/final intensive intervention lesson shadow/observation		

OTHER CHECKLIST ITEMS UNIQUE TO YOUR SCHOOL DISTRICT

_____

_____

_____

ALSO FOR THIS MONTH

- [ ] Well-Being Goal _____
- [ ] **Collaborate on Mentoring Activities**
- [ ] **Suggested Resources: follow up?**

SPECIAL EDUCATION FOCUS

To support your goal setting, this section is meant for you to jot down one focus area/question in each of your primary roles.

- [ ] IEP: _____

- [ ] Intensive Intervention: _____

- [ ] Collaboration: _____

Note that anything italicized in the checklist is referring to a template in the back of this guidebook.

February Monthly Checklist

This checklist provides a roadmap for mentor discussions and timely special education roles and responsibilities typically occurring around this time of the year. There are spaces to add your own checklist items and goals within the three primary roles and responsibilities of special education professionals related to IEP caseload management, collaboration, and teaching specifically designed instruction also referred to as intensive interventions.

Key Learning Goals

1. Define the key terms associated with dis/crit, ableism/anti-ableism, neurodiversity, neuroplasticity, and disability studies, emphasizing the significance of these concepts as they relate to K–12 special education programs.

2. Understand the impact of societal attitudes and beliefs on the inclusion of individuals with disabilities, focusing on how the social construction of disability impacts policies and practices.

PART I: PERSON-FIRST LANGUAGE AND DISABILITY FRAMEWORKS

What Is Person-First Language?

Using person-first language—for example, referring to "a person with a visual impairment" versus disability-first language such as referring to "a blind person"—is a neutral approach that identifies the person before their disability. Encouraging a student or colleague to advise you on the best language to use is a next step when/if in doubt. For some individuals, person-first language is an important way to ensure that they are identified first as a person and second as a person with a disability. For other individuals, their self-identification within a specific disability culture is a meaningful counterpoint to societal stigmatization of disability. Additionally, written language related to "disability" can also reflect the intention of the information being shared. Using "dis/ability" or "disABILITY" is meant to deemphasize the deficit-based language used to describe disabilities with the goal of emphasizing abilities/strengths.

Disability Frameworks

Let's take a closer look at some overarching frameworks that guide our special education programs and practices. Our special education K–12 school systems/districts can have more or less restrictive programs—that is, they might have separate special education classrooms and programs versus completely inclusive special education programs where there are no separate classrooms in a school building. In this month's "Going Deeper," we will review current frameworks that can guide special education programs. Many special education teacher preparation programs may not include coursework related to disability studies, which may be partly due to K–12 being a system of "entitlement" where all students are entitled to a free and appropriate public education (FAPE). In contrast, disability studies considers the larger context of disability in society from a wide range of perspectives. After students graduate from K–12 public schools in the United States, postsecondary and adult services are advocacy-based, which means it is up to the person with a disability to advocate for what is needed to access their community, employment, and other activities of daily life.

Let's use a helpful learning tool as you review disability frameworks and strengths-based models. Please take a moment to jot down what you already know about the questions posed on the KWL chart (figure 14) and what you hope to learn about. We have used KWL charts once previously in this Guidebook, and there are innumerable strategies to help recall background knowledge, make predictions, and so on. Other activity resource suggestions are listed at the end of this month.

KWL Chart: Disability Frameworks

K — What do I already know?	W — What do I want to learn?	L — What did I learn?
☐ Person-first language?		
☐ Disability Studies?		
☐ Anti-Ableism?		
☐ Dis/Crit?		
☐ Neurodiversity & neuroplasticity?		

Jot down any notes within columns K & W before getting started with the going deeper reading.

Figure 14. KWL Chart: Disability Frameworks
This chart includes a list of disability frameworks and space to jot down what you already know about the frameworks listed. After reviewing the "Going Deeper" information, take a moment to jot down any key ideas you learned.

Consider common disability models in education (shown in table 3.1) to help frame the discussion of disability frameworks. This section of the Guidebook is combining special education and disability studies schools of thought to provide a more comprehensive context of disability in schools and society.

Table 3.1. Common Disability Models in Educational Environments

	Medical Model	**Social Model**	**Cultural Model**
Focus:	Disability is a deficiency and something that needs to be fixed and considered to be wrong with the person.	Disability is a difference.	Disability is a valuable element of human diversity.
Instructional focus:	Remediation and correcting for deficits.	Accommodation that is inclusion-focused with recommendations for intensive interventions.	Accommodations, inclusive and strengths-building steps, undertaken with the belief that diversity in ideas and thinking is the norm and is advantageous for all students.
Disability is caused by:	A condition someone is either born with or acquires adventitiously and which needs to be fixed or remediated.	A condition that is the result of social and/or environmental factors.	A social construct that is created by societal norms, attitudes, and barriers.

Source: Olkin (2002).

GOING DEEPER

PART II: WHAT ARE DISABILITY STUDIES? (MEDICAL, SOCIAL, AND CULTURAL MODELS)

Disability studies is an interdisciplinary academic field that studies social, cultural, political, and historical aspects of disability and seeks to understand and challenge patterns that are negatively impacting people with disabilities. It aims to promote a more inclusive and equitable society by challenging discrimination, stereotypes, promoting disability rights, and fostering a better understanding of the diverse experiences and needs of individuals with disabilities. It sees disability as "diversity" and a natural part of the human experience. It serves as a platform for advocacy and enhanced policy development to improve the quality of life for people with disabilities. It includes a critical look at accessibility, such as exploring architectural, technological, and communication barriers faced by individuals with disabilities, and it centers on the concept of universal design, which aims to create products, environments, and systems that are accessible to all. Disability studies also includes research in health care and disability, with a focus on addressing health care disparities, challenges to accessing health care services, and the intersection of disability issues related to health care ethics, policies, and practices—that is, ensuring consideration of the rights and consent of a person with disabilities in their health care decision-making. Another area of concern is related to employment and disability. People with disabilities are protected under the Americans with Disabilities Act (ADA), and the protections under that law provide a foundation for investigating issues related to employment opportunities, workplace accommodations, and the inclusion of individuals with disabilities in the workforce. Additionally, this research focuses on understanding the challenges specific to independent living and activities of daily life, which can include aging, social and emotional needs, and assistive technology needs and devices.

Example areas of disability advocacy can be seen in how people with disabilities are represented in popular media, for example, a person with a disability playing a character versus someone pretending to have a disability playing that same character. Another example can be found in enhanced policy implementation that creates more access and support for people with disabilities. An excellent example of this work in action is one of the continued trends since the worldwide pandemic of COVID-19 in 2020: since then, workplaces have continued to allow more hybrid and remote working configurations, which has had a particularly positive impact on people with disabilities having more flexibility and autonomy in their workplaces.

WITHIN DISABILITY STUDIES, WHAT ARE THE CURRENT FRAMEWORKS?

Dis/Crit (Cultural Model)

Within disability studies, many frameworks have emerged that are summarized here. "Dis/Crit" is a term that combines "disability" and "critical" and is often used in the context of disability studies; it most often includes a critical look into how disability intersects across multiple groups of students. For instance, there are disproportionate rates of students of color served in special education programs. It seeks to deconstruct and analyze the social, cultural, and political systems within communities and aspects of disability, much like other critical approaches in various fields where a systems approach can be used to understand how each element in a situation impacts the others.

Anti-Ableism (Cultural Model)

Anti-ableism is a social justice movement that seeks to create a more inclusive and equitable society by challenging the assumptions, discrimination, and prejudice that individuals with disabilities face in their communities, workplaces, and schools. It involves recognizing and challenging the systemic and individual biases, attitudes, and practices that discriminate against people with disabilities. It aims to promote the full participation and empowerment of people with disabilities in all aspects of life. Anti-ableism sees societal inaccessibility as the primary barrier in the daily lives of people with disabilities. This view of disability is that it is a natural form of diversity in the human experience, and it is but one identity along with other possible identities such as race, gender, religion, sexuality, socioeconomic status, and more.

Neurodiversity/Neuroplasticity (Social and Cultural Models)

Neurodiversity is a framework in special education that emphasizes that the brain is always growing and changing, for example, by growing dendrites, and disability is just a natural variation in human experience. The neurodiversity framework is also a social movement that views neurological differences as natural differences in the human population rather than something that is wrong with the person and needs to be fixed, as is commonly associated with an approach that views difference in terms of disorders or deficits. It is based on the idea that neurological diversity, including conditions such as autism, attention-deficit/hyperactivity disorder (ADHD), dyslexia, and others, are a valuable and integral part of human diversity. It adopts a social model view of disability, believing that disability is the result of social and environmental factors that should instead be addressed through accommodation and acceptance of disability as diversity. Similarly, neuroplasticity is a concept in brain research that highlights the brain's capacity for change and adaptation throughout an individual's lifespan. It helps explain how we learn and remember information. When we acquire new skills or knowledge, our brain forms new neural connections—dendrites—and it strengthens existing connections, which enhances our ability to recall and apply what we've learned. Neuroplasticity is connected to Hebb's Law (1949), which states that "neurons that fire together wire together." Other components of neuroplasticity include the brain's ability to recover (in some or many ways) after experiencing an injury such as a traumatic brain injury (TBI). Another component is "experience-dependent plasticity," which means that the brain's ability to learn can be enhanced through the proven benefits of many early intervention efforts in special education. Understanding neuroplasticity has led to numerous therapeutic interventions in speech, vision, rehabilitation, physical and occupational therapy, and so on.

Why Should Special Education Teachers Learn about these Disability Frameworks?

Special education teachers can consider the social, cultural, political, and historical aspects of disability in order to better understand the challenges that are negatively impacting people with disabilities. Having an understanding of how your students can advocate for themselves and the communities that can provide support, partnership, and connectedness is an important way to support your students' future success.

Consider the disability models you learned about this month. Which ones were familiar to you? What did you wonder about each and how do they relate to the special education programming in your school building and district/system?

Nothing about Me without Me

Having an understanding of the medical, social, and cultural models in disability studies helps special education teachers consider disability issues, services, supports, and access that will impact students when they graduate from K–12 school systems. Additionally, considering the disability frameworks and advocacy undertaken in our society helps K–12 special educators be more sensitive to the issues and lived experiences that are present for students and their families across their lives.

 **WELL-BEING**

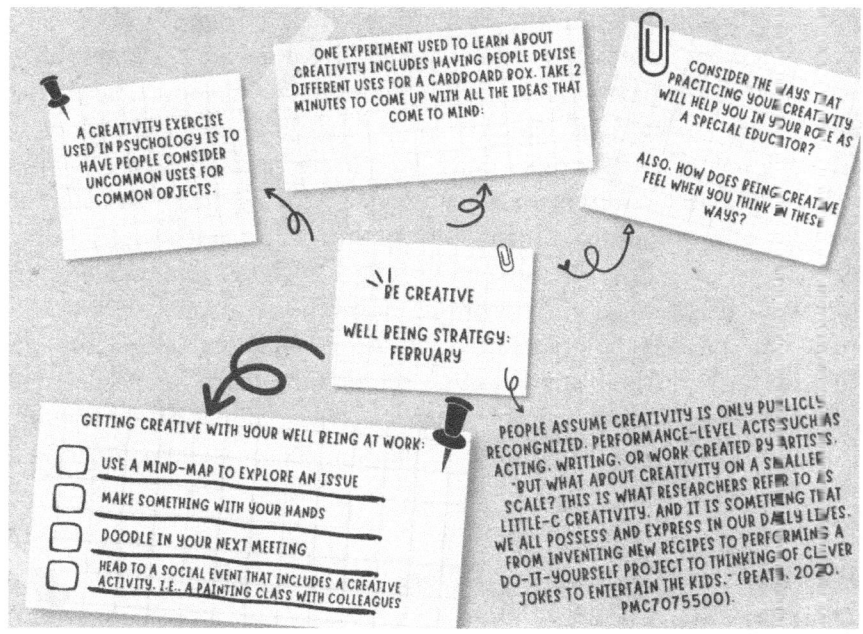

February Plan for Well-Being

For February, enlisting more creativity into your teaching practice has the dual purpose of cultivating your own curiosity and also helps you reimagine student learning. Are there opportunities for more creativity in your teaching practice? Creative representations of information and ways to demonstrate understanding—students can write a paper or create a visual representation of the content—promotes Universal Design for Learning (UDL).

Share your well-being goal each month with one another to support making it happen!

 **COLLABORATE ON**

With your mentor, learn about disability advocates who can serve as models and champions for your students. Using the mantra *nothing about me, without me*, consider the difference of serving students when guided by the approaches of "doing for your student" or "doing with your student." Take a critical look at your program and determine whether you are able to highlight stories of people with disabilities for your students to learn from. Give thought to the curated list of selected voices in disability advocacy below and include those stories that would benefit your students.

1. Judy Heumann was a lifelong advocate for the rights of people with disabilities. She played a key role in the passage of the Americans with Disabilities Act (ADA) and was a global leader in disability rights. https://judithheumann.com/.

2. Haben Girma is a lawyer who is deafblind and an advocate focused on disability rights, accessibility, and inclusion. She is the first deafblind graduate of Harvard Law School. https://habengirma.com/.

3. Alice Wong is a disability activist, writer, and founder of the Disability Visibility Project, which amplifies the voices of people with disabilities. https://disabilityvisibilityproject.com/.

4. Andrew Pulrang is a disability rights advocate and co-founder of the #CripTheVote campaign, which promotes political engagement and disability rights issues. https://disabilitythinking.com/.

5. Rebecca Cokley is a disability rights advocate who has worked on policy and advocacy issues related to disability, civil rights, and social justice. https://www.fordfoundation.org/about/people/rebecca-cokley/.

6. Mia Ives-Rublee is a disability advocate known for her work in disability justice and intersectionality. She has been involved in various disability rights initiatives. https://www.americanprogress.org/people/ives-rublee-mia/.

7. Vilissa Thompson is a social worker and disability rights advocate who is known for her work on issues related to race, disability, and intersectionality. https://www.vilissathompson.com/.

8. Stella Young was a disability advocate, broadcaster, comedian, and writer. In a letter to herself, she noted, "Able-bodiedness is not the Holy Grail. The body that you're in is perfectly fine, perfectly beautiful." https://stellayoung.com.au/.

9. Temple Grandin is an American academic and animal behaviorist. She is a prominent proponent for the humane treatment of livestock for slaughter and the author of more than sixty scientific papers on animal behavior. https://www.templegrandin.com/.

10. Xian Horn is a joyful half-Asian woman with cerebral palsy who serves as a beauty and disability advocate, speaker, educator, *Forbes* contributor, and founder of the nonprofit Give Beauty Wings. https://xianhorn.com/.

SUGGESTED RESOURCES

If you have not already had a chance to review *Your Students, My Students, Our Students*, which has been listed as a resource in the previous months, it would be a great resource to use to continue thinking about the ideas we have been discussing. In chapter 1, see the discussion of challenges regarding students' academic struggles being traditionally seen as a problem with the individual rather than a problem with instruction. To counteract this cycle of underachievement for students, consider using an approach aligned with Universal Design for Learning (UDL) where proactive supports are implemented to support a wide range of student learning needs. Additionally, with UDL the social model of special education would encourage us to consider additional elements of the curriculum and instruction to identify more ways to support student learning.

Beaty, R. E. (2020). *The creative brain*. Cerebrum.
Birdsong, M. (2020). *How we show up: Reclaiming family, friendship, and community*. Hachette UK.
Cordell, A. (2020). The implications of disproportionate individualized education plan classifications in New York City schools. *Columbia Social Work Review, 18*(1), 1–11. https://doi.org/10.7916/cswr.v18i1.5925.
Dewey, J. (2013/1902). *The school and society and the child and the curriculum*. University of Chicago Press.
Dintersmith, T. (2018). *What school could be: Insights and inspiration from teachers across America*. Princeton University Press.
Duncan-Andrade, J. M. (2022). *Equality or equity: Toward a model of community-responsive education*. Harvard Education Press.
Freire, P. (1996). *Pedagogy of the oppressed* (revised edition). Continuum.
Fritzgerald, A. (2020). *Anti-racism and universal design for learning: Building expressways to success*. CAST.
hooks, b. (2014). *Teaching to transgress*. Routledge.
Hoover, J. J., & Patton, J. R. (2017). *IEPs for ELs: And other diverse learners*. Corwin Press.
Kendi, I. X. (2019). *How to be an antiracist*. One World.
Ladau, E. (2021). *Demystifying disability: What to know, what to say, and how to be an ally*. Ten Speed Press.
Olkin, R. (2002). Could you hold the door for me? Including disability in diversity. *Cultural Diversity and Ethnic Minority Psychology, 8*, 130–137.
Rufo, J. M., & Causton, J. (2022). *Reimagining special education: Using inclusion as a framework to build equity and support all students*. Brookes Publishing Company.
Santos, L. (n.d.). *The science of well-being* [MOOC]. Coursera. https://www.coursera.org/learn/the-science-of-well-being.
Thorpe, H. (2017). *The newcomers: Finding refuge, friendship, and hope in an American classroom*. Simon & Schuster.
Vernikoff, L. (2021). *Disabling the school-to-prison pipeline: The relationship between special education and arrest*. Rowman & Littlefield.
Wong, A. (Ed.). (2020). *Disability visibility: First-person stories from the twenty-first century*. Vintage.

Internet Resources

Disability Visibility, podcast and web resource: https://disabilityvisibilityproject.com/.
Classroom protocols for active learning, web resource link: https://curriculum.eleducation.org/sites/default/files/curriculumtools_classroomprotocols_053017.pdf

March

An Inclusive Classroom Requires a Juggling Act

CASE STUDIES

How can a special education teacher ensure that the goals outlined in a student's Individualized Education Program (IEP) are met while balancing the needs of the entire class?

Stacy is a special education teacher who has a student named Tommy in her class. Tommy has attention-deficit/hyperactivity disorder (ADHD) and an emotional disturbance (ED also called, SED), which both require an IEP to ensure he receives the support he needs to succeed emotionally and academically. Stacy must balance the goals outlined in Tommy's IEP with the needs of the other students in the inclusive class she teaches. This requires careful planning and creativity on Stacy's part.

The class is studying a unit on American history, and the students are required to create presentations about a historical figure of their choice. Tommy is interested in Martin Luther King Jr. and has expressed interest in creating a video for his final project. His primary accommodations on his IEP are extra time, executive functioning supports to break projects down into chunks, support around emotional well-being using coping strategies, and taking breaks, as needed, with teacher support. Stacy must ensure that Tommy has the time he needs to complete his final presentation while also ensuring that he doesn't fall behind on other classwork. Tommy loves working on projects but can become hyper focused on a project and be challenged to prioritize and organize his work so he can complete a project by the due date. He also becomes invested in the plan for the project over the criteria—that is, the video production will become the most important aspect and Tommy can become extremely frustrated when a needed technology tool does not work out as planned. Stacy is curious about how to support these executive functioning challenges that Tommy exhibits when trying to organize for lengthier projects. Additionally, Stacy is considering how she can differentiate the project planning to serve multiple students in her class since she knows that organizational support not only benefits Tommy but also most of the students in her class.

In previous projects, when organizational systems had not been put in place, Tommy had requested additional help from Stacy, which also resulted in tension in the class when other students had questions. Stacy must strike a balance between meeting the needs of Tommy, ensuring he understands the content, and making sure that the other students are engaged and are learning. She has some decisions to make and planning to do.

Case questions:

- What long-term planning methods could Stacy teach to support student projects and teach them executive functioning skills? What ways could she enhance those to add some additional support for Tommy knowing he prefers (and can become dependent on) having a teacher sit with him to support his process?
- Should Stacy try another approach, such as using peer tutoring or different teaching methods? How can she ensure that Tommy still receives the necessary support while not neglecting the rest of the class as the project timeline gets more complicated?
- What adaptations could she make to ensure the task is accessible to Tommy and that he is progressing towards the goals outlined in his IEP?

Special Education Mentoring
MONTHLY CHECKLIST: MARCH

TO DO...	DONE	NOTES
Revisit family communication and discuss how it is going for caseload students		
Review *Evaluation Template* and go over any questions that emerged		
Review *Intensify Intervention Taxonomy* and brainstorm an example of how a current intervention curriculum could be intensified		
Review a new method for assessing and progress monitoring a student(s) IEP goal. Outline the procedure for progress monitoring and analyze student data collaboratively		
Learn about task analysis and conduct a task analysis together for an academic task that supports a student on your caseload.		
Check-in on well-being goals: how are they going? Where are you feeling overwhelmed?		
Talk about how to get through a challenging issue related to collaboration whether on the teaching team, a parent, or other team member		
Discuss what evaluation or meetings have not been shadowed yet, make a plan to observe those (annual, evaluation, MTSS, behavior...)		

OTHER CHECKLIST ITEMS UNIQUE TO YOUR SCHOOL DISTRICT

_____

_____

_____

SPECIAL EDUCATION FOCUS

To support your goal setting, this section is meant for you to jot down one focus area/question in each of your primary roles.

☐ IEP: _____

☐ Intensive Intervention: _____

☐ Collaboration: _____

Note that anything italicized in the checklist is referring to a template in the back of this guidebook.

ALSO FOR THIS MONTH

☐ **Well-Being Goal**
☐ **Collaborate on Mentoring Activities**
☐ **Suggested Resources: follow up?**

March Monthly Checklist

This checklist provides a roadmap for mentor discussions and timely special education roles and responsibilities typically occurring around this time of the year. There are spaces to add your own checklist items and goals within the three primary roles and responsibilities of special education professionals related to IEP caseload management, collaboration, and teaching specifically designed instruction also referred to as intensive interventions.

Key Learning Goals

1. Interpret the benefits and challenges of different least restrictive environments (LREs) for students with disabilities in addition to the aspect of teacher considerations in determining the best LRE for student learning needs.

2. Specifically consider the impacts on academic achievement, socialization, self-esteem, and self-determination related to different LREs for students.

3. Weigh the advantages and disadvantages of different curricular and LRE models used in special education, such as resource models, co-teaching, and full inclusion programs, and evaluate their potential for promoting LRE.

4. Consider the impact of strengths-based and UDL-framed approaches in supporting students with disabilities in contrast to deficit-based programs.

PART I: UNDERSTANDING LEAST RESTRICTIVE ENVIRONMENT (LRE) AND SPECIAL EDUCATION PROGRAM MODELS

Special education programming has come a long way from the Education of All Handicapped Children Act in 1975 (Public Law 94-142). Recall that PL 94-142 was the foundational law that led to IDEA, launched in 1990 and then reauthorized in 1997, 2000, and 2004. There have been regulations incorporated into IDEA in 2006, 2008, 2011, 2013, 2015, and 2017. As we discussed previously, many of these were created due to legal cases having been decided by a state or national supreme court that reinterpreted the law. (Learn more at "A History of the Individuals with Disabilities Education Act," US Department of Education.)

Over this first year as a special education professional, you have seen the procedural safeguards outlined in IDEA (2004) firsthand as they are implemented in your program. During this month, we are going to take some time to discuss LRE. Ideally, the most frequently used LRE in your school district is designated as general education. There is overwhelming support for inclusive education settings in the research literature across student disability areas and level of learning needs. (See "Suggested Resources" list of recommendations for inclusive education research.) With that said, having a continuum of services to support a range of LREs is critical since we know that students will have evolving student needs due to developmental, behavioral, emotional, and academic reasons. On your caseload, there are likely students with more intensive needs who need more service minutes, and depending on the level of need, some students may need to spend some or a significant portion of time outside of general education to support their learning needs in a more restrictive environment (i.e., a special education classroom). What is critically important is that we don't decide an LRE and see that determination as a permanent decision to be continued year after year. IDEA mandates that LRE be discussed at every annual IEP meeting. This means that each year, teams should consider how to support student success in less restrictive LREs. Additionally, it is critical that teams weigh the pros and cons of the LRE decision that has been made considering the student learning, social, and behavioral needs.

Special education employs various instructional models and approaches to support the diverse needs of students with disabilities. These models are designed to provide appropriate support, accommodations, and interventions for students to help them succeed academically and develop essential skills for their success in school, life, and independence. Let's review some common models:

- **Inclusion model**: Inclusion means that students with disabilities are served in general education classrooms alongside their typically developing peers. Special education teachers and support staff collaborate with general education teachers to provide necessary accommodations and support within the general education classroom setting.

- **Resource room model**: In this model, students with disabilities spend part of their school day in a separate resource room (i.e., special education) where they receive specialized or specifically designed instruction (i.e., interventions), typically in small groups. They also participate in general education classes with their peers. This model is indicated on the IEP as instruction that is "outside of the general education classroom."

- **Self-contained classroom model**: Many school districts/systems will have programs that serve students with more intensive needs that are considered "self-contained" or "intensive learning needs" programs. Students with more significant disabilities—multiple disabilities—may benefit from a self-contained classroom, where they receive instruction from a special education teacher in a separate classroom setting for some or much of their school day. These programs are also indicated as instruction being done "outside of [the] general education classroom." Unfortunately, it is often this LRE decision that is not revisited enough in annual IEP meetings. It is critical to consider student learning needs and goals and collaborate with the teaching team to determine ways to promote a less restrictive learning environment for students with multiple disabilities.

- **Co-teaching model**: Co-teaching involves a general education teacher and a special education teacher working together in the same classroom. We discussed co-teaching configurations in January, and co-teaching configurations can toggle across those models. Teachers in these models will collaborate to provide differentiated instruction, support, and accommodations to all students, including those with disabilities.

- **Consultation model**: In this model, special education teachers or specialists provide consultation and support to general education teachers. They offer advice, strategies, and resources to help general education teachers meet the needs of students with disabilities in their classrooms. They are primarily working with the teaching team with some specialized support provided to students that is usually one-on-one or small groups. This approach is common for related-service providers who do not require as many service minutes with students.

- **Collaborative team teaching model**: This model emphasizes collaboration among multiple professionals, including special education teachers, speech therapists, occupational therapists, and others, who work together as a team to address students' diverse needs. This model is common within intensive/self-contained classrooms or specialized residential school placements, where special education teachers routinely work with related-services team members on a weekly basis.

- **Response to Intervention (RTI)/ Multiple Tiered Services and Supports (MTSS) Models**: RTI and MTSS are similar models, and they both include multi-tiered approaches to identifying and supporting students with learning difficulties and other academic challenges. They involve early intervention, ongoing assessment, collaboration with a wide support team within school buildings, and the adjustment of instruction based on students' responses to interventions with the goal to improve academic success in a way that leads the student to no longer need an evaluation for inclusion within the special education program.

- **Behavioral or autism-based center-based interventions**: These programs are designed to meet the unique needs of students with autism or significant behavioral needs related to their disability area(s) and meant to be transitional so students receive intensive support with the goal to return to a general education setting when/if possible. They are typically characterized by having increased resources, intensive program supports, generalizable skill practice, supportive socialization, unique specializations in their services (e.g., applied behavior analysis [ABA] therapists, potentially specialized classrooms, and more staffing support, such as lower ratios of students to adults).

- **Transition services model**: For students who are eighteen and older, school districts/systems are required to have transition program support, whether embedded in a high school program or a standalone program. These programs focus on preparing students with disabilities for career, college, and independent living beyond K–12 schooling. IDEA requires postsecondary goals to be included in the IEP by age sixteen, while many school districts include postsecondary goals to be included in the IEP by age fourteen or earlier. Transition programs typically include planning for postsecondary education, employment, independent living, and community participation. They can employ job coaches and other specialized staff to support postsecondary goals.

- **Specialized schools and programs**: In some cases, students with a severe or low-incidence disability, such as a sensory impairment, are eligible to attend a specialized school or program, which are considered to be the most restrictive placement for a student. These schools can be state schools for students who are blind or visually impaired or who are deaf or hard of hearing. Specialized schools and programs like these are meant to be transitional supports that are intensive and prepare students to return to their home school district or system after receiving intensive, specialized services. An additional component of these specialized schools is they typically include a mission to collaborate and guide the local school district or system through collaborative consultation—that is, local team members are typically invited to annual IEP meetings to discuss student transition on an annual basis. Additionally, special education professionals from these specialized schools will often visit the local school district/system to provide local support along with outreach consultants if they are available in the state as well.

Within any of these models, special education teachers will likely be required to professionally develop in some, or many, additional areas related to their caseload student learning needs and type of program. For example, you may be required to completed training related to: general education content differentiation, specialized intervention programs or curriculum related to literacy and math, interventions unique to language learners, disability-specific interventions and programs, behavior-specific programs, and curriculum/program components unique to the grade level such as early childhood education, elementary school, middle school, high school, transition, and other unique special education–related programs. As you consider the professional learning you will need to add to your busy schedule, don't be afraid to advocate for (1) professional learning opportunities and (2) professional development time (such as paid leave) to learn new skills in order to support your ability to implement any of these program types and components listed here.

Reflect with one another about these program types as they relate to your school building.

- What are the various special education programs within your school building and district/system?
- Discuss the pros and cons of more or less restrictive environments for students in your school.
- What does a more restrictive environment look like at your school, and are there students who need more support than your school building can provide?

Part II: Creating a Strength-Based Special Education Program

Strengths-based special education programs and deficit-based special education programs represent two different approaches to educating students with disabilities. These mindsets focus on student abilities and challenges differently. Let's consider the differences between these special education program approaches.

Strengths-Based Special Education Programs

- Strengths-based programs focus on the whole student, not just the disability area; they honor the abilities of the student, including their interests, goals, and assets.

- Specifically, they are assets-oriented in emphasizing, identifying, and nurturing a student's value, strengths, talents, and interests. The goal is to build upon what the student is good at rather than focusing solely on their deficits.
- They include a growth and positive mindset, meaning that strengths-based programs promote a positive mindset, both for students and educators, emphasizing possibilities and opportunities for student success. They believe that by fostering a sense of achievement and self-worth, students are more motivated to learn and overcome challenges or barriers.
- This type of program orientation acknowledges that the brain is always growing and that neurodiversity—that is, differences in how we think and behave—are the norm not the exception. They understand that there is no "average brain or student" (Rose, 2016) and configure program supports that celebrate difference and UDL.
- They are individualized, recognizing that each student has unique strengths that need tailored instruction to empower and support them to harness those strengths. This approach can include personalized learning plans, goal setting, and differentiated instruction that is data driven.
- They know that labels matter and can hurt students. Once a student has been identified as having a disability this can color the way the student is perceived by the school, their peers, and teaching teams. For this reason, strength-based programs de-emphasize the disability in order to amplify the person.
- Finally, strength-based programs recognize that students will have big, small, and everything-in-between behaviors that can be seen as a natural part of being human. They seek to teach students strategies to communicate their feelings and frustrations in a way that will work more universally in different learning contexts.

DEFICIT-BASED SPECIAL EDUCATION PROGRAMS

- These programs are deficit-oriented and tend to focus on identifying and addressing a student's weaknesses, challenges, or disabilities. The goal is often to remediate or, when possible, "fix" deficits.
- Deficit-based programs are primarily oriented toward problems and difficulties, potentially leading to a negative mindset for both students and educators. Even if the special education

program within a school building is strengths-based, the building culture across the teaching team may be more aligned with a deficit-based culture. Unfortunately, this type of school building culture can be common.

- Within these programs, there will often be standardized approaches to learning in which a handful of interventions or supports are provided to students; these approaches can have a one-size-fits-all strategy that may not be effective for all students. There may be limited resources, staffing, and administrative support to personalize instruction for students needing something tailored to their learning challenges and barriers.
- The academic emphasis in deficit-based programs will often prioritize academic achievement over other aspects of a student's development, potentially neglecting social and emotional needs. It will also focus on remediation of deficit skills, which can, at times, lead the students to feel badly about their deficits (for example, a student who needs to work on a fundamental math skill may be using an intervention that is meant for elementary-aged students while they are in high school with the goal of remediating the skill).
- As a result, deficit-based programs can create dependency in students inadvertently. These student dependencies may emerge due to students feeling the focus is on what they cannot do and will look to their teachers, peers, or others to do for them because they may not feel empowered to try. That positioning of the program can have a negative impact on student independence and self-advocacy.

In practice, many special education programs incorporate elements of both approaches, recognizing the importance of addressing challenges and reteaching areas that are critical for student academic success, while also leveraging students' strengths, independence, and empowerment. However, there is a shift toward more strength-based approaches gaining momentum as research and experience show that focusing on what students can do well will lead to more positive outcomes, improved self-esteem, and increased engagement in the learning process. Additionally, with a proliferation of assistive and educational technology supports, students have increased opportunities for accessibility to general education content—for example, students who are struggling readers or writers can use technology supports to access grade level literacy activities (such as using text-to-speech and speech-to-text to write and read at grade level with little assistance). These tools and shifts toward more inclusive educational practices can also have the effect of increasing independence, particularly for students with multiple disabilities, and providing more access to age-appropriate accommodations to support growth in learning.

- How would you classify the program configuration of your special education program: Is it primarily configured as a strengths- or deficit-based program or a combination of both approaches?
- What would you say is the overarching culture in your school building as it relates to your program configuration?
- How has it evolved over time?

LRE AND STUDENTS WITH MULTIPLE DISABILITIES

Students with multiple disabilities approximately comprise "1 percent" of all students with disabilities served in special education programs. Best practices for creating fully inclusive programs for students with multiple disabilities is an area that continues to make slow progress despite research supporting the benefits for students in both special and general education when schools work to promote fully inclusive programs. Recall overarching recommendations in this mentoring Guidebook such as teachers making the least dangerous assumption (LDA) and presuming competence of students. Using those two recommendations, consider how the programs in your school building and district/system could be more inclusive. A few resources are provided here for you to learn more and weigh how to promote more fully inclusive LREs for students with multiple disabilities:

- Agran, M., Brown, F., Hughs, C., Quirk, C., & Ryndak, D. (2014). *Equity and full participation for individuals with severe disabilities: A vision for the future.* Paul H. Brookes.
- Rogers, W., & Johnson, N. (2018). Strategies to include students with severe/multiple disabilities within the general education classroom. *Physical Disabilities: Education and Related Services, 37*(2), 1–12.
- Rapp, W., Arndt, K., & Hildenbrand, S. (2019) *Picture inclusion! Snapshots of successful diverse classrooms.* Brookes Publishing Co.

 WELL-BEING

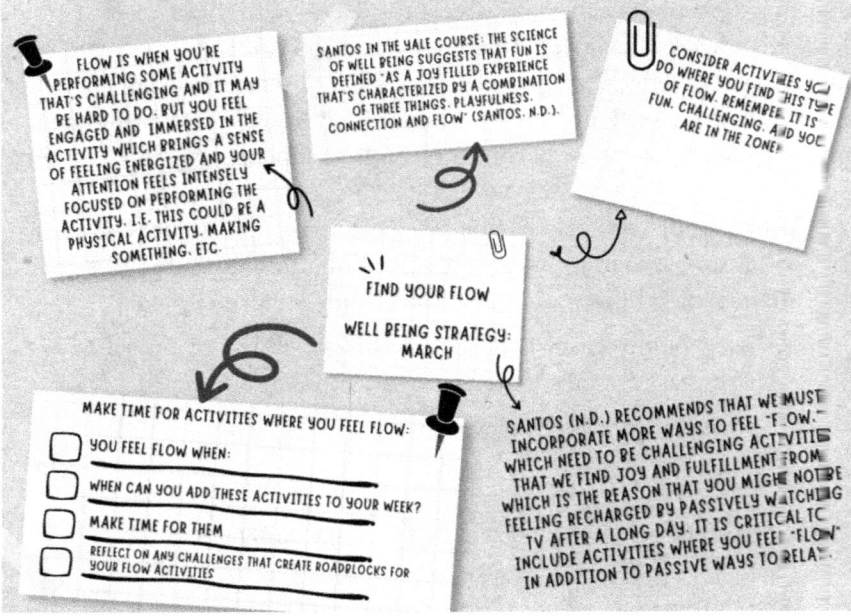

March Plan for Well-Being

For March, we are thinking about "flow." Flow was originally described by early educational researchers. Csikszentmihalyi (1990/1996) described flow as the merging of an action and a person's awareness in which the individual loses track of both time and self due to the flow being experienced. A key component to flow is that the challenge of the task is balanced with the person's skill level of the tasks at hand—meaning, essentially, the experience of "flow" is dependent on us being adept at the task we are engrossed in doing (note, this does not mean we are masterful at the task; adept can mean we know how to do it well enough to be considered adept). It can happen during mundane tasks, such as when we are cooking or gardening, but it can also happen when we embark on creative or highly technical tasks, such as art-making or fixing a machine that is broken, that we are intimately familiar with its inner workings. It is shown to be a deeply satisfying feeling and experience. Current research (Santos, n.d.) suggests that we must have instances of flow to cultivate our happiness and joy. So, identify where you find flow and be sure to incorporate those activities in your life!

Share your well-being goal each month with one another to support making it happen!

 COLLABORATE ON

A suggested collaborative activity for this month is to consider the challenges of developing and implementing an inclusive plan for a student on your caseload. Consider an inclusive plan for a student who has been struggling this year and needs more support. The support needed could be behavioral, academic, or something else. How could you make a plan that includes (1) the content that the student needs and how to differentiate it; (2) the process(es) that the student needs to be successful; (3) the elements that need to be or could be incorporated in the learning environment that will help the student be more successful—for example, sensory supports or breaks; (4) and the final project—the way the student demonstrates their understanding and how that can be adapted, modified, and so on?

Another helpful resource to review together when considering inclusive plans and intensive intervention is Swift Education Center, swiftschools.org. Their "Ten Point Paradigm" captures much of our discussion throughout this Guidebook where you are encouraged to think proactively (UDL, interrupt bias, intensify interventions, promote inclusion) and then implement further interventions and collaborate across teaching teams to support individualized students' learning needs.

Learn more about inclusive special education programs. Have you watched *Including Samuel* (https://includingsamuel.com/)? It is an excellent documentary film that grapples with the questions we all may be asking as we consider the triumphs and challenges of inclusive special education programs in relation to students' learning needs. Another set of great resources to begin learning more about inclusive special education are Understood.org and Cast.org.

Agran, M., Brown, F., Hughs, C., Quirk, C., & Ryndak, D. (2014). *Equity and full participation for individuals with severe disabilities: A vision for the future.* Paul H. Brookes.
Armstrong, T. (2012). *Neurodiversity in the classroom: Strength-based strategies to help students with special needs succeed in school and life.* Association for Supervision and Curriculum Development (ASCD).
Baines, A. (2014). *(Un) learning disability: Recognizing and changing restrictive views of student ability.* Teachers College Press.
Cooper, J. O., Heron, T. E., & Heward, W. L. (2007). *Applied behavior analysis.* Pearson.
Csikszentmihalyi, M. (1990). *Flow: The psychology of optimal experience.* HarperPerennial.
Csikszentmihalyi, M. (1996). *Creativity: Flow and the psychology of discovery and invention.* HarperCollins.
Downing, J. E., & Peckham-Hardin, K. D. (2007). Inclusive education: What makes it a good education for students with moderate to severe disabilities? *Research and Practice for Persons with Severe Disabilities, 32*(1), 16–30.
Downing, J. E. (2005). Inclusive education for high school students with severe intellectual disabilities: Supporting communication. *Augmentative and Alternative Communication, 21*(2), 132–148.
Downing, J. (2010). *Academic instruction for students with moderate and severe intellectual disabilities in inclusive classrooms.* Corwin Press.
Friend, M., & Bursuck, W. D. (2002). *Including students with special needs: A practical guide for classroom teachers.* Allyn & Bacon.
Erickson, K. A., & Koppenhaver, D. A. (2020). *Comprehensive literacy for all: Teaching students with significant disabilities to read and write.* Brookes Publishing Company.
Habib, D. (2008). *Including Samuel: A documentary.* DH Photography.

Hennessy, N. L. (2021). *The reading comprehension blueprint: Helping students make meaning from text*. Brookes Publishing Company.

Heumann, J., & Joiner, K. (2021). *Rolling warrior large print edition: The incredible, sometimes awkward, true story of a rebel girl on wheels who helped spark a revolution*. Beacon Press.

Hoover, J. J., & Love, E. (2011). Supporting school-based response to intervention: A practitioner's model. *Teaching Exceptional Children, 43*(3), 40–48.

Hoover, J. J. (2012). *Linking assessment to instruction in multi-tiered models: A teacher's guide to selecting reading, writing, and mathematics interventions*. Pearson.

Hosp, M. K., Hosp, J. L., & Howell, K. W. (2016). *The ABCs of CBM: A practical guide to curriculum-based measurement*. Guilford Publications.

Olmstead, J. E. (2005). *Itinerant teaching: Tricks of the trade for teachers of students with visual impairments*. American Foundation for the Blind.

Rapp, W., Arndt, K., & Hildenbrand, S. (2019) *Picture inclusion! Snapshots of successful diverse classrooms*. Brookes Publishing Co.

Reinke, W. M., Sprick, R., & Knight, J. (2009). Coaching classroom management. In J. Knight (Ed.), *Coaching: Approaches and perspectives* (pp. 91–112). Corwin Press.

Rogers, W., & Johnson, N. (2018). Strategies to include students with severe/multiple disabilities within the general education classroom. *Physical Disabilities: Education and Related Services, 37*(2), 1–12.

Rose, T. (2016). *The end of average: How to succeed in a world that values sameness*. Penguin UK.

Ruppar, A., Kurth, J., Bubash, S., & Lockman Turner, E. (2023). A framework for preparing to teach students with extensive support needs in the twenty-first century. *Teacher Education and Special Education, 46*(1), 26–43.

Sharpe, V. S., & Strosnider, R. (2022). *Everyday executive function strategies: Improve student engagement, self-regulation, behavior, and learning*. Corwin Press.

Schwartz, D., Blue, E., McDonald, M., Giuliani, G., Weber, G., Seirup, H., & Perkins, A. (2010). Dispelling stereotypes: Promoting disability equality through film. *Disability & Society, 25*(7), 841–848.

Vaughn, S., & Bos, C. S. (2012). *Strategies for teaching students with learning and behavior problems*. Pearson.

Internet Resources

High-Leverage Practices: https://highleveragepractices.org/.

April

CULTIVATING STUDENT INDEPENDENCE

What adaptations can be made to the classroom environment to ensure full access, achievement, and participation for students with physical disabilities?

Gabriela is a fourteen-year-old student with cerebral palsy. She uses a power wheelchair and has limited mobility of her upper body. Gabriela is very bright and has demonstrated a strong interest in math and science, and a particular interest in the physics of momentum. She has an advanced understanding in physics and is currently taking an advanced placement physics course, earning dual high school and college credit. However, she has faced significant barriers to access and participation in her classes due to the inaccessibility of many elements of her classroom, particularly in her general education science and math classes. For example, she has difficulty navigating through the narrow walkways in the science room, as well as the multiple hallways she must navigate to get to math class, resulting in her both being late to class and missing the last five minutes of the class prior to math. She struggles with accessing materials, lab equipment, and technology arranged on high shelves or tables. Her participation can also be limited in class discussions due to issues with wait time for her to finish sharing her ideas and also when teachers don't have systems implemented to be sure all students are able to participate in discussion in various ways, for example, polling or other technology-rich methods, it is even worse since students will just blurt out ideas before she has a chance to participate.

Despite these challenges, Gabriela's teachers and support staff have worked to create a more accessible and inclusive classroom environment. They have implemented a number of adaptations, such as shelves placed at lower levels in science and math classes, providing a variety of seating when transferring out of her wheelchair, and positioning options for Gabriela's wheelchair in classrooms. The team also provides adapted materials and technology, as well as paraprofessional or peer support during group work and discussions to support increased participation for Gabriela. Additionally, they have worked to educate Gabriela's peers and the broader school community about the importance of accessibility and diversity in the classroom and in society as a whole. They emphasize the importance of hearing everyone's contributions to class, noting that diverse perspectives help ideas grow and be enhanced.

Gabriela faces competing pressures to prioritize her educational goals and interests, while also advocating for her rights and needs as a person with a disability. She must navigate complex legal, school, and social systems, be able to communicate effectively with her teachers and peers, and be able to articulate her needs and goals in a way that is respectful and persuasive. She must also confront and overcome societal attitudes and biases that may restrict her access to education and other opportunities. At the same time, Gabriela is a teenager who wants to socialize and do other activities that her friends are doing, making her feel frustrated that she must always be advocating for herself to access her educational program instead of just getting to be a teenager like everyone else.

Case questions:

- How can the access issues that Gabriela is experiencing be made better? What other supports could be available so she can focus on her academics and feel that access to her academics is not always an afterthought that she needs to advocate for?

- Should Gabriela use an assistant or mentor in the classroom to have an increased voice to share ideas in class and other supports, when needed? Would a peer volunteer work, or would it be better to use a professional support staff? How would this intervention impact Gabriela's full participation, socially in front of her peers, and engagement in her learning—that is, would it impact how other students see her or her self-confidence to have someone helping her in classes?

- Gabriela is an advanced student in the sciences. What other transition-related resources and activities could the team bring into her academic program?

Special Education Mentoring
MONTHLY CHECKLIST: APRIL

TO DO...	DONE	NOTES
Connect standardize assessment results to student learning needs and programming		
Review how an *intensifying intervention plan* went from last months collaboration		
Review end-of-year procedures for progress monitoring, parent communication, and transition planning		
Create a new/adapted/enhanced *paraprofessional schedule* building upon the current scheduling of building/program paraprofessionals		
How can collaboration across paraprofessionals and other support team members be better implemented?		
Discuss methods for gradually releasing support for students to become more independent		
Review and discuss mentor observations across the year, how did they go? Reflect on teaching in the fall and now, how has it evolved over time?		
Outline a birdseye view of district programs from child find through transition. Consider different roles of special educators in each.		

OTHER CHECKLIST ITEMS UNIQUE TO YOUR SCHOOL DISTRICT

_____

_____

_____

ALSO FOR THIS MONTH

☐ **Well-Being Goal**

☐ **Collaborate on Mentoring Activities**

☐ **Suggested Resources: follow up?**

SPECIAL EDUCATION FOCUS

To support your goal setting, this section is meant for you to jot down one focus area/question in each of your primary roles.

☐ IEP: _____

☐ Intensive Intervention: _____

☐ Collaboration: _____

Note that anything italicized in the checklist is referring to a template in the back of this guidebook.

April Monthly Checklist

This checklist provides a roadmap for mentor discussions and timely special education roles and responsibilities typically occurring around this time of the year. There are spaces to add your own checklist items and goals within the three primary roles and responsibilities of special education professionals related to IEP caseload management, collaboration, and teaching specifically designed instruction also referred to as intensive interventions.

Key Learning Goals

1. Identify the roles and responsibilities of teaching teams, paraprofessionals, and related service professionals as a collaborative team.

2. Summarize the characteristics of effective collaboration in a special education setting, including strong communication, trust, and respect among team members.

3. Develop a plan for creating a positive and inclusive learning environment that involves collaboration among paraprofessional team members, addressing factors such as schedules, routines, and community building activities.

Part I: We Work as Collaborative Professionals

As a special education professional, it is common for you to work with one or more paraprofessional team members, who are sometimes called instructional aides, paraeducators, or assistant teachers. The role of the paraprofessional is critical to the success of your special education program. Teachers and paraprofessionals are partners in an education program, working together to provide the best educational experience possible for each student. The special education paraprofessional's role is to assist the teacher and allow more effective utilization of the teacher's abilities, support for students, and professional knowledge. With paraprofessionals, the teacher functions in a leadership role and is ultimately responsible for the implementation of each student's Individualized Education Program (IEP). Paraprofessionals serve under the direction and supervision of the teacher to assist in carrying out the IEP, but school districts/systems will have varying hierarchical configurations for classroom/program aides in which the paraprofessionals may be under either teacher or administrator supervision. In order for paraprofessionals to provide direct instruction to the student, special education teachers must plan and prescribe the learning environment and instruction for the student. It is critical that special education teachers instruct paraprofessional(s) in the specifics of the individualized instructional techniques—namely, how to evaluate student progress, promote inclusion in general education settings, and monitor the effectiveness of the paraprofessional's implementation of the instructional strategies. A summarized list of paraprofessional duties and responsibilities may include the following:

- Paraprofessionals generally work in an inclusionary setting, which can be the general or the special education classroom, supporting one or more students with academic, behavioral, social-emotional, or other individual needs.
- Most states require a minimum of a high school diploma or associate's degree, or higher for paraprofessionals.
- Typical paraprofessional duties include addressing student health, personal, and wellness care; behavior supports, peer or social supports; student independence or safety; and supporting academic tasks (i.e., not implementing interventions that require more specialized instructional techniques).

What is the special educator's role in supporting paraprofessionals?

The special educator's role includes:

- supervising the paraprofessional's instructional support through assessing and planning instruction for individual students served in special education;
- facilitating the plan for services directly related to implementing the goals and objectives of the IEP;
- creating a schedule to help supervise and coordinate the work of paraprofessional and other support staff;
- training, communication, collaboration, and all other supports of the professional team that are necessary to implement programs and services related to all students on the caseload that are being served by the paraprofessional; and
- providing feedback to assist the paraprofessional in continuing to refine skills in supporting students.

Key considerations when professionally developing a paraprofessional team is to teach them about:

- prompt hierarchies—that is, going from highest level of prompt to lowest level of prompt to allow for more student independence;
- how to scaffold supports for students—namely, to start with more support and gradually implement less and less support while students feel more comfortable and confident with the concepts;
- gradual release, where paraprofessionals slowly provide more space for student independent learning and socializing;

- how to be objective- and data-driven in student skill observation in order to collaborate with the special education team to determine best supports to continue to grow student independence;
- how to work with teaching team members in collaborative general education classroom environments; and
- collaborative advocacy where paraprofessionals can support student access, participation, and accommodations using best practices of learning, communication, and teaming.

This list is not exhaustive. It includes the primary areas of paraprofessional support, teacher collaboration, and areas to consider in your collaborative work. What is missing?

Brainstorm together what the other roles and responsibilities of paraprofessionals are in your building. Are there any areas that are underutilized? Conversely, are paraprofessionals overworked in your building and is there evidence of burn out?

Part II: Build Up Your Team! How Can Special Education Teams Amplify the Support Paraprofessionals Can Provide?

If you are working with paraprofessionals, you know how invaluable they are in supporting the program, students, and school community. Oftentimes, they are truly unsung heroes but should be more celebrated since the program could not run without them! What are some ways to amplify their incredible work, plan more effectively for partnership, and encourage them in ways that support their strengths on the team?

Five categories—*communication*, *leadership*, *gradual release*, *contingency*, and *empowerment*—are listed below to expand on the questions posed in this "Going Deeper, Part II," along with an opportunity to stop and jot with one another as you consider these suggestions.

1. Communication

It is important to set up consistent ways to communicate with the team such as daily logs, weekly student journaling, or other ways to share happenings and progress with one another. Having consistent communication systems will help you progress monitor student growth and also catch issues before they become a bigger problem needing conflict resolution. Additionally, establishing expectations for how team members will share out related to student progress toward IEP goal areas and other academic, social, behavioral, and individual goals will help you monitor IEPs and support student success. Consider discussing and establishing communication norms in the beginning of the year and don't hesitate to revisit norms if team communication is breaking down.

Along with other team norms, share out what type of "conflict" style each team member has when working on a team. A social psychologist, Johnson (2006), identifies five types of conflict personas. He argues that our responses and strategies in conflict resolution tend to involve an attempt to balance our own concerns (our goals) with the concerns of the other people involved (their goals and preservation of the relationship). Johnson outlines five main styles or approaches to this conflict resolution balancing act. See a checklist and description of each area in figure 15.

Which animal describes you best when you are in a conflict with a team member?

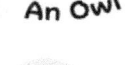

Avoiding **turtles withdraw into their shells to avoid conflicts.** They give up on their personal goals and relationships and will do anything they can to stay away from conflict (including not having an opinion on an issue that has come up). They believe it is easier to withdraw (physically and psychologically) from a conflict than to face it.

Collaborating **owls highly value their own goals and relationships.** They view conflicts as problems to be solved and seek a solution that achieves both their own goals and the other person's goals. Owls see conflicts as a means of improving relationships by reducing the tension between two persons when conflicts arise. They try to begin a discussion that identifies the conflict as a problem. Owls maintain the relationship by seeking solutions that satisfy both themselves and the other person, but they will only be satisfied once the tension and negative feelings have been resolved.

Compromising **foxes are moderately concerned with their own goals and their relationships with others.** Foxes seek a compromise: they give up part of their goals and persuade the other person in a conflict to give up part of her/his goals. They seek a conflict solution in which both sides gain something – the middle ground between two extreme positions for the common good.

Accommodating **teddy bears, the relationship is of great importance while their own goals are of little importance.** Teddy bears want to be accepted and liked by others and they believe that conflict should be avoided in favor of harmony and that people cannot discuss conflicts without damaging relationships. They are afraid that if the conflict continues, someone will get hurt.

Competing **sharks try to overpower opponents by forcing them to accept their solution to the conflict.** Their goals are highly important to them and they may seek to achieve their goals at all costs. Winning gives sharks a sense of pride and achievement and losing makes them feel badly. They may try to win by attacking, overpowering, overwhelming, and intimidating others.

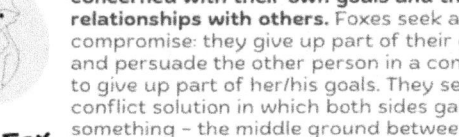

Figure 15. Conflict Management Styles
This figure depicts five primary conflict management styles and their descriptions.

 **STOP & JOT** What style are you? Consider learning about the conflict resolution styles of your paraprofessional team members as well.

2. Leadership

Providing opportunities for more leadership and agency in the special education program will have a beneficial impact on both students and paraprofessional team members. Consider that paraprofessional team members may spend more time with students, depending on program configuration and size of program, than you do on any given day. Encouraging their involvement in program development will promote more buy in and collaboration. Give some thought to undertaking some Q & A with your team members to learn about student progress and ideas for enhancing support.

Question examples could be:

- What has been working well in your work with students within inclusive class settings?
- What supports have been provided and what do you feel could be improved?
- From your perspective, how independent are students within their inclusive environments? What scaffolding or accommodations could encourage more independence for students?
- What more can I (the special education teacher) provide to support your (the paraprofessional) work with students? Training? Co-teaching? Further explanation regarding a particular accommodation or strategy?

3. Gradual Release

Teaching how to implement gradual release of paraprofessional support will increase student independence. A common issue that can occur in special education programs where students need support from paraprofessional team members can be that we "overdo" for students. It is easy for any team member to fall into patterns where we (1) over-prompt, (2) overdo, (3) speak for, or (4) impede student independence in other ways. What are some strategies for cultivating teamwork toward student independence? Some example strategies are listed below, though it is not an exhaustive list. You are encouraged to discuss more with one another and jot down what other strategies have worked well to encourage more student independence.

- *Over-prompting*—Teach paraprofessional teams prompt hierarchies and make a plan for how they will be implemented progressively, allowing for more student independence. For example, prompting a student with multiple disabilities can start with a physical prompt where we might do the activity together with full hand-under-hand physical support. The next set of prompts gradually provide less prompting, which increases student independence (i.e., this hierarchy could be from 5, the most obtrusive, to 1, the least: [5] physical, [4] model, [3] visual, [2] gestural, [1] verbal). One issue that can come up with over-prompting is when there is not a plan for how to progressively prompt less so, as in the example scenario, we always provide a physical prompt. Another common issue is not allowing enough wait time for students to proceed with the activity being prompted. In this instance, special education teachers can develop a wait time recommendation and then have paraprofessional team members document time before or beyond the wait time plan that a student needed (this is called "latency recording"— tracking where we can document how long the student takes from prompt to task).

- *Overdoing*—Work as a team to plan for how supports can be progressively lessened so students are doing more on their own. For instance, a student with a physical disability may be sitting idly while a team member does the entire task sequence for them because it is assumed there are no elements that the student can do on their own. Watch for these opportunities for more independence and capitalize on them. This can be a challenging issue sometimes where team members will disagree on the best ways to support a student (recall our conflict personas and special education teachers sometimes shell up like a turtle not wanting to push the issue). Creative solutions might be to enlist paraprofessional support in collecting data on what steps can be completed independently by students, for example, "Please take data on the level of independence of our student during her personal hygiene routine and where she needs a verbal prompt to move to the next step." Collecting data serves two purposes, it creates a replacement task for the team member so they will not overdo and also serves as a progress monitoring tool for students' IEP goals.

- *Speak for*—This is another common issue for students who use augmentative alternative communication (AAC) devices, where paraprofessionals will speak and answer for them because they understand what the student is saying, but this is an instance of us speaking for a student instead of allowing for more independent voice. It is critical that we outline communication plans and follow them to increase communication success for students using AAC. Look to your speech-language pathologist to guide the team on how much we should support communication and how we can provide prompts with the AAC device to support increased student independent communication.

- *Impede student independence*—Another issue that can emerge is being an "in between" presence when students are interacting with their peers. It is important that we stand back and allow students to interact with peers independently as is appropriate for their goals and support needs. There will be instances where students need supportive peer interactions and it is okay to support those interactions, but we want to always be looking for how our supports, prompts, and interventions can be progressively lessened to increase student independence and socializing.

4. Contingency

Paraprofessional support is an instrumental component in most special education programs. Over the past several years, there have been growing concerns about shortages of both special education teachers and paraprofessionals (Billingsley & Bettini, 2019). Many programs are running on shoestring budgets and can struggle throughout the school year due to these shortages, team member absences, or team member sharing between multiple programs. Special education teachers report that one of the most challenging issues is developing a schedule on the fly when one of these instances happens and student support needs to be reconfigured quickly at the start of the day. These staffing issues also impact student programming and can lead to advocacy challenges from families. A suggested solution is to devise multiple schedule configurations at the start of the school year, for example, an "A," "B," and "C" schedule or something similar. These schedules can outline support when all team members are present and alternative plans for instances when team members are absent or other issues that can arise unique to student needs in your program (i.e., if a team member is commonly pulled to support a unique student situation, make a plan for it that can be easily implemented when it happens). Contingency plans can outline action plans in the event that something disrupts the "usual" plan. Disruptions to the schedule are likely going to be the norm, not the exception, so planning for them will also be a proactive practice to have in place.

5. *Empowerment*

Related to the concerns over special and general education teacher shortages, paraprofessionals are ideal candidates to complete their teaching license. Several school districts/systems will have paraprofessional "pipelines" or "pathways to teaching" to help solve shortage issues. Encourage your paraprofessionals to consider becoming licensed teachers. Having a team member training to be a general or special education teacher working in your program is only going to enhance your program support. Learn about ways to support teachers in training and advocate for paraprofessional pathways in your school district/system (Mason & Choate, 2023).

In this section, we discussed five growth areas to consider when working with paraprofessional team members. Consider each and discuss with one another.

1. Communication
2. Leadership
3. Gradual Release
4. Contingency
5. Empowerment

Working across the Team

Special education teachers are required to supervise, train, and manage paraprofessional staff members in addition to their daily lesson/intervention planning, direct instruction, assessment, and caseload management. Some effective strategies for training and collaborating with your paraprofessional team is to professionally develop together, as a team. Consider ways to implement annual professional development learning with your paraprofessional team. For example, at the beginning of the year, consider a pre-fall survey to learn what instructional or IEP implementation professional learning topics are emerging for your team. Some examples of items to include on the pre-survey are: (1) communication devices or systems, (2) behavior management strategies, (3) supports for safety risks such as behavior or medical needs, (4) inclusive practices within general education, or (5) systems for progress monitoring IEP goals. From the top areas of learning need, create a monthly professional learning calendar. Potentially solicit support from the district/system to have guest speakers to instruct, or another option is to enroll as a team to complete a professional development workshop. A step further would be to set professional development goals with your team after learning new strategies and include a system for monitoring your progress such as videoing teaching snippets and discussing new strategy implementation as a team. With this final suggestion, be willing to include teaching snippets of your instruction to promote collaboration and discussion across the team including your work toward implementing new strategies.

 WELL-BEING

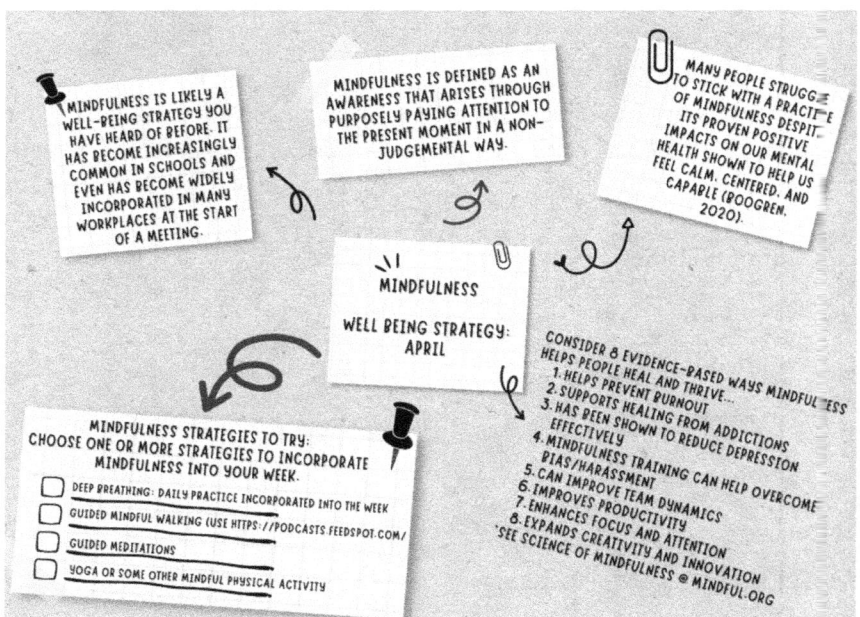

April Plan for Well-Being

For April, enlist mindfulness in your well-being goals and weekly practices. People will say that mindfulness can feel like something they simply do not have time for. This is a common issue across professionals in the field of education. Teachers lament they are just too busy to incorporate well-being practices into their weekly schedules. Recall that a primary goal of this Guidebook is to help you create a *sustainable* special education teaching practice, and in order to do that you must take care of yourself! Mindfulness will truly help with that goal. Simply put, if you feel that you are currently running on empty or have functioned that way this year, it may have worked for that moment, but it will not work forever.

Share your well-being goal each month with one another to support making it happen!

Using the schedule templates (see Resource 13) provided in this Guidebook, collaborate on a revised or new paraprofessional schedule. Consider the needs that have been identified to determine which schedule template is best—student focused? team focused? contingency focused?

COLLABORATE ON

Take a look at the Council for Exceptional Children (CEC) Paraeducator Core Competencies and discuss how these are implemented in your team and program. https://exceptionalchildren.org/paraeducators.

SUGGESTED RESOURCES

Americans with Disabilities Act of 1990 42 U.S.C. §§ 12101 et seq.
Billingsley, B., & Bettini, E. (2019). Special education teacher attrition and retention: A review of the literature. *Review of Educational Research*, *89*(5), 697–744.
Boogren, T. (2020). *180 days of self-care for busy educators*. Solution Tree Press.
Causton-Theoharis, J. (2009). *The paraprofessional's handbook for effective support in inclusive classrooms*. Brookes Publishing Company.
Council of Exceptional Children (CEC). (n.d.). *Paraeducator competencies*. https://exceptionalchildren.org/paraeducators.
Fair Housing Amendments Act of 1988 42 U.S.C. §§ 3601 et seq.
Griffin-Shirley, N., & Matlock, D. (2004). Paraprofessionals speak out: A survey. *Re:view*, *36*(3), 127–136.
Johnson, A. P. (2006). *Making connections in elementary and middle school social studies*. Sage.
Mason, T., & Choate, J. (2023). A tale of two grant-funded special education recruitment and training projects focused on assistive technology. *Journal of Special Education Preparation*, *3*(2), 66–74.
Mason-Williams, L., Bettini, E., Peyton, D., Harvey, A., Rosenberg, M., & Sindelar, P. T. (2020). Rethinking shortages in special education: Making good on the promise of an equal opportunity for students with disabilities. *Teacher Education and Special Education*, *43*(1), 45–62.
Section 501 of the Rehabilitation Act of 1973, as amended 29 U.S.C. § 791.
Section 503 of the Rehabilitation Act of 1973, as amended 29 U.S.C. § 793.
Section 504 of the Rehabilitation Act of 1973, as amended 29 U.S.C. § 794.
Section 508 of the Rehabilitation Act of 1973, as amended 29 U.S.C. § 794d.
Walker, V. L., Douglas, K. H., Douglas, S. N., & D'Agostino, S. R. (2020). Paraprofessional-implemented systematic instruction for students with disabilities. *Education and Training in Autism and Developmental Disabilities*, *55*(3), 303–317.

Internet Resources

Paraeducator Core Competencies: https://exceptionalchildren.org/paraeducators.
Texas Education Agency (TEA), working with paraprofessionals guide: https://spedsupport.tea.texas.gov/.
Understood.org, working with paraprofessionals at a glance: https://www.understood.org/en/articles/paraprofessionals-what-you-need-to-know.

Section IV
Reflection, Revitalization, Regrowth

Teachers can engage in multiple activities to support their reflection and revitalization at this point in the year. Recall from the first-year teaching graphic, the later spring semester brings in reflection, rejuvenation, and anticipation for the next year. Capitalize on this time of year when you are naturally inclined to reflect and consider how you might proceed differently the next time a student issue or program situation arises. You have learned so much this year and using this time to your advantage will help you enhance your program in many ways for next year. Some ways to implement a reflective teaching practice are to journal, enlist peer observations, and self-assess your teaching practice. You have been doing these activities this year already! Hopefully, you were able to have one another observe teaching and evaluation procedures over the course of the year and reflect on how you improved your teaching. You also have journaled in this Guidebook each month, answering case study questions, collaborating with your mentor, and completing innumerable "Stop and Jots" throughout the book. Let's take stock on some of that growth now as we embark on the final section of this book.

Consider the journaling you have done this year in this Guidebook. Flip back through Sections I to III and think about themes in your thinking. What do you notice that you were thinking the most about? List your top five themes and/or key takeaways from Sections I to III:

1.

2.

3.

4.

5.

Did you and your mentor observe one another teaching? Observe evaluation procedures such as student testing? Consider how those went and what you learned from observing and reflecting:

-

-

-

Finally, let's take stock on where you were and where you are now. If you mentored this year, it has likely been a year of tremendous learning for you in different ways than for your mentee. You may have been reflecting on your own teaching or infused new ideas into your practice. That is common when mentoring new teachers, and it revitalizes our own teaching practice. If you are working as a new special education teacher this year, it was likely a bit of a whirlwind! You may feel that it has gone much faster than you expected, and it may feel overwhelming to finally be here in May (and a relief as well). Rate where you feel that you were in the beginning of the year and where you are now in the three primary roles we discussed in the beginning of this Guidebook.

Caseload Manager

Rating: 1 to 10, with 10 being the highest level of understanding and implementation.

Where were you at the beginning of the year?

How would you rate yourself now?

Why?

Intensive Intervention and Teaching

Rating: 1 to 10, with 10 being the highest level of understanding and implementation.

Where were you at the beginning of the year?

How would you rate yourself now?

Why?

Collaborator

Rating: 1 to 10, with 10 being the highest level of understanding and implementation.

Where were you at the beginning of the year?

How would you rate yourself now?

Why?

During this section of the book, we will discuss other ways to capitalize on this time of the school year as it is coming to a close. It is a time to reflect and renew your practice as you anticipate your plan for next year. Other ways to capitalize on this time are to consider professional development opportunities for this month or over the summer that you can take part in (skip to July in this Guidebook to review a list of professional organizations in special education). Also, consider online networking and professional learning communities that can help broaden your ideas and strategies toolkit. This time of year can also be a good time to incorporate something new into your teaching such as experimenting with a technology tool or implementing a final project-based learning activity with your students to wrap up the school year. May is an ideal time to solicit student, parent, and team feedback, and upon reviewing feedback, consider some goals for next year while this year is still fresh in your mind. Finally, it is time to celebrate! You did it! Acknowledge this huge accomplishment of the first year coming to a close and look back on all that you have done this year. It was likely a mix of happiness, anticipation, stress, and uncertainty throughout the year. Congratulations on getting through it together in your mentoring partnership! Take a moment to thank one another for the support provided this year.

May

Transitioning to College

CASE STUDIES

What are the unique challenges and opportunities facing students with disabilities as they navigate the transition to adulthood, and how can we promote equity and inclusion in the transition process?

Mark is a nineteen-year-old student with a specific learning disability, traumatic brain injury (TBI), and cerebral visual impairment (CVI) who is about to transition from high school to college. Mark uses they/them pronouns and has been living with a new foster family this year after the sudden loss of their primary guardian, an aunt who they had lived with for the past five years. They are passionate about advocating for disability rights and have been actively involved in local advocacy groups for years. Mark is excited to use their experiences to help other students with disabilities navigate the complex transition process, but they are also apprehensive about the challenges and barriers that they may face.

Mark has recently discovered that there are many transition supports to help students with disabilities as they transition to college and beyond. They are a student athlete in track and field and goalball and hope to continue competing on intramural leagues at the university level where students can be successful in both academics and other university-level activities with the right accommodations in place.

Mark is struggling with the idea that they may face significant barriers and obstacles as they enter adulthood considering how involved they have been at the high school level and obstacles that have been overcome. Despite the many resources and opportunities available to them, they worry that they will not be able to fully participate in society due to the continued societal stigmas and injustices that confront people with disabilities. Mark is committed to advocating for themself and others, but they need guidance and support in channeling their passion, athleticism, and energy into effective action. Additionally, Mark has significant trauma in their life, and it is critical that they have caring adult team members who recognize their strengths and passions so they can thrive.

Case questions:

- How can Mark leverage their own experiences and the experiences of other students with disabilities to advocate for greater equity and inclusion in educational, recreational, and employment settings?
- Should Mark's special education teacher help them explore more assistive technologies (AT) that can enhance accommodations to prepare for enrolling in college? What AT could be helpful?
- What transition activities would be especially helpful to support Mark's success and advocacy goals? How can special education team members further support Mark to be successful in working toward their goals?

Special Education Mentoring
MONTHLY CHECKLIST: MAY

TO DO...	DONE	NOTES
It is nearly the end of the year; reflect on your mentoring partnership and acknowledge one another- specifically, what worked well? What were the challenges and how did you get through them? Celebrate each other!		
Review end-of-year procedures for progress monitoring, parent communication, and transition planning (review *transition plan template*)		
Review planning for next year's program implements: have student caseloads been determined and discussed, supplies needed, curriculum programs being adopted?		
Review opportunities for pofessional development over the summer and at the beginning of the year		
Discuss favorite end of the year activities with students and families		
Make plans for collaborations next year related to goals from this year and develop a checklist for what is needed to implement (i.e. co-teaching or new programs to implement)		
Review any end-of-year data collection tasks, monitoring, IEP reporting, and program reviews for school district/system		

OTHER CHECKLIST ITEMS UNIQUE TO YOUR SCHOOL DISTRICT

_____

_____

_____

ALSO FOR THIS MONTH

☐ Well-Being Goal _____

☐ Collaborate on Mentoring Activities

☐ Suggested Resources: follow up?

SPECIAL EDUCATION FOCUS

To support your goal setting, this section is meant for you to jot down one focus area/question in each of your primary roles.

☐ IEP: _____

☐ Intensive Intervention: _____

☐ Collaboration: _____

Note that anything italicized in the checklist is referring to a template in the back of this guidebook.

May Monthly Checklist

This checklist provides a roadmap for mentor discussions and timely special education roles and responsibilities typically occurring around this time of the year. There are spaces to add your own checklist items and goals within the three primary roles and responsibilities of special education professionals related to IEP caseload management, collaboration, and teaching specifically designed instruction also referred to as intensive interventions.

Key Learning Goals

1. Interpret the role of families, schools, and communities in supporting students with disabilities transitioning to adulthood and identify key factors that can affect their success.

2. Develop innovative strategies to engage and empower students in the transition process by leveraging technology, peer mentoring, and other resources to promote self-advocacy, independence, and informed decision-making.

PART I: TRANSITION PLANNING

The transition into the adult world can present challenges for all young people. The process of transition from K–12 is more difficult for students with disabilities and requires unique strategies to enable each student to achieve the most independence when working, living, and participating in the community as adults. Students with disabilities often have a difficult time deciding what they want to do and knowing what they will be able to do once they have completed high school. Upon graduating, they move from a supportive and familiar entitlement program within their school (FAPE) to a world of adult services based on varying eligibility requirements. They must become their own self-advocates to be provided with the support and accommodations needed for independence and access. Making the transition from school to the adult world requires careful planning and a cooperative effort among families/guardians, school teams, and community service providers. Further, planning transition services cannot be done in isolation and must reach beyond the school boundaries into the community. Planning must also reach beyond a student's limitations to explore the student's strengths, interests, hopes, and dreams.

The transition into adulthood is not a separate plan developed in isolation from a student's other services or academic needs. It is a collaborative effort aimed at ensuring the student's academic program is directly tied to their future aspirations and objectives, thereby making it more meaningful and effective in helping students reach their goals and dreams for the future. Individualized transition planning should be viewed as an opportunity to focus attention on what services, coursework, experiences, and supports are necessary in order for a student to achieve success and independence as an adult.

The Individuals with Disabilities Education Act (IDEA, 2004) regulations require transition planning and services. School districts/systems are responsible for initiating transition planning and services to ensure that each student with a disability is prepared for their post-school life before leaving K–12 school, and it is critical that special education teams consider the urgency of connecting students, families, and guardians with community agencies that will be able to provide services and supports for students in their adult lives.

Family/Guardian Focus

Parents and guardians can be a great resource to learn about their students' hopes for the future. They can be influential and critical partners in the successful transition of their students. Primary areas to consider when inviting families/guardians to transition planning activities include:

- Opportunities for reflection on the student's interests, traits, strengths, abilities, and so on. They know their student's strengths and challenges in different ways than school-based teams and they can provide a fuller story regarding student motivations, challenges, dreams, and hopes for the future. These opportunities can be provided as questionnaires, surveys, or Q & A during an annual transition planning meeting.
- Linkages to community agencies, transition planning programs and services, and state/federal funding opportunities for supporting their student's postsecondary programs. Many parents/guardians will continue as a financial planner, guardian, and/or in other supportive roles for their child and will need collaboration and advice on community agencies that can support those services in adulthood.
- Advisement on rights of adults with disabilities in community, workplaces, and college postsecondary plans. Encourage parents/caregivers to join a parent group, listserv, or organization if they are not already involved with one in their communities.

While parents/guardians are a critical partner in transition planning, challenges can arise for the team to discuss related to student supports, eligibility for services, and so on. Consider possible issues families/guardians may be facing as they embark on transition planning. Check all that apply to students on your caseload:

— Acceptance of child's disability by family members
— Agreement/disagreement on proper media for students to use in order to accommodate their needs for learning, communication, differentiation, modification, or something similar

- Issues around overprotectiveness by family/caregivers
- Issues of teasing or bullying by peers
- Student challenges with social interactions and feelings of isolation
- Family understanding of the limitations of the disability in areas that will need support and empowerment for student independence—that is, instances where family or students do not have realistic expectations for needs to support independence, career, and/or college planning
- Learning how to accept or reject help in a healthy way—namely, student struggles to self-advocate
- Issues around help-dependency
- Student feels overly stressed and pressured to perform
- Challenges around sexuality, for example, lack of awareness of student's sexuality
- Lack of age-appropriate interests and experiences—meaning, student has not had enough exposure to age-appropriate activities and gravitates toward activities that are at a younger level developmentally than the student's age
- Have not considered or planned for future goals, hopes, and dreams
- Assumed student will always live with family/parents not planning for the event that it is not possible
- Low grades and limited opportunities for college or career next steps
- Intensive behavior issues that can limit opportunities in the transition
- Personal hygiene or care issues that need to be addressed
- Student exhibits limited interest areas
- Issues related to lack of progress or slow progress

(List curated from Understood.org and Pogrund, 2014)

Consider the issues you checked and brainstorm ways to embed supports for parents/guardians to learn more about each area of need.

Postsecondary College Focus

K–12 services are entitlement services while postsecondary services require self-advocacy. Table 4.1 is included here to consider the differences across special education, 504 Plans, and university-level policies.

Table 4.1.

Component	K–12 Special Education	K–12 504 Plan	University Level
Student records	All records are accessible to student and parent/guardian.	All records are accessible to student and parent/guardian.	University-level records are only accessible to the student. Governed by FERPA, information cannot be released to anyone, including the parent, without a written release by the student.
Emotional/behavioral supports	Consideration, planning, and support for behavioral needs.	Student must follow a code of conduct for behavior.	Student is held to the *Student Code of Conduct* and is not entitled to any special consideration.
Eligibility	District evaluates and identifies disabilities. Students must have an educational need for intervention and services.	Parent provides documentation of disability. Another difference is 504 Plans do not require intensive invertions and services as included in special education.	Student is responsible to provide documentation of disability and need for reasonable accommodations to the student disability services office.
Student success	IDEA requires an Individual Education Plan (IEP) to be reasonably calculated to enable a student to make progress in light of the child's circumstances and teachers must monitor progress.	Plans don't guarantee student success, they are primarily for access and accommodations.	Student is responsible for their own academic success.
What is provided?	Special education services, supports, interventions, and related services are provided.	Regular class curriculum with accommodations that do not change target skills.	Disability support office's role is to accommodate the student in university-level classes with no fundamental alteration of the content.

(continued)

Table 4.1. *Continued*

Component	K–12 Special Education	K–12 504 Plan	University Level
Possible fees	Free evaluation of disability and the guarantee of a free and appropriate public education (FAPE).	Parents can provide an evaluation of disability, but the district can also evaluate.	Student is responsible for disability evaluation and submits to the office of disability services for consideration.
Who develops the plan?	The IEP team develops an IEP as a collaborative team.	Services determined by the 504 Plan team.	Student initiates requests for reasonable accommodations. There are no IEPs or 504s in postsecondary education.
Who ensures the plan is implemented?	District ensures that the IEP is implemented and FAPE.	District/parent/student responsible.	Student is responsible for their own academic progress.
How are services seen?	Entitled services identified on the IEP.	Services determined by 504 Plan.	Providing reasonable accommodations is not an automatic process; university services for a student with disabilities determines eligibility and what reasonable accommodations will be provided based on the disability documentation provided.
How are accommodations and modifications seen across these plans?	Accommodations, modifications, and other intensive support to the program of study are permitted as identified on IEP dependent on eligible disability areas.	Only accommodations to programs of study that do not alter target skills are permitted as identified in 504 Plan.	No fundamental alterations allowed: accommodations may not result in a fundamental alteration to course content or academic program; nor impose an undue burden on an institution to provide accommodation. *Universities must be ADA and WCAG Compliant (which may create undue burden, but they are required to comply).*

Component	K–12 Special Education	K–12 504 Plan	University Level
Who advocates?	Teacher, student, parent, and other team members can advocate for student	Parent/student advocates.	Student advocates for self.
What else is included?	Personal, academic, and behavioral services: for example, transportation, personal attendant, nurse, and inclusive education support such as working with a paraprofessional.	No personal services provided.	No personal services; however, supports will be identified on accommodation letters such as orientation and mobility, sign language interpreters, proctoring for testing, support for notes (i.e., for a student with physical access challenges) that will then be implemented in support of the student accommodations.

FERPA (Family Educational Rights and Privacy Act of 1974): All students over the age of eighteen are free to access their own student records, request changes to their student records, and "to have some control over the disclosure of personally identifiable information from these records." Parents of children over the age of eighteen are not permitted to access their child's student records, as protected under FERPA.

Postsecondary Career Focus

Consider activities that can expose and orient students to careers when they graduate from high school and/or college. Activities that can help students plan for transition include:

1. "All about me" questionnaires and activities

2. Career inventories, see O*Net to support student career exploration

3. Considering areas of adult life such as questionnaires about independent living, transportation, healthy lifestyle, budgeting, hobbies and interests, socializing, and other independent living responsibilities

It is helpful to teach students about the law that governs their access to workplace accommodations. The Americans with Disabilities Act (ADA) outlines three groups of people whose rights are protected.

1. People with an actual disability—physical or mental impairment—that substantially limits one or more life activities. This is meant to be a functional definition, not a medical definition. It is all about how the disability affects this person and it is determined on a case-by-case basis.

2. People with a record of disability.

3. People that are regarded as a "person with a disability." This one can be confusing: it can be someone who is diagnosed with a disease, for example being diagnosed with AIDS, and this diagnosis means they cannot be discriminated against. It can also protect a parent or caregiver who cares for someone with a disability (ada.gov).

What are some activities that are currently included in your special education program and/or within your school that expose students to college/career information? Are there college visits scheduled in your program (if high school)? Are there career shadow opportunities or other learning activities for students to learn about careers they may be interested in?

Independent Living Focus

The ADA also protects persons with disabilities within areas of community and living access and required infrastructure. Exploring stories of advocacy and access within communities with students will launch discussions and support student understanding of their rights. An additional law protecting housing is the Fair Housing Act, as amended in 1988, which prohibits housing discrimination on the basis of race, color, religion, sex, disability, familial status, and national origin. As educators, keep in mind that IDEA governs K–12 schooling. When students graduate from K–12, the ADA, Rehabilitation Act of 1973, which includes Sections 501, 503, 504, and 508, and other laws are what guarantee rights to persons with disabilities in adulthood.

Part II: Transition Planning: Systems versus Person Planning

A person-centered planning approach encourages teams to frame planning by the student's needs, focus on the student's individual strengths and capacities, and acknowledge disability-specific issues related to community and funding resources that can support student well-being, access, and independence. The student and the student's family/guardians are highly involved in the transition process. Person-centered planning is not a one-shot meeting—that is, only discussed at the IEP meeting each year. It is ideally ongoing, iterative, and invites a shared support focus. A system-framed transition planning is typically more focused on what community supports are available in the geographical area and finding ways to fit student needs into what is available. Learn more about advances in person-centered planning from state-level resources such as New Jersey's Person-Centered Approach in Schools and Transitions; Perkins School for the Blind, "The Power of Person-Centered Planning"; and MAPS from Inclusive Solutions.

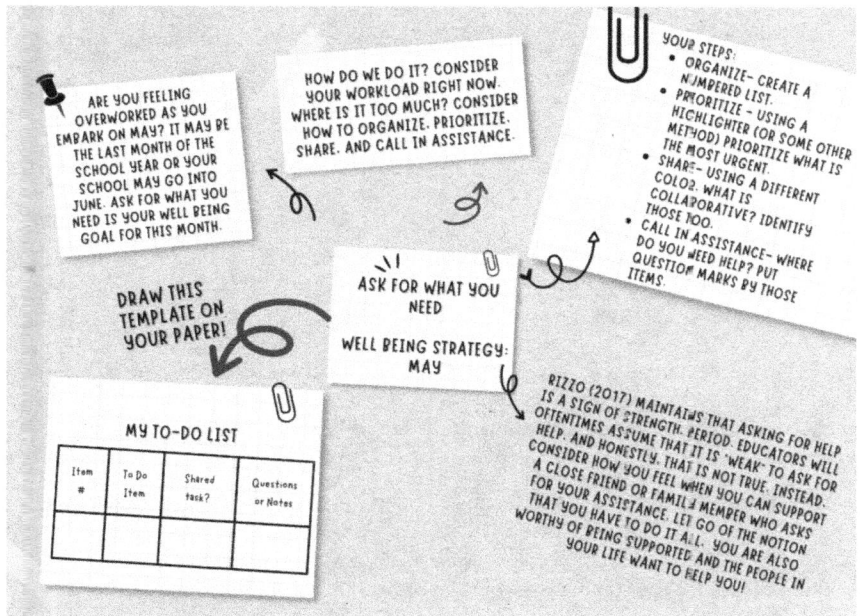

WELL-BEING

May Plan for Well-Being

For May, it can be incredibly difficult to ask for help. At times, we can feel so overwhelmed that we don't even know what to ask for when asking for help! Has that happened to you? Remember, it takes courage to ask for help. This month, consider asking for help with something that has been too much to complete on your own.

Share your well-being goal each month with one another to support making it happen!

Having realistic expectations of future independent plans can be challenging for students to imagine. This can be hard for any high school student and acutely challenging for students with disabilities who may have unrealistic expectations for independent living—that is, students may suggest that they will live the dream in another state with a full-time

COLLABORATE ON

personal care attendant but not consider how they will fund those experiences, travel, and other supports they may require to live independently. Check out the resources provided by the National Technical Center on Transition: The Collaborative (NTACT:C) to find and download student activity resources to help support discussions and training opportunities to guide comprehensive transition planning with your students. https://transitionta.org/.

SUGGESTED RESOURCES

Bridgeo, W., Caruso, B., D'Andrea, L., Fitzgerald, D., Fox, S., Gicklhorn, C., & Zatta, M. (2014). *Total life learning: Preparing for transition*. Perkins School for the Blind.

Morningstar, M., & Clavenna-Deane, B. (2018). *Your complete guide to transition planning and services*. Paul H. Brookes Publishing Company.

Pogrund, R. L. (2014). "Book review: *ECC essentials: Teaching the expanded core curriculum to students with visual impairments.*" *Journal of Visual Impairment & Blindness, 108*(6), 519–522.

Rizzo, K. (2017, September 15). Why asking for help is a strength (and three ways to do so effectively), *Forbes*.

Internet Resources

National Technical Assistance Center on Transition (NTACT): https://transitionta.org/.
O*Net: https://www.onetonline.org/.
MAPS, Inclusive Solutions: https://inclusive-solutions.com/person-centred-planning/maps/.
Person-centered planning guidance at PACER: https://www.pacer.org/transition/learning-center/independent-community-living/.
Vanderbilt IRIS Center, Transition Planning: https://iris.peabody.vanderbilt.edu.

Supporting students with intensive learning needs/multiple disabilities:

Texas School for the Blind: https://www.tsbvi.edu/programs/transition.
Perkins School for the Blind: https://www.perkins.org/transition-center/.

June

WORKING IN EARLY CHILDHOOD

How can early intervention programs be implemented and assessed using data-based decision-making?

Meet Jack, a special education teacher who has been working with students with autism spectrum disorder (ASD) for more than a decade. Jack loves to stay up to date on the latest evidence-based early intervention practices. He wants to ensure that his team's interventions are effective, aligned with current interventions to support students with ASD, and support students' successful transition going into kindergarten.

Jack has recently begun to use a data-based decision-making approach to assess the curriculum and instruction in the early intervention programs that he and his team implement. By gathering and analyzing data on the effectiveness of different interventions, Jack hopes to make informed decisions about which strategies to keep, modify, or replace. Currently, Jack is researching strategies to engage in more "joint attention" with his young students. He has learned about a literacy strategy that has been proven effective: adding words during periods of joint attention to help students pair words with objects and activities resulting in helping them learn new words while working on joint attention. He is trying out different strategies to incorporate this strategy into both the literacy block and periods of play during the school day.

Related to this strategy and others, Jack has been analyzing various interventions and gathering data on their effectiveness. He is keeping up with these observations by jotting down anecdotal notes at the end of each day and keeping a tally system of successful instances of various student goals. A challenge that he realizes is not all interventions work for every student with ASD, which is for a continuum of reasons, one being unique interests of his students that are different for each one of them. Jack must balance the need for individualized interventions with the need for research-based practices to continue to develop his planning each week. Another challenge is keeping up with each paraprofessional and related services team member across the week to note their observations of student learning.

Case questions:

- Explore ways that Jack can be efficient in planning and collaborating on individualized interventions for each student in his preschool program, which has eighteen students enrolled with four paraprofessional aides and four related service professionals (SLP, SLP Assistant, OT, and PT) supporting the program.
- How can Jack measure the effectiveness of an intervention and gather appropriate data for decision-making? How can he work as a team with his paraprofessional and related services team to collect individual student data and make adjustments to interventions and strategies each week?

Special Education Mentoring
MONTHLY CHECKLIST: JUNE

TO DO...	DONE	NOTES
School is out for summer (sometime this month!) Discuss Extended School Year (ESY) programs. If you are out of the building consider connecting with one another for lunch or coffee to discuss ESY and other summer planning		
Summer time is an ideal time to reflect and renew your curriculum planning for the year. Using the curriculum planning template, think through an intervention program you hope to launch next year. Use the vertical plan (across a couple of years) and horizontal plan (across one school year) to develop goals and plan		
During the year, you likely had little time to review special opportunities available in your district for students served in special education. Are there adaptive sports, tutoring, TriO programs (for first-generation college students), etc.		
Plan for your caseload for next year. Potentially use this time to get organized, jot down reflections on students who will continue in your program while their progress is still fresh on your mind.		

OTHER CHECKLIST ITEMS UNIQUE TO YOUR SCHOOL DISTRICT

_____

_____

_____

ALSO FOR THIS MONTH

☐ Well-Being Goal _____

☐ **Collaborate on Mentoring Activities**

☐ **Suggested Resources: follow up?**

SPECIAL EDUCATION FOCUS

To support your goal setting, this section is meant for you to jot down one focus area/question in each of your primary roles.

☐ IEP: _____

☐ Intensive Intervention: _____

☐ Collaboration: _____

Note that anything italicized in the checklist is referring to a template in the back of this guidebook.

June Monthly Checklist

This checklist provides a roadmap for mentor discussions and timely special education roles and responsibilities typically occurring around this time of the year. There are spaces to add your own checklist items and goals within the three primary roles and responsibilities of special education professionals related to IEP caseload management, collaboration, and teaching specifically designed instruction also referred to as intensive interventions.

Key Learning Goals

1. Define the concept of early intervention within special education and its importance in providing support to students and their families.

2. Analyze, evaluate, and justify the effectiveness of different strategies for engaging families/caregivers in early intervention practices, including the use of technology, home visits, cultural brokers, and family support networks.

3. Understand benefits of horizontal and vertical curriculum planning to support special education program development.

Part I: Early Intervention in Special Education

Early intervention is an ecosystem of support and collaboration put in place to support a child with an identified developmental delay or other eligible disability such as a physical, sensory, motor, or social disability, or a disability in another area. The two common pathways for flagging a need for early intervention services are (1) genetic or congenital factors that have been identified at birth or during infancy; and (2) children identified later by parent, guardian, medical professional, or caregiver as having a form of developmental delay that is preventing the child from reaching developmental milestones.

- What do you already know about early childhood special education services? (You may be working as an early childhood special education teacher in which case you know a ton about this topic.)
- What services and programs are provided in your school district/system?
- What are the Child Find procedures in your school district?

Early childhood programs will typically include the five areas listed in figure 16 below. Early childhood plans are constructed by a multidisciplinary team with a unique focus on home and school partnerships. Goals are designed to be implemented both at school and home with consistent communication systems included as part of the early childhood Individualized Family Service Plan (IFSP). Eligibility areas of disability can be associated with a congenital disability such as a visual impairment, hearing impairment, cerebral palsy, or a disorder associated with a syndrome, such as CHARGE or Rett's syndrome. If a disability has not been identified but a child is determined as having a develop-

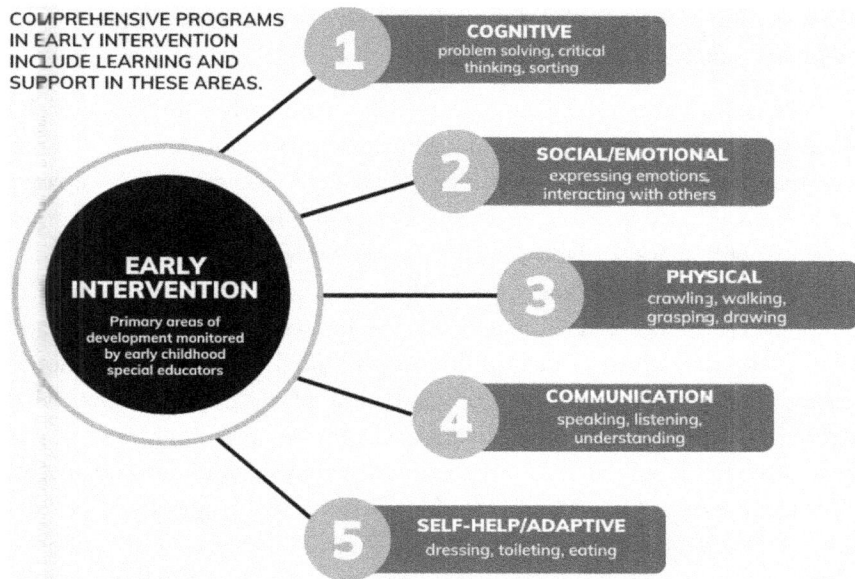

Figure 16. Early Childhood Program Overview
This figure depicts five primary areas of early childhood education.

mental delay, their disability area is categorized as "developmentally delayed." This designation can stay in place on the IEP until third grade. It is important to keep in mind that the unique needs of students with sensory impairments, multiple impairments, autism, speech/language impairments, and physical impairments have been widely researched in areas of early intervention.

Let's discuss the research base on early intervention benefits. There are a wide range of benefits for students who receive early intervention support, such as developmental gains that can provide accommodations and support to enhance targeting skill areas within cognition, physical adaptations, communication, and more. Also, early intervention has been shown to dramatically improve learning potential for students and increase academic and behavioral success in K–12. From a five-year study implemented in Washington, they observed that students with autism who were nonverbal received early intervention services to support their communication, and fewer than 10 percent of the students remained nonverbal following the early intervention program (University of Washington Autism Center, n.d.). Other areas of success: preventing academic/behavior challenges by teaching adaptation and self-regulation skills, enhancing social/emotional well-being, increased family involvement and support, cost-saving, improved independence, increased school readiness, inclusivity, and positive long-term outcomes in adulthood.

What are the primary roles of special education professionals in early childhood education and development?

There are some notable areas that distinguish early childhood special education professionals from K–12 education professionals. The field has a tremendous growth outlook but can have a reduced salary as compared to K–12 special education teachers. Early childhood special education teachers will work collaboratively across a multidisciplinary team for most of the school day and may work much more closely with families and caregivers than educators who work with students from other grade levels. The curriculum in early childhood is linked to the five areas noted earlier and will typically be designed as a play-based program with structures included that are individualized to the students served in the programs. A primary area of satisfaction noted by early childhood special education teachers is watching students grow and being part of collaborative teams all working together to support our youngest students. Working closely with families is also counted as another reward area in early childhood education. Special education professionals will lead the team to design and implement the IFSP which defines the goals, services, and collaborative supports that will be implemented across the family and multidisciplinary team.

Learning Partnerships between Home and School in Early Childhood

A distinguishing feature in early childhood education is the high level of parent/guardian collaboration and communication. The Office of Early Childhood Development provides a robust list of early childhood embedded strategies that are specific to students with autism but can benefit any student. The tips in their guidance are based on concepts of learning and early childhood development that can be embedded into everyday routines at both home and school. In their tips for early care and education providers guide, concepts are described with information about why they are important, and a step-by-step description of how to embed concepts into home and school routines. Examples of these concepts are engaging children in play, using children's interests in activities, using visual cues to make choices, shared book reading, and predictable spaces and routines. In your role as an early childhood special educator, you could practice strategies together with students and their parents/guardians to model and collaborate on the strategy, language used in teaching, and prompting being used to keep it consistent across school and home settings.

Part II: Map Out a Curriculum Plan for Next Year

We are switching gears from the overview of early childhood to consider curriculum planning strategies. As you launch into summer and reflect on what went well this year, it is an ideal time to consider how you might sequence an intervention or curriculum unit differently. Without the distraction of students, once you have more time to rest and recoup from the year, considering how to map out a curriculum intervention is a worthwhile activity to consider completing. Within the Section V "Resources" in this Guidebook, you will see horizontal and vertical curriculum maps to use as launching points for curriculum planning. Let's define some curriculum terms in case any of these strategies are new for you.

- **Horizontal curriculum**: The goal of horizontal curriculum is to plan learning across the year in order to ensure enough scaffolds and concept exposure is included to support student learning. Horizontal curriculum can also refer to teachers teaching the same standards to create uniformity in their curriculum so students will be exposed to the same content across different teachers.
- **Vertical curriculum**: The goal of vertically aligned curriculum is to consider the knowledge, skills, and standards students are expected to know at lower grade levels and also be aware of what knowledge, skills, and standards students are expected to know at higher grade levels. Understanding how concepts are building off one another can support your work as a special education professional since you are either differentiating or accommodating academic content at grade level and/or providing remediation of academic content from previous grade levels in the form of intensive intervention or review to support student learning needs.

When mapping curriculum, whether it be general education standards or intensive intervention learning goals, the steps are broadly the same, which are to create a plan that organizes the learning concepts and outcomes for the student. First, identify the standards or sets of standards. Depending on your state, standards may already be organized to have overarching learning goals with several objectives underneath each goal/standard. That organization system is helpful to consider underlying skills within each standard/goal that must be mastered as students learn new knowledge and skills. Next, consider your student caseload abilities. This step can be aided by creating a visual map to brainstorm such as a mind-map with the standard/goal in the middle and prerequisite skill areas that students need to know and be able to do surrounding it. A web resource is listed in the selected resource section of this month, *Achieving the Core*, which includes "Coherence Maps" of the math standards from K–12. The Coherence Map represents a visual map of the standard at any given grade level allowing the user to view underlying skills across all grade levels. Consider your learner's abilities, any additional special education–specific learning objectives, the district/system/school expectations for mastery, and curriculum materials you have access to.

Use the brainstorming template, figure 17, to consider a standard or learning goal. Add it to the middle of the diagram and then brainstorm as many ideas as you are able to within each branch. See the "tips" box in the lower right-hand corner of the brainstorming template. It suggests you can number both the prerequisite and skills listed to help you create a horizontal map of your instructional plan.

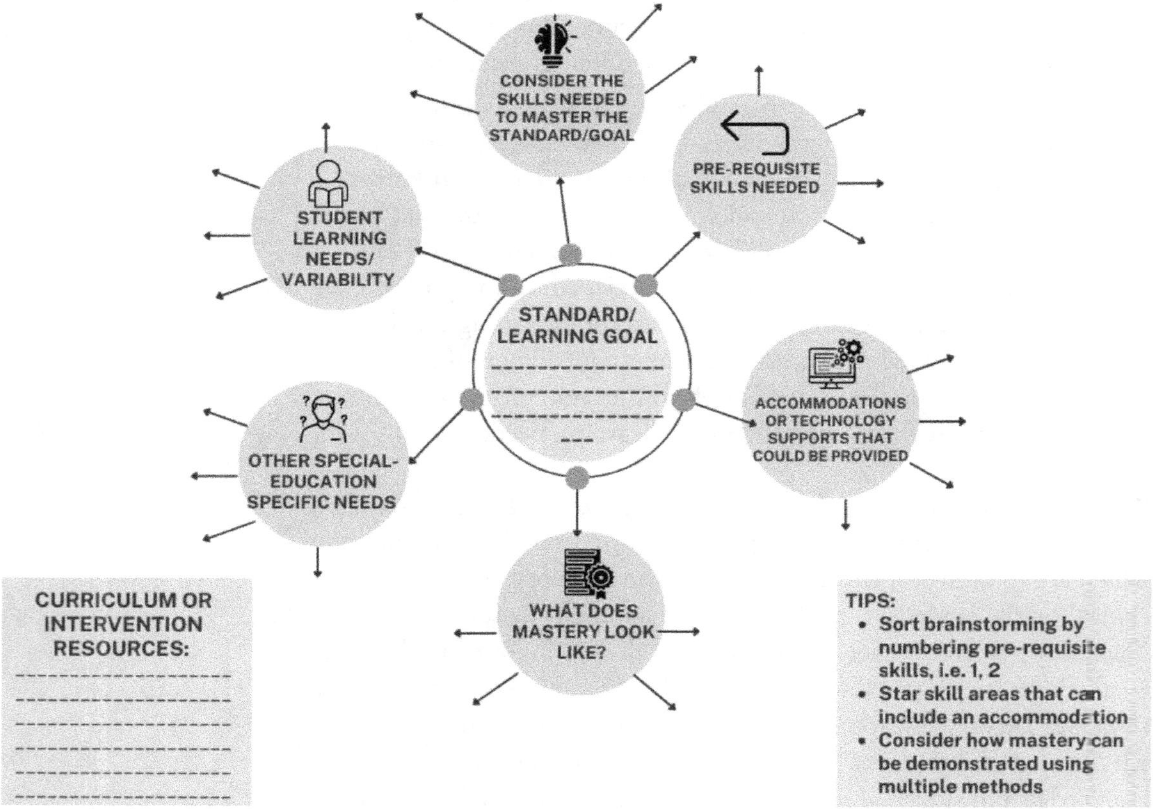

Figure 17. Curriculum Mapping Brainstorming Map

This figure is a concept map for considering factors that impact the horizontal curriculum mapping of a standard or learning goal.

Using the templates provided in resource 14 from Section V of this Guidebook can help you outline a horizontal or vertical curriculum map linked to what you have brainstormed above. Keep in mind that curriculum maps aim to:

- be purposefully developed and well organized;
- be organized to identify alignment (or misalignment) between skill areas, learning objectives, gaps in transition from grade levels, and subject areas to support our students in the special education programs we implement;
- clearly define learning goals and outcomes so we can better design differentiated instruction;
- work toward identifying educational gap(s); and
- be well aligned with the curriculum and learning targets within our school building/district/system.

WELL-BEING

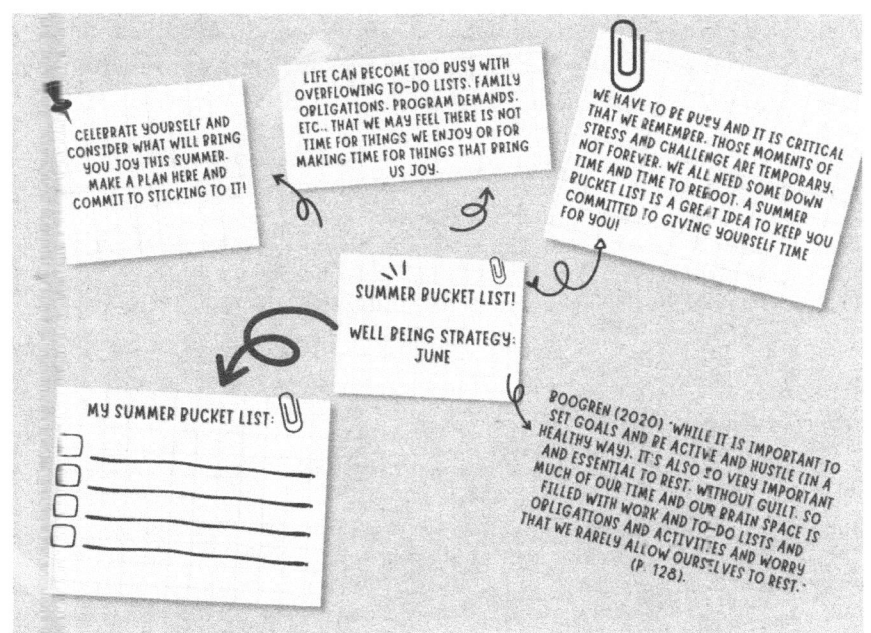

June Plan for Well-Being

For June, the summer bucket list! Please consider ways to celebrate your incredibly hard work this year! Bucket list items for the summer do not have to involve splurging on a big trip or an epic adventure that is local. They can be big or small, but what is essential is that they are activities that bring you joy, fun, and a recharge.

Share your well-being goal each month with one another to support making it happen!

COLLABORATE ON

Find time to check in and reflect on the year. It is June, so you may be finished for the year and meeting with one another may not be possible this month. Take a moment to reflect. Consider jotting down a note to one another, see the prompts below, and share when you get back to your school buildings.

Dear _____,
    Our work together this year was _____ and impacted me in these ways: _____.
    I am grateful for your _____. You always _____, and that is a strength you possess that is such an asset to our school community. Thank you.
    I want to add this final thought: _____.

Sincerely,

_____

SUGGESTED RESOURCES

Helpful resources for early childhood can be found on the Centers for Disease Control and Prevention and Center for Parent Information and Resources website (parentcenterhub.org).

Flinders, D. J., & Thornton, S. J. (Eds.). (2021). *The curriculum studies reader*. Routledge.
Lickey, D., & Powers, P. (2011). *Starting with their strengths: Using the project approach in early childhood education*. Teachers College Press.
Pogrund, R. L., & Fazzi, D. L. (2002). *Early focus: Working with young blind and visually impaired children and their families*. American Foundation for the Blind.
Reichow, B., Boyd, B., Barton, E., & Odom, S. (Eds.) (2016). *Handbook of early childhood*. Springer.

Internet Resources

Achieve the Core, coherence map, math: https://tools.achievethecore.org/coherence-map/.
The Lettered Classroom: https://www.youtube.com/channel/UCFebmxJBh559c-8BEcnxL-DQ. (*Note*: this is a vlog of a fourth-grade teacher who delves into ways to build curriculum planning.)
Office of Early Childhood Development, autism awareness and acceptance in early childhood: https://www.acf.hhs.gov/archive/ecd/child-health-development/asd
Teacher Lesson Planner at Common Curriculum: https://www.commoncurriculum.com/.
University of Washington Autism Center (n.d.). *On-time autism intervention (OTAI) / early recognition*. https://depts.washington.edu/uwautism/.

July

Putting It All Together

How can a special education teacher seamlessly differentiate, individualize, and scaffold instruction to support students with various disabilities within an inclusive classroom?

Jordyn is a special education teacher who works at a public middle school. He has a caseload of twenty-five students ranging from sixth to eighth grade. His middle school is fully inclusive, and he pushes into six classes a day with two planning periods for interventions and IEP caseload management. Recently, he has noticed that one of his students, Emma, has been struggling to keep up with the rest of the class in math. Emma has a diagnosis of dyscalculia and attention-deficit/hyperactivity (ADHD), which makes it difficult for her to solve basic math problems. While Jordyn knows that he needs to differentiate his instruction to meet Emma's needs, he is not sure what the best approach is. He wants to create a math assistive technology (AT) plan that will support Emma's math work (while not missing out on learning important math knowledge and skills by using comprehensive technology support). Additionally, Emma's family immigrated from India, and her mom is a mathematician working at the university in their city. Jordyn's perception is that Emma's mom struggles to support Emma at home because it is hard for her to understand why Emma does not make the same connections she does when solving math problems.

Emma's math class is currently working on multiplication and division. Jordyn designs a math lesson that involves creating visual models to help students understand the concepts. He provides several different examples and writing prompts for the students to practice. He also paired Emma with a classmate who is strong in math and encouraged them to work together on the assignment. Jordyn asks Emma to explain to her partner what she understands from the reading, emphasizing that it's okay to ask questions and work through problems slowly.

The central conflict Jordyn faces is that Emma needs lessons catered to her individualized needs, but Jordyn isn't sure how to execute this without creating a completely new lesson just for Emma every time. How could Jordyn infuse technology support, peer mentoring, and other recurring accommodations so Emma can be successful without one-on-one support? Jordyn's competing pressures include keeping up with the pace of the class material and ensuring that Emma is making adequate progress to meet her Individualized Education Plan (IEP) goals in addition to the planning he needs to implement across his entire caseload.

Case questions:

- Consider Jordyn's intensive intervention "hat." How can Jordyn design individualized instruction for Emma? What are tools and resources that will help him design ongoing interventions and differentiated supports for her in math?
- Think of Jordyn's collaboration "hat." What are the ways he can collaborate with his teaching team to create a team effort that supports Emma and other students in the same middle school math class as Emma?
- Finally, think of Jordyn's IEP caseload management "hat." How can he learn about technology tools that will support Emma's math accommodations? How can he track her progress relative to her IEP goals and invite more partnership with her family to support her learning goals?

Special Education Mentoring
MONTHLY CHECKLIST: JULY

TO DO...	DONE	NOTES
July is a great month to rest, relax, and reset! You will likely not be working this month, even if you taught ESY, you will be wrapping that up and have most of July off (hopefully!). Enjoy this time and reconnect with your well being.		
This month provides some breathing space for you to R & R. Consider reading an inspirational book or story about a person with a disability. Suggested novels to consider- look to library staff curated lists for a book that is right for you! The Boston Library has an excellent list entitled, In Their Own Words: Memoirs About Living With Disabilities and Chronic Illnesses		
Learn about your professional organizations and join one! Check out July's *Professional Development Self-Reflection* template to choose an organization and imagine future goals for your development and leadership opportunities.		
Plan for your caseload for next year. Potentially use this time to get organized, jot down reflections on students who will continue in your program while their progress is still fresh on your mind.		

OTHER CHECKLIST ITEMS UNIQUE TO YOUR SCHOOL DISTRICT

_____

_____

ALSO FOR THIS MONTH

- [ ] **Well-Being Goal**
- [ ] **Collaborate on Mentoring Activities**
- [ ] **Suggested Resources: follow up?**

SPECIAL EDUCATION FOCUS

To support your goal setting, this section is meant for you to jot down one focus area/question in each of your primary roles.

- [ ] IEP: _____

- [ ] Intensive Intervention: _____

- [ ] Collaboration: _____

Note that anything italicized in the checklist is referring to a template in the back of this guidebook.

July Monthly Checklist

This checklist provides a roadmap for mentor discussions and timely special education roles and responsibilities typically occurring around this time of the year. There are spaces to add your own checklist items and goals within the three primary roles and responsibilities of special education professionals related to IEP caseload management, collaboration, and teaching specifically designed instruction also referred to as intensive interventions.

Key Learning Goals

1. Identify the key professional skills required in special education teacher leadership roles, such as communication, problem-solving, and decision-making, and explain how they contribute to effective teaching team management.

2. Plan and create a professional development plan that is aligned with your future professional goals in special education.

3. Develop a visionary statement about your role in special education teacher leadership in promoting equity and inclusion, outlining specific goals and strategies that align with the professional standards in the field of special education.

PART I: MAKING A PLAN FOR YEAR TWO, LEADERSHIP, AND PROFESSIONAL ORGANIZATIONS

Becoming a leader in special education involves a combination of gaining expertise in the field, building leadership skills, and advocating for inclusive practices. There are endless opportunities to consider for next steps in your career after becoming a special education teacher. Why? Because special education teachers are incredibly adept in many areas of student learning, making them uniquely qualified to become learning leaders in their school buildings as well as within their districts or school systems. There are several paths toward leadership development, such as adding more licenses or credentials; for example, adding your administrator license will enable you to consider an administrative position. Another professional development path could lead toward scholarship and district- or system-level roles by obtaining a master's or doctoral degree. Let's start with how to ensure you are continuing to grow in the field, and next, we can discuss different career paths to consider for your career advancement.

Here are the next steps for teachers to become leaders in special education:

1. An important activity for teachers is to undertake continuous professional development. For example, you can create continuous learning opportunities by joining professional organizations, attending conferences, joining professional listservs and professional learning networks (PLNs), and more. Being a member of a professional organization is an ideal way to stay current with research, trends, and best

practices in special education. Each state has varying rules related to maintaining your probationary or professional teaching license, and there is typically a professional development component with a certain number of hours required over a period of time; for example, your state may require ninety professional development "seat" or "workshop" hours over a five-year period to maintain a professional license, or something similar. Professional development opportunities within your school district/system will also count toward this time, but one issue that is sometimes problematic for special education professionals and related service team members is that this professional development is not aligned with their teaching license/certification areas (since it may be geared toward general education professional development). A list of organizations to learn about and consider is included in this month's "Suggested Resources" section.

2. Another important leadership and collaborative activity in special education is to become involved with special-education-focused parent, teacher, and community engagement activities. There may be school- or district/system-level teachers or parent/teacher organizations that advocate and support special education or related programs, which can be a great way to become more involved and increase your leadership skills. By fostering strong relationships with parents and the local community, you will enhance your professional skills and grow more sensitive to the concerns, needs, and ideas of team members who can help broaden your perspective and understanding. Conversely, you also have an opportunity to be a resource for parents related to topics such as learning strategies, cultivating student independence, and strengthening the connections between home, community, and school.

3. Consider advanced degrees, licenses, and certifications. Another next step in leadership and learning for special education professionals is to consider pursuing advanced degrees (e.g., a master's or doctorate) or additional certifications in special education, administration, psychology, applied behavior analysis (ABA specialist), or other related field areas, to deepen your knowledge and expertise. With an advanced degree, you will be entitled to a higher salary in most school districts/systems, and it can also advance you within the school building or district/system to a higher salaried position. Working at the district/system level as a coach, interventionist, mentor, or other role could be achieved with an advanced degree and years of experience within the school district or system. Both master's and doctoral degrees will entitle you to work at the university level

or with other professional development organizations to support new special education teachers. With a terminal degree in special education or something similar, you are entitled to be a director and design a teacher preparation program, and potentially research best practices in the field, thus exponentially impacting future generations and students in K–12. Finally, preparing for work in higher education will be strengthened by professional activities such as leadership training, presenting at conferences or within the school district/system, participating in action research with colleagues or partnering with university-level collaborators, as well as pursuing professional writing opportunities such as authoring peer-reviewed journal articles and other publications.

4. Another area of special education that is important to note for future leadership is training to be an advocate or work in other law-related fields that support a student's right to free and appropriate public education (FAPE) and other procedural safeguards included in the Individuals with Disabilities Education Act (IDEA).

Part II: Learning Leaders

Becoming a leader in special education is a journey that requires dedication, ongoing professional learning, and a commitment to improving educational outcomes for all students, particularly those with disabilities. Your advocacy and leadership can have a significant impact on creating inclusive and equitable learning environments by coming to know, first-hand, how to proactively cultivate those types of learning environments. Remember, it is important to learn from the perspectives of both your fellow educators and the students you serve. Note organizations below that are "for" versus "of," which is one way to distinguish how an organization is situated in the field of special education—that is, is it an organization that "does for" or is it an organization that "does with"? Work to include both types of organizations in your professional development.

Create a professional development plan for yourself. First, consider your short- and long-term goals. Take a moment to think about them now and jot down some ideas.

Where do you see yourself this coming year and over the next few years?

Create one to three short-term goals (1–3 years):

-

-

-

Now, look to the future, in five years or more from now, where do you see yourself? Imagine some considerations such as your workday or calendar year: do you want to be working a particular school schedule (e.g., have a shorter or longer day depending on outside-of-school factors or to allow time for afterschool activities)?

Mid-range goals (5–6 years):
Any changes to your calendar year or schedule that you want to include in this longer-term planning?

-

-

-

Finally, think about ten years or more from now. I can imagine that might feel very far away. But imagining a professional development plan in this way can be a manifestation of future goals—that is, it can inspire and plant the intention so they will become a reality. It can also be interesting to look back at your previously imagined goals at a later time even if that path was not the one you ended up taking.

Long-term goals (10 years):

-

-

-

Give yourself a hand! It can be challenging to plan for the future, and it benefits your professional goals to note goal ideas and planning. Nice job!

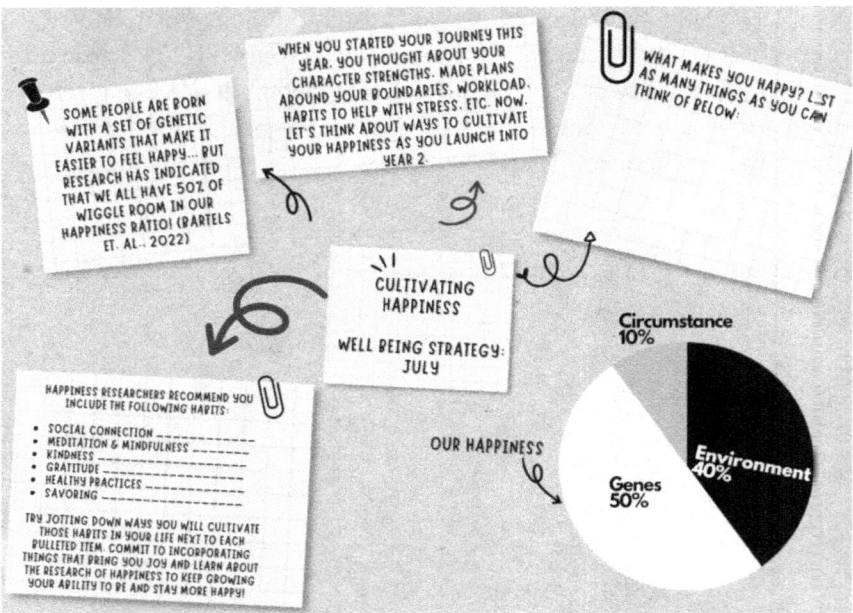

July Plan for Well-Being

For July, you are considering a year's worth of well-being goals that will help you continue to cultivate happiness in your life. We have come back to the importance of taking care of yourself, particularly essential in the field of special education, where we can have unique challenges that can create stress and overwhelm. Noted by well-being advocates, you may have heard the phrase "put on your own oxygen mask before helping others," like we hear on airplanes. This sage wisdom is critical in the field of special education. We cannot be at our best if we are exhausted, overwhelmed, overworked, and unhealthy. We will not make our best decisions and feel grounded in challenging moments with students or teaching teams. Those challenges will happen. Why? Because we are fierce advocates for our students and when they struggle, we may also feel it! Take care of yourself and cultivate happiness in your life. You deserve joy.

Share your well-being goal each month with one another to support making it happen!

You are likely starting to get ready for the upcoming school year. A great collaborative activity at this point in the summer is to connect with one another. Sharing the professional learning goals that you developed would be a great way to launch a check-in conversation. Other items to add to your list might be: (1) Student caseloads for this coming year—have they been determined? If so, share IEPs. (2) Are there any curriculum or district/system-level changes coming to special education this year? (3) Are there any professional development opportunities coming up in August? (4) Are there any building or team changes to note and discuss?

COLLABORATE ON

You have come to the end of the Guidebook. Wow, what a year, huh? Congratulations on finishing this first year of special education teaching and mentoring. Working in a mentoring partnership is truly a gift. It is a space for all the joy, laughter, tears, and frustration along with everything that comes in between. Remember the first-year teacher cycle you reviewed together back in August? There will be newbie teachers coming into your building this year without a doubt, and they will be full of anticipation and excitement for the upcoming year along with feeling like a ball of nerves! Knowing what you know now . . . consider being their "marigolds" and sending some care and support their way. Thank you for choosing to be a special education teaching professional. We are a fierce and loyal bunch who are not afraid to advocate for our students' right to access, achievement, and inclusion.

Go be amazing, and don't forget to take care of yourselves. You deserve supportive teams, along with time to plan, learn, and develop, as well as manageable workloads and caseloads. Don't be afraid to advocate for yourself and your students. You are both worthy of the fight.

The list of professional special education–related organizations below is not exhaustive. The most common organizations are listed below with websites included. If you are a student teacher while completing this guidebook, it's good to know that most organizations will have a reduced student rate. Benefits of joining a professional organization are numerous, including professional development, collaboration, and networking opportunities.

SUGGESTED RESOURCES

1. National Disability Rights Network (NDRN): NDRN is a national organization that provides protection and advocacy services for individuals with disabilities. They work to protect the legal rights of people with disabilities through advocacy and litigation. https://www.ndrn.org/.

2. American Association of People with Disabilities (AAPD): AAPD is the largest cross-disability advocacy organization in the United States. They work to advance the economic and political power of people with disabilities. https://www.aapd.com/.

3. National Council on Disability (NCD): NCD is an independent federal agency that promotes policies and practices that support the inclusion and full participation of people with disabilities in all aspects of society. https://ncd.gov/.

4. Disability Rights Education and Defense Fund (DREDF): DREDF is a national law and policy center focused on advancing the civil and human rights of people with disabilities. They provide legal advocacy and resources. https://www.dredf.org/.

5. Autistic Self Advocacy Network (ASAN): ASAN is an organization run by and for autistic people. They advocate for the rights of autistic individuals, focusing on self-advocacy, empowerment, and inclusion. https://autisticadvocacy.org/.

6. National Federation of the Blind (NFB): NFB is an organization of blind and visually impaired individuals working to promote equality, opportunity, and independence for blind people. https://www.nfb.org/.

7. The Association for Education and Rehabilitation of the Blind and Visually Impaired (AER) is a professional membership organization dedicated to professionals who provide services to persons with vision loss. https://www.aerbvi.org.

8. United Cerebral Palsy (UCP): UCP is a nationwide network of affiliates providing support and advocacy for individuals with cerebral palsy and other disabilities. They focus on promoting inclusion and independence. https://www.ucp.org/.

9. Easterseals: Easterseals provides a wide range of services, support, and advocacy for individuals with disabilities and their families. They focus on promoting independence, inclusion, and wellness. https://www.easterseals.com/.

10. National Spinal Cord Injury Association (NSCIA): NSCIA advocates for individuals with spinal cord injuries and disorders. They provide support, resources, and education. https://www.spinalcord.org/.

11. Little People of America (LPA): LPA is an organization that provides support and advocacy for people with dwarfism and their

families. They work to raise awareness and promote inclusion. https://www.lpaonline.org/.

12. TASH advances equity, opportunity, and inclusion for people with disabilities, with a focus on those with the most significant support needs in the areas of education, employment, and community living through advocacy, research, and practice. https://tash.org/.

13. Council for Exceptional Children (CEC): CEC is one of the largest professional organizations dedicated to special education. It offers resources, conferences, publications, and advocacy efforts to support educators, researchers, and other professionals in the field. https://www.cec.sped.org/.

14. National Association of Special Education Teachers (NASET): NASET provides resources, publications, professional development, and legal support for special education teachers and professionals. They also offer a certification program. https://www.naset.org/.

15. Council for Learning Disabilities (CLD): CLD focuses on the needs of individuals with learning disabilities. They offer research, professional development, and advocacy to improve educational outcomes for students with learning disabilities. https://council-for-learning-disabilities.org/.

16. Autism Society: The Autism Society is a leading advocacy organization for individuals on the autism spectrum. They provide resources, support, and advocacy efforts to improve the lives of those with autism and their families. https://autismsociety.org/.

17. National Down Syndrome Society (NDSS): NDSS focuses on advocating for the rights and inclusion of individuals with Down syndrome. They provide resources, support, and promote research related to Down syndrome. https://www.ndss.org/.

18. American Speech-Language-Hearing Association (ASHA): ASHA is dedicated to professionals in the field of speech-language pathology and audiology, including those who work with individuals with communication disorders and special education professionals. https://www.asha.org/.

19. Association for Positive Behavior Support (APBS): APBS promotes the use of positive behavior support techniques in special education and related fields. They offer resources, conferences, and training. https://www.apbs.org/.

20. National Association of the Deaf (NAD): NAD is an advocacy organization for the deaf and hard of hearing community. They work to protect the civil rights and promote the inclusion of deaf and hard of hearing individuals. https://www.nad.org/.

21. Learning Disabilities Association of America (LDA): LDA provides support, resources, and advocacy for individuals with learning disabilities and those who work with them. They also offer publications and conferences. https://ldaamerica.org/.

22. Cast: Cast is a multifaceted organization with a singular ambition: "Bust the barriers to learning that millions of people experience every day." https://www.cast.org.

23. Assistive Technology Industry Association (ATIA): ATIA's mission is to serve as the collective voice of the assistive technology industry so that the best products and services are delivered to people with disabilities. https://www.atia.org/.

24. ASCD: ASCD is a nonprofit educational organization combined with ISTE (International Society of Technology in Education). Its goal is to empower educators to reimagine and redesign learning through impactful pedagogy and meaningful technology use. https://www.ascd.org/.

Bartels, M., Bang Nes, R., Armitage, J., van de Weijer, M., Vries, L., & Haworth, C. (2022). *Exploring the biological basis for happiness*. World Happiness Report.
Berlinghoff, D. & McLaughlin, V. L. (Eds.) (2022). *Practice-based standards for the preparation of special educators*. Council of Exceptional Children.
McLeskey, J., Maheady, L., Billingsley, B., Brownell, M. T., & Lewis, T. J. (Eds.). (2022). *High leverage practices for inclusive classrooms*. Routledge.
Sayeski, K. L. (2018). Putting high-leverage practices into practice. *Teaching Exceptional Children, 50*(4), 169–171.

Internet Resources

Council for Exceptional Children, "State of the Profession" (2019): https://exceptional-children.org/improving-your-practice/state-profession.
Keltner, D., & Simon-Thomas, E., The Science of Happiness (online course): https://ggsc.berkeley.edu/what_we_do/event/the_science_of_happiness.
Santos, L., The Science of Well-Being [MOOC] (online course), Coursera: https://www.coursera.org/learn/the-science-of-well-being.

Section V
Resources

Resource 1

Who Is Who

This guide is meant to be a template to use for connecting with your team in a new school building. Typical IEP team members are listed, and there are blank spots for adding additional team members unique to your school and district.

Team Member	Preferred Collaboration Method (email, meetings, text)	Contact Info	Team Meeting Info (add consistent meeting time and location)
General education team member(s)			
Administrators			
Psychologist and other evaluators			
Related Service Team Members			
Speech-language pathologist			
Teachers of students with visual impairments (TSVI) and deaf and hard of hearing			
Behavior analyst/ABA specialist			
Physical therapist			
Occupational therapist			
Nurse			
Social worker			
Transition specialist			

Resource 2

Intensive Lesson Plan Template

Lesson Title:

Grade Level/Class Description:

Weekly Outline:

Weekly Outline				
M	**T**	**W**	**Th**	**F**

Standards addressed in this lesson:

Big Ideas

Student Understandings	Essential Questions	Big Idea(s)

- Student-friendly lesson objective (an LO to write on the board for students):

- Students will know:

- Students will be able to do (knowledge and skills):

- How will you differentiate in relation to students' prior knowledge and level of independence with lesson objectives?

- Consider IEP and CLD specific supports needed: What will you include?

Consider Universal Design for Learning

Engagement in Learning Activities	Demonstration of Learning Objective (i.e., project, paper, test)	Representation of Learning Materials

Assessment Plan: Explain How Progress toward Objectives Will Be Measured

	Pre-Assessment	Formative Assessment	Planned Summative Assessment
Assessment accommodations (universal and individualized)			
Anticipated difficulties for students			
Behavior management expectations (motivation, engagement, frustration, transitions, positive reinforcement)			
Materials/resources needed			

Learning Plan/Lesson Outline		Notes
Lesson procedures. What learning experiences and instructional strategies will enable students to achieve the desired results?		
Scaffold learning. Explain how learning will be broken down into parts or how you can guide students through challenging components. What will need to be directly and explicitly taught using step-by-step instructions? Identify guided and independent practice.		
Identify specific high leverage practices (HLPs) being focused on.		
Lesson closure		

Resource 3

Annual IEP Calendar

Use this simple annual calendar to plot out when student IEPs are due. A rule of thumb is to plan IEP meetings to discuss the annual IEP one to two weeks before the IEP is officially up for renewal. Each school district/system/state will have their own procedures for conducting IEP meetings in compliance with the federal laws governing special education programs. Always default to the school district/system procedures for IEPs.

IEP Calendar

August	September	October
November	December	January
February	March	April
May		

Resource 4

IEP Sections Template

Individualized Education Plan (IEP) Report Outline

Visit https://www.understood.org for resources including the "Anatomy of the IEP" workbook to guide your caseload-management professional learning.

- Demographic data/enrollment/eligibility areas
- Dates: The dates of our current meeting and when the triennial evaluation is.
- Procedural safeguards: Offer a copy of the procedural safeguards? These are offered each year in English or another home language.
- Present levels of performance: How is your student doing? This section includes teacher feedback, grades, evaluation data, progress monitoring, and strengths/challenges at school.
- Consideration of special factors: Are there any special factors such as using assistive technology or being a dual language learner, visual impairment, and so on?
- IEP goals.
- Accommodations and modifications.
- ESY predictive factors.
- Extended school year (ESY).
- Assessment participation: What accommodations are needed on standardized assessments?
- Services: The minutes your student meets with a special education teacher or any other specialist in the building inside or outside (special education) each week—this can be called specially or specifically designed instruction (SDI).
- Least restrictive environment (LRE): The percentage of time spent in general education and/or special education.

- Prior written notice (PWN): Anything to add to this document to be sure it is documented as a concern or need. This can include questions or parental rejections needing to be followed up.
- Student/parent participation.
- Meeting participants: Anyone who was part of the meeting is included in meeting participants.

Resource 5

Case Law Review Template

Case Law Review Template

Case	Summarized Legal Precedent	Impacts IEP Implementation How?
Brown v. Board of Education, 347 US 483 (1954)	Separate educational facilities are inherently unequal (this case was determined regarding racial segregation).	This case determined that any "separate but equal" programming choice is inherently unequal.

There have been countless cases that have interpreted IDEA since it was originally written into law in the 1990s. Review more caselaw here: https://www.wrightslaw.com/caselaw.htm.

The sections proposed on this table could be used to help (1) review the case; (2) summarize the findings, which will usually be stated as "the court held . . ."; (3) indicate how this case changes the way that special education programs should be implemented. A common example is listed below, and extra rows are provided to fill in some notes from further case law explorations.

Case	Summarized Legal Precedent	Impacts IEP Implementation How?
Endrew F. v. Douglas County School District RE-1 (No. 15-827) (2017)	In his opinion, Chief Justice Roberts wrote, "a student offered an educational program providing 'merely more than de minimis' progress from year to year can hardly be said to have been offered an education at all."	This case suggests that special education teams must strive to support student growth and success beyond just the bare "minimum" of growth. It means that teams cannot idly allow for a student experiencing either a lack of progress or no progress: teams must instead intensify interventions, support student progress in other ways as well, and clearly document progress monitoring toward goals.

Resource 6

Student One-Pager Template

IEP software will typically provide "one-pagers" regarding students for teaching teams to share with one another. These can often be several pages long. It is recommended that special education caseload managers create a one-page summary of pertinent information as a "one-pager." As with any recommendations in this Guidebook, check your district/system policy on whether these are standard procedure and how they can be shared—that is, over email or only printed/distributed, as well as other protections that are aligned with FERPA and student privacy concerns.

Student Name: IEP goals:	Grade level/current programs/electives/schedule:	Picture of the student
Areas of educational need:	Strengths, interests, and motivators:	Triggers or specific challenges:
Instructional strategies that work well:	Accommodations needed:	Assistive technology or other differentiated supports:

Resource 7

AT Evaluation and Template

Assistive Technology Evaluation

Date:

Evaluator: [name], Assistive Technology Specialist

Overview and Purpose

Assistive technology (AT) devices are identified in IDEA 2004 as: "Any item, piece of equipment or product system, whether acquired commercially off the shelf, modified, or customized, that is used to increase, maintain, or improve the functional capabilities of children with disabilities." This definition includes training and implementation of AT. This evaluation aims to determine the most effective AT tools and strategies for students served by an IEP or 504 Plan.

Birthdate:

Age:

Grade level:

School:

Disability areas:

Percentage of time in general education:

Receives special education support for:

Referring teacher:

Resource 7

AT Assessments Used and Results

	Results Analysis	
Accommodations Needed	**Assessment Results Specific to Reading, Writing, Math (etc.)**	**Additional Items**

Summary of assistive technology (AT)/accommodation supports needed:

AT trialing needed:

Recommended AT Implementation		
Within School	Outside School	Collaborative Team Members
Services needed:		
Team members providing services:		
Instruction needed:		Who will provide:

Resource 8

Bias Self-Reflection Guide

EXPLORING OUR BIAS: SELF-REFLECTION

STEP 1
Visit: https://implicit.harvard.edu/

Choose one or more Implicit Association Tests (IAT)

STEP 2
In the space below, using any art-making media you choose, reflect on what you learned about implicit associations you are unconsciously making.

STEP 3
Create 1-2 self-awareness goals around your IAT results. Fill these in below.

I became aware that _____, to talk back to this unconscious bias, I will/try/wonder _____.

I became aware that _____, to talk back to this unconscious bias, I will/try/wonder _____.

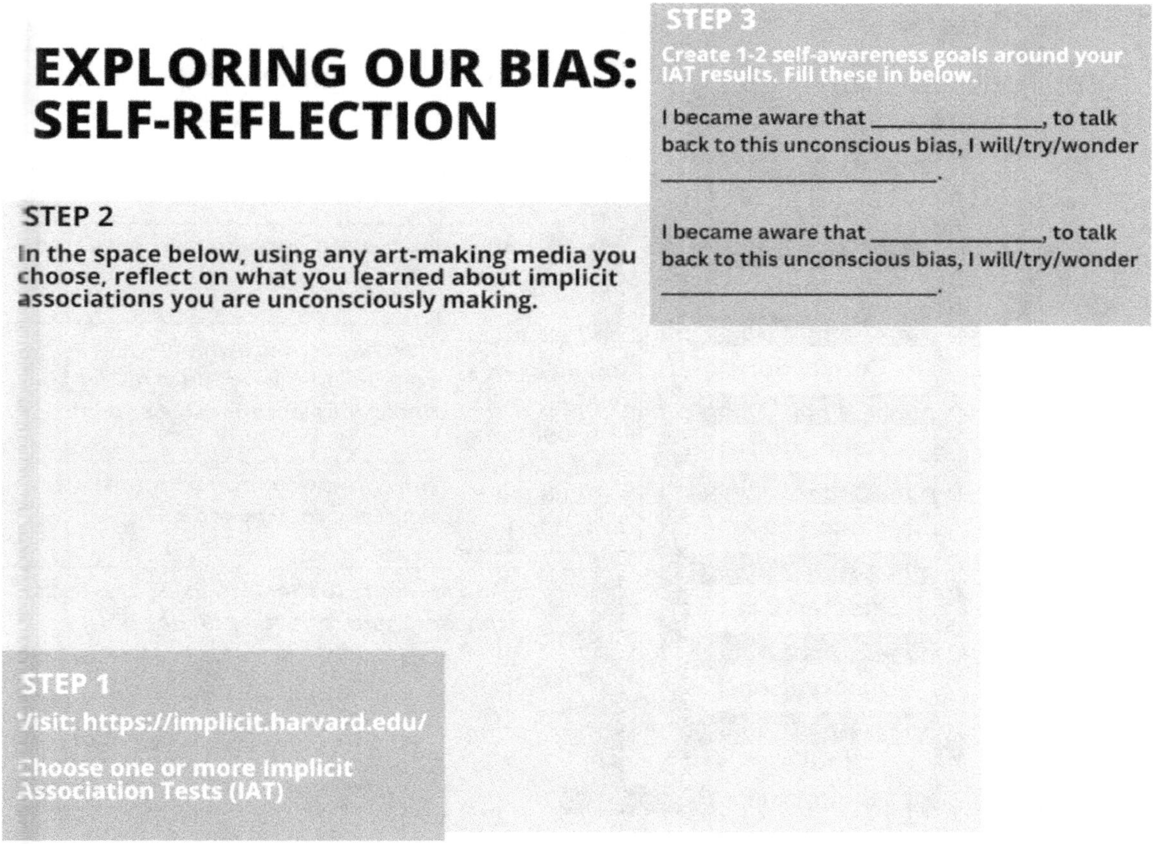

Figure 18. Bias Self-Reflection Guide

This guide provides instructions on using arts-based reflection to consider areas of bias you uncovered in the implicit bias tests. Consider areas that emerged and goals for how you can interrupt those areas of bias in your teaching practice.

Resource 9

Coming Down the Ladder

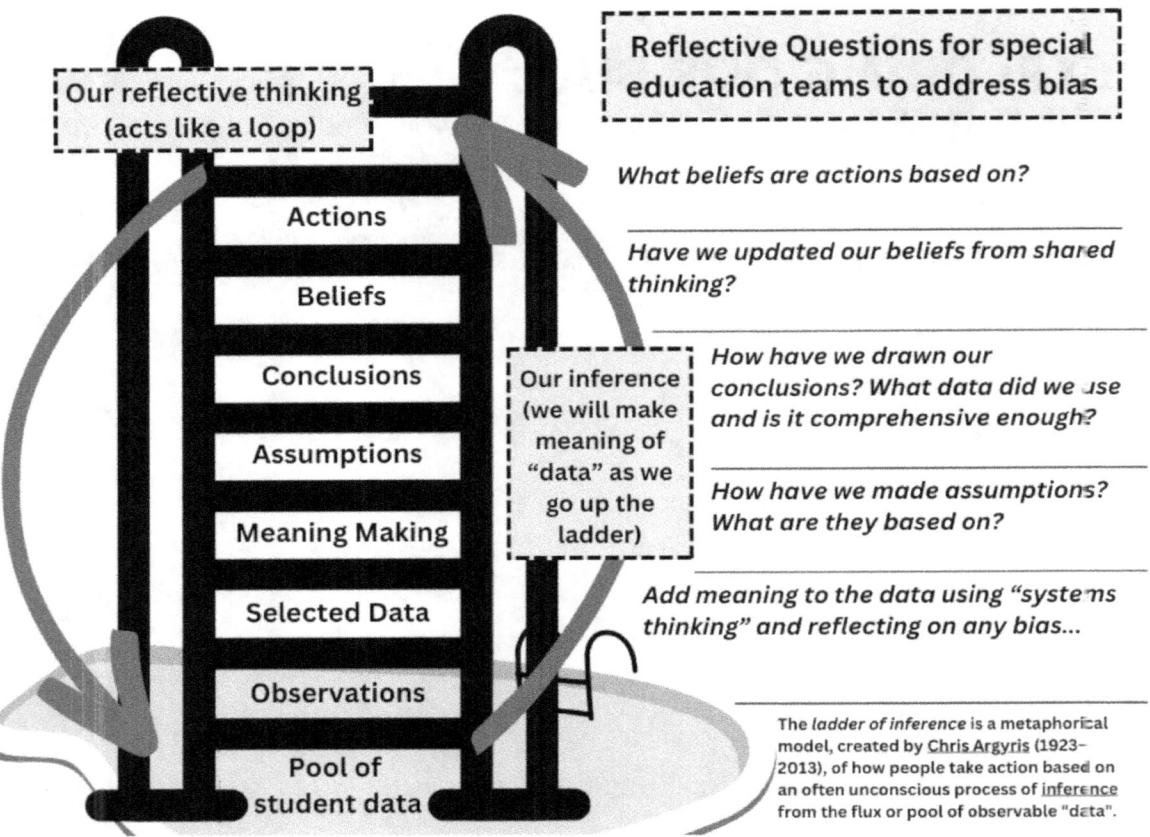

Figure 12. Ladder of Inference
This figure depicts a visual of the Ladder of Inference, originally created by Argyris (1982), to help teams consider the assumptions that may be affecting their thinking and planning for students.

Resource 10

Co-Teaching Modalities and Guide

Co-Teaching Modalities Guide

Co-Teaching Configuration	Internet Resource	Notes
One Teach, One Support	Understood.org has a comprehensive resource defining co-teaching configurations, checklists to implement them, and suggested use cases: https://www.understood.org/en/articles/6-models-of-co-teaching. Cult of Pedagogy provides practical tips for co-teaching configurations to support student learning and teacher communication: https://www.cultofpedagogy.com/co-teaching-push-in/. Visit https://www.cultofpedagogy.com/co-teaching-push-in/ for co-teaching tips, strategies, and professional learning opportunities.	
One Teach, One Assist		
Station Teaching		
Parallel Teaching		
Supplemental Teaching		
Team Teaching		

Resource 11

Evaluation Template

EDUCATIONAL EVALUATION

Name: Birthdate:

School: Grade:

Examiner/Evaluator: Evaluation Date(s):

Report Date:

Introduction (describe student and reason for evaluation):

Present Levels (specific to the areas being evaluated and reported):

Records Review:

Summary of Previous Evaluations (if a reevaluation):

Testing Behavior (provide some description for each category):

Student level of conversational proficiency:

Student level of cooperation/engagement with the evaluation:

Student level of activity:

Observable student attention and concentration:

Perceived student self-confidence:

Perceived student care in response:

Behaviors or responses to difficult tasks:

Description of Tests Administered (include formal names for assessments administered):

Description of Evaluation Findings (include graphs or other visual descriptions of findings):

Validity of Test Results:

Academic Areas:

Parent/Student Feedback:

Summary of Evaluation:

Recommendations of Evaluator:

Resource 12

Intensify Intervention Taxonomy

Discuss the systematic method for using data to determine when and how to provide more intensive interventions as recommended by the National Center for Intensifying Interventions (NCII). The NCII emphasizes the method is an ongoing process, not a single intervention, and is especially beneficial for students with severe and persistent learning and behavioral needs. Use the thinking guide below (see table 5.13) to help you consider a unique student instance needing increased support and intervention.

Table 5.13.

Data-based Individualization	Describe student and challenge needing intensive intervention	Using the DBI process, outline the current intervention, progress monitoring, diagnostic data, intervention adoption (see more below) and continued progress monitoring efforts
www.intensiveintervention.org		1. 2. 3. 4. 5.

Next, consider how to intensify and individualize the intervention. See NCII for more resources to implement the taxonomy of intervention strengthening. The steps are included below (see table 5.14) to support your problem-solving process.

Table 5.14. Breaking Down the Steps in the Taxonomy of Intervention Intensity

Dimensions	Description	Notes
Strength	How well the intervention program has worked for students similar in need to your student(s) (effect size, results from research studies).	
Dosage	Number of opportunities the student has to respond to or interact with the intervention. (Could this be increased?)	
Alignment	How well does the program align with student learning needs (grade level, deficit areas)?	
Attention to Transfer	The extent that intervention is designed to transfer to other areas of academic need.	
Comprehensiveness	The number of explicit instructional principles incorporated in the intervention.	
Behavioral or academic support	Does the program include student self-regulation or other executive functioning supports?	
Individualization	Validated, data-based process for individualizing the intervention to match student needs.	

Fuchs, L. S., Fuchs, D., & Malone A. S. (2017). The taxonomy of intervention intensity. *Teaching Exceptional Children, 50*(1), 35–43.

The *Taxonomy of Intervention Intensity* found in more detail on the NCII website (Fuchs, Fuchs, & Malone, 2017) can be helpful to select or evaluate an intervention aligned with student learning needs and the data-based intervention (DBI) process. The taxonomy criteria can also be utilized to guide the special education team in adaptations of an intervention during the intervention adaptation step of the DBI process (see more recommendations related to the DBI process).

Resource 13

Paraprofessional Schedule

There are several ways to create paraprofessional schedules. The three examples below are configured in different ways that each could work better or differently in various program configurations. Some considerations when choosing how to organize a schedule could be how many students and paraprofessionals need to be scheduled each day or how many grade levels are represented in the program. Recall, creating "contingency" schedules is recommended so you have an "A" and "B" schedule that can be swapped in the event that team members are out, or a unique student issue arises. Any of these schedule examples could be duplicated and then adapted to create an "A" and "B" version allowing for team members to be absent in the event of illness or other circumstance.

Paraprofessional Schedule

	Monday	Tuesday	Wednesday	Thursday	Friday
Student:					

Schedule Explanation: In this schedule, you will plan for each student each day of the week. Paraprofessionals can be assigned to the student, which can potentially be indicated through highlights of different colors.

	Monday	**Tuesday**	**Wednesday**	**Thursday**	**Friday**
Transportation/bus pick up					
First Period or 8–9 a.m.					
Transitions					
Second Period or 9–10 a.m.					

Schedule explanation: In this schedule, you will plan for students across the school day using time increments. Students can be highlighted in a color that corresponds to the paraprofessional assigned to support *or* names could be added in parentheses next to the student. In all schedules, don't forget to plan for transitions, supervision, and paraprofessional breaks/lunches. One issue that can come up is when team members want to take a break at the same time. Remember, that the first priority is student support, which can mean, for instance, that adults may not be able to have a break at the same time since that does not allow enough support for students.

Paraprofessional Schedule

	Team Member #1	**Team Member #2**	**Team Member #3**	**Team Member #4**
Time increments or students	*8 a.m.* *9 a.m.* *And so on . . .*	*Student A* *(9–11)* *Student B* *(11:30–1:30)* *And so on . . .*		

Schedule Explanation: In this schedule, you will outline the paraprofessionals' schedules and add students or time increments down the first column. This could also be done using one sheet per team member and would be a simple way for a team member to see just their schedule instead of the entire grid, which includes all of the students and team members.

Resource 14

Transition Plan Template

In addition to an annual Individualized Education Plan (IEP), students aged sixteen or older (in many states fourteen or older) will be required to have a transition plan included in their IEP. Typically included sections are listed below.

Postsecondary Transition Plan

- Transition assessment conducted (by whom/what transition needs were indicated?)
- Projected date of graduation
- Projected type of completed program (standard high school diploma or adapted high school diploma)
- Postsecondary goals:
    - Career employment goal
    - Postschool education/training goal
    - Independent living skills goal (where applicable)
- Planned course of study (high school years will be listed and credits added either as a list or narrative explanation)
- Transition services and activities
- Education/instruction and related services needed to support transition services and activities
- Career/employment and other post-school adult living objectives
- Community experiences
- Agency linkages

Note, as students graduate from high school special education teachers are also responsible for creating a "Summary of Performance" (SOP). It is completed the year of high school graduation, even if students are transitioning to an eighteen-plus transition program in the school district. An overview of the sections typically included in a SOP is included below.

Summary of Performance (SOP)

Part I: Student Information

Typically included in this part are student demographic information, contact information for the school, and primary disability areas. A one to two paragraph introduction to the student can also be added here that summarizes student interests, strengths, and high school activities engaged in, such as, student Y enjoyed being on yearbook staff and supporting events by volunteering for the events committee.

Part II: Summary of High School Performance

This section is based on age-appropriate skills and assessments tied to the students' post–high school goals.

Academic Achievement and Cognitive Performance	Strengths	Challenges	For each content area, include a brief description of the current level of performance (strengths, needs, grade level, assessment summary).
Science			
Industrial arts/arts/other electives			
Academic advisory/student support			
Career exploration course(s)			
Math			
Social studies			
English			
Health			
Other			
Other			

Part III: Independent Living and Transition Skills

Functional Performance	Strengths	Challenges	If marked strength or challenge, describe functional capacities and how they may relate to post–high school performance work, community, or educational setting.
Social, interpersonal, behavioral skills			
Independent living skills			
Self-care, personal hygiene			
Environmental access/ motor and mobility skills			
Self-determination, advocacy, self-direction			
Communication			
Career and vocational			
Work tolerance and work skills			
Recreation and leisure skills			
Additional important considerations that can assist in making decisions about disability determinations for adult services and needs accommodations.			

Based on age-appropriate abilities, assessment, and tied to the student's post–high school goals

Part IV: Recommendations

Post–High School Area	Recommendations to Assist the Student in Achieving Measurable Post–High School Goals	
	Recommendations (to assist the student in meeting post–high school goals)	**Agency(s) Contact Information** (name and/or title, phone number, address, or email)
Employment		
Education		
Training		
Independent living (if applicable)		

Part V: Document Summary (Transition-Related Assessments)

Part VI: Student and Parent/Guardian Input

Resource 15

Curriculum Planning Template

Instructional and intensive intervention planning—horizontal and vertical maps. Curriculum mapping can be helpful as you think about the steps toward achieving student individualized goals (IEP or other academic goals) and also for organizing an instructional plan across the calendar year or over several years for your students and special education program(s). Use these two templates to fill in simple goals and instructional plan focus areas. The vertical plan will help you think of goal areas for four years from today and how they impact your curriculum and instruction. Vertical mapping could be particularly helpful when considering student transition planning, whether it's from one grade band to the next, for example, elementary school program transitioning to middle school, or transition planning for students in high school to postsecondary college/career/independent living.

Horizontal Plan

Month	Goal Area(s)	Instructional Focus
August		
September		
October		
November		
December		
January		
February		
March		
April		
May		
June		
July		

Vertical Plan

Year 1	Year 2	Year 3	Year 4
Fall:	Fall:	Fall:	Fall:
Winter:	Winter:	Winter:	Winter:
Spring:	Spring:	Spring:	Spring:
Summer:	Summer:	Summer:	Summer:

Index

AAC. *See* augmentative alternative communication
AAPD. *See* American Association of People with Disabilities
ABA. *See* applied behavior analysts
ableism: bias with, 108; disability justice and, 131. *See also* anti-ableism
absenteeism of teachers, 20
accommodations: in conflict management, *163*; curricular adaptations as, 70; in health care plan, 62–63; in IEP, 57, 62–63, 67, 69–72, *72*; for LEP, 63; for neurodiversity, 138; paraprofessionals and, 162; in transition planning, *182*; in vertical curriculum, 193
action and expression, in UDL, 84
action research, 202
active listening, 17
ADA. *See* Americans with Disabilities Act
ADHD. *See* attention-deficit/hyperactivity disorder
AER. *See* Association for Education and Rehabilitation of the Blind and Visually Impaired
African Americans. *See* Blacks
American Association of People with Disabilities (AAPD), 206
American Sign Language (ASL), 80; co-teaching with, 126; in IEP, 62
American Speech-Language-Hearing Association (ASHA), 207
Americans with Disabilities Act (ADA), 51, 54; Heumann and, 141; independence in, 184; transition planning and, 183–85
Angelou, Maya, 51, 107
anti-ableism, 130, 131, 134; in disability studies, 138; in EBPs, 40, 41

anti-racism, 115; in EBPs, 41
APBS. *See* Association for Positive Behavior Support
applied behavior analysts (ABA), 121; for autism LRE, 149
April: collaboration in, 160–69; independence in, 157–60; monthly checklist for, 159, *159*; special education in, 157–69; well-being in, 168, *168*
Archer, Anita, 41–42, 46
Arndt, K. L., 39–40, 46
art, for Down syndrome, 31–32
ASAN. *See* Autistic Self Advocacy Network
ASCD. *See* Association for Supervision and Curriculum Development
ASD. *See* autism spectrum disorder
ASHA. *See* American Speech-Language-Hearing Association
Asians: bias against, 108; disproportionality of, 109
ASL. *See* American Sign Language
assessment: bias in, 86; disproportionality and, 111; in HLPs, 43, 44; in IEP, 57; in LRE, 148
assistive technology (AT): for ADHD, 197; co-teaching with, 126; defined, 64–65, 91–93; funding for, 93; in HLPs, 44; in IEP, *61*, 64–65, 94; specialist in, collaboration with, 122; for TBI, 176; UDL and, 3, 79–82, 94–96, *96*; users of, 93–94
Assistive Technology Industry Association (ATIA), 92–93, 208
assistive technology service, 92
Association for Education and Rehabilitation of the Blind and Visually Impaired (AER), 206

243

Association for Positive Behavior Support (APBS), 207
Association for Supervision and Curriculum Development (ASCD), 208
AT. *See* assistive technology
ATIA. *See* Assistive Technology Industry Association
attention-deficit/hyperactivity disorder (ADHD): AT for, 197; IEP for, 197, 198; inclusive education for, 143–44; mathematics and, 197–98; neurodiversity of, 138
audiologist, collaboration with, 122
augmentative alternative communication (AAC), 93; gradual release and, 165–66; in IDEA, 92; in IEP, 64; for literacy learning, 95–96; specialist in, collaboration with, 122
August: monthly checklist for, 15, *15*; special education in, 11–29; well-being for, 28, *29*
autism, 48–49; disability justice and, 132; LRE for, 148–49; neurodiversity of, 138; special transit for, 65
Autism Society, 207
autism spectrum disorder (ASD), 187–88
Autistic Self Advocacy Network (ASAN), 206
average person, 82–83

Behavioral Intervention Plan (BIP), in IEP, *61*, 62
belonging, 86; disability justice and, 132
bias: against Asians, 108; in assessment, 86; in December, 107–9; in EBPs, 41; stereotypes in, 108; against students of color, 102; systems thinking for, 113–15; types of, 107
bilingual education: in IEP, 64; poverty and, 102
BIP. *See* Behavioral Intervention Plan
Blacks (African Americans): bias against, 109; disproportionality of, 109; in special education, 85–86
brain: dynamic development of, 85–91. *See also* neuroplasticity; traumatic brain injury
brain stem, 89, *89*
Brown v. Board of Education of Topeka, 52
bullying, 105

case management: for autism, 49; of IEP, 25–26, 68, 81, 129
Cast, 208
CEC. *See* Council for Exceptional Children
CEEDAR. *See* Collaboration for Effective Educator Development, Accountability, and Reform
Center for Literacy and Disability Studies, 95
cerebral visual impairment (CVI), 175–76
certified orientation and mobility specialist (COMS): collaboration with, 122; LMA by, 62
certified teacher of students with visual impairments (CTVI): collaboration with, 122; LMA by, 62
CHARGE, 190
Civil Rights Act of 1964, disproportionality and, 111
civil rights movement, 52
classroom management, 21
CLD. *See* Council for Learning Disabilities; culturally and linguistically diverse
Coherence Maps, 194
Cokley, Rebecca, 141
collaboration: with AAC specialist, 122; with ABA, 121; in April, 160–69; with audiologist, 122; with COMS, 122; conflict management in, *163*, 164; with co-teaching, 123–26, *124*; co-teaching and, *37*; with counselors, 122; with CTVI, 122; with deafblind specialist, 122; with disability, 40; in early childhood, 192; with educational diagnostician, 121; with general education, 123–26; with HLPs, 43, 44; with IEP, 118, 121, 123, 129; in January, 117–27; LRE and, 127, 148; in monthly checklist, 81; with nurse, 123; with paraprofessionals, 160–67; roles in, 120–21; with sign language interpreters, 122; with SLP, 121; with social workers, 122; in special education, 26–27; with special education coordinators, 123; with special education directors, 123; with AT specialist, 122; with specialist support staff, 121; in

specialized schools and programs, 149; with transition planning specialist, 122; well-being in, 120
Collaboration for Effective Educator Development, Accountability, and Reform (CEEDAR), 43
communication: in early childhood, *191*; with paraprofessionals, 162–64, *163*; plans, 21, *61*, 62; style, 18, *18*. *See also specific topics*
COMS. *See* certified orientation and mobility specialist
confidentiality, in IDEA, 8
confirmation bias, 107
conflict management, *163*, 164
constructive feedback, 21
consultation model, for LRE, 148
contextual influence, in UDL, 85–91, *89*, *90*
contingency, paraprofessionals and, 166
co-teaching, 13; with AT, 126; with ASL, 126; collaboration with, 123–26, *124*; dos and don'ts of, 125–26; in general education, *37*; in LRE, 67, 146, 148
Council for Exceptional Children (CEC), 43, 207; Paraeducator Core Competencies of, 169
Council for Learning Disabilities (CLD), 207
counselors, collaboration with, 122
#CripTheVote, 141
Csikszentmihalyi, M., 154
CTVI. *See* certified teacher of students with visual impairments
Cult of Pedagogy, 45
culturally and linguistically diverse (CLD): disproportionality of, 110; in IEP, *61*; for LEP, 64
culturally responsive teaching, 115; for autism, 49; disproportionality and, 111
cultural model (Dis/Crit), for disability, *136*, 137–38
curriculum: adaptations in, in IEP, 70; materials, 16; planning, 193–95, *194*
CVI. *See* cerebral visual impairment

deafblind specialist, 122
December: bias in, 107–9; disproportionality in, 109–15; monthly checklist for, 101, *101*; parent/guardian input in, 99–102; special education in, 99–115; special education systems thinking in, 102–6, *104*, *106*, 113–15; well-being for, 114, *114*
deficit-based programs, 40, 52; in March, 151–53; person-first language and, 134
differentiation: accommodations and modifications in, 71–72; in transition planning, 179; in vertical curriculum, 193
disability: adverse educational impact of, 60; in EBPs, 40; frameworks for, 134–36, *135*, *136*, 139; stereotypes of, 52; studies, 136–39; system thinking on, 104–6, *106*. *See also specific topics*
disability justice: in February, 131–34; movement, 52
Disability Rights Education and Defense Fund (DREDF), 206
Disability Visibility Project, 141
Dis/Crit (cultural model), *136*, 137–38
disproportionality: causes of, 110–11; Civil Rights Act of 1964 and, 111; in December, 109–15; in disability studies, 138; in EBPs, 41; IDEA and, 111; of students of color, 138; systems thinking for, 113–15
diversity, in EBPs, 40
Downing, J., 46
Down syndrome, 31–32; executive function with, 118
DREDF. *See* Disability Rights Education and Defense Fund
dynamic brain development, in UDL, 85–91
dyscalculia, 197
dyslexia, neurodiversity of, 138

early childhood: IFSP and, 190, 192; in June, 187–92, *191*
EBPs. *See* evidence-based practices
ECC. *See* Expanded Core Curriculum
educational diagnostician, collaboration with, 121
Education for All Handicapped Children Act, 51, 54, 55
Einstein, Albert, 102
ELA. *See* English language arts

ELL. *See* English language learner
emotional disorder. *See* serious emotional disorder
empowerment: paraprofessionals and, 167; in transition planning, 180
The End of Average (Rose), 82–83
engagement: disability justice and, 131; in early childhood, 192; in HLPs, 44; in UDL, 83, 91
English as a second language (ESL), in IEP, 62, 63
English language arts (ELA), 13
English language learner (ELL): bias against, 109; in IEP, *61*, 62
equity, in EBPs, 40
Erickson, Karen, 95
ESL. *See* English as a second language
ESY. *See* Extended School Year
ethnicity: bias with, 108; stereotype threat and, 109
Every Student Succeeds Act, 54
evidence-based practices (EBPs), 2; HLPs and, 34, *35*, 41–46, *42–43*; implementation of, 39–41; in KWL chart, 34, *35*; UDL and, 40
examples, in EBPs, *42*
executive function: with Down syndrome, 118; in UDL, 83
Expanded Core Curriculum (ECC), 122
experience-dependent plasticity, 139
explicit instruction, 3; in EBPs, *43*; in HLPs, 34, 44
Extended School Year (ESY), 69

facilitative roles, in collaboration, 120
Fair Housing Act, 184
Family Education Rights and Privacy Act (FERPA), 8; transition planning and, *181*, 183
FAPE. *See* free and appropriate public education
FBA. *See* Functional Behavioral Assessment
February: disability justice in, 131–34; disability studies in, 136–39; monthly checklist for, 133, *133*; person-first language in, 134–42, *135*; special education in, 131–42; well-being for, 140, *140*
feedback: constructive, 21; in EBPs, *43*; in HLPs, 44
FERPA. *See* Family Education Rights and Privacy Act

"Find Your Marigold" (Gonzalez), *45*
504 plan, 53; on accommodations and modifications, 69; on transition planning, 180, *181–83*, 184
504 sit-in, 53, *53*
free and appropriate public education (FAPE), 5; accommodations and modifications for, 69; disability frameworks for, 135; Education for All Handicapped Children Act and, 55; ESY for, 69; health care plan and, 63; in IDEA, 51; leadership for, 202; special transit and, 65; transition planning for, 178, *182*
Functional Behavioral Assessment (FBA), 44, 62
Functional Vision Assessment (FVA), 72

gender: bias with, 107, 108; stereotype threat and, 109
general education: collaboration with, 123–26; co-teaching in, *37*; curriculum planning for, 193; IEP in, 16, 67; paraprofessionals in, 162; service delivery statement for, 67; in UDL, 84
Girma, Haben, 100, 141
Gonzalez, Jennifer, *45*
Google Docs, 12
grading bias, 107
gradual release: for IEP, 23, *23*; paraprofessionals and, 161, 165–66; special education in, 21–23, *22*
Grandin, Temple, 141
grit, 40
growth mindset, 40

health care plan, *61*, 62–63
Hebb's Law, 139
Heumann, Judith, *53*, 100, 141
hidden disabilities, 52–53
High-Leverage Practices (HLPs): EBPs and, 34, *35*, 41–46, *42–43*; KWL chart and, 34, *35–39*; RBPs and, 43
horizontal curriculum, 193, 195
Horn, Xian, 141

IDEA. *See* Individuals with Disabilities Education Act
IDEIA. *See* Individual with Disabilities Education Improvement Act
IEE. *See* Independent Educational Evaluation

IEE. *See* Individual Education Plan
IFSP. *See* Individualized Family Service Plan
implicit bias, 107
inclusion model, for LRE, 147
inclusive education: disproportionality and, 111; for Down syndrome, 118; early childhood and, 191; IEP for, 143–44; LRE for, 130, 146; in March, 143–50; paraprofessionals in, 161; for SED, 143–44; UDL and, 54
independence: in ADA, 184; in April, 157–60; early childhood and, 191; gradual release and, 166; in transition planning, 180, 184
Independent Educational Evaluation (IEE), 8
individual differences, in UDL, 83–84
Individual Education Plan (IEP), 2, 5; AT in, *61*, 64–65, 93, 94; academic achievement in, 57; accommodations in, 57, 62–63, 67, 69–72, *72*; for ADHD, 197, 198; adverse educational impact of disability in, 60; assessment in, 57; behavior plan in, *61*; bilingual education in, 64; BIP in, 62; case management of, 25–26, 68, 81, 129; CLD in, *61*; collaboration with, 118, 121, 123, 129; communication plans in, *61*, 62; contents of, 57; developer of, 56; early childhood and, 191; Education for All Handicapped Children Act and, 55; ELL in, *61*, 62; ESL in, 62, 63; ESY in, 69; FBA in, 62; in general education, 16, 67; gradual release for, 23, *23*; health care plan in, *61*, 62–63; in IDEA, 7–9, *9*, 58, 149; for inclusive education, 143–44; informed consent for, 8; intensive intervention for, 27–28; interview for, 60; introduction of, 59; LEP in, *61*, 62–63; LMA in, 62; LRE in, 8, 57, 58–59, 67, 69–70, 147; in mild-to-moderate middle school resource program, 12, 13, 15; modifications in, 57, 67, 69–72, *72*; in October, 56–73; paraprofessionals and, 160, 161, 163; parent/guardian input for, 7, 58, 59–60; PBSP in, 62; person-centered planning and, 185; present levels section of, 59; processes of, *58*; progress monitoring in, 57, 59; PWNs for, 8; review of, 73; service delivery statement in, 67; shelter and develop model in, 17; SLP and, 68; SMART in, 57, 66; special factors in, *61*, 61–65, *66*; special transit in, *61*, 65; strengths-based instruction and, 41; student input section of, 59–60; student participation in, 58–59; timing of, 56; transition planning in, 60, *61*, 149, *181*, *182*; UDL and, 3
Individualized Family Service Plan (IFSP), 190, 192
Individuals with Disabilities Education Act (IDEA), 3, 51, 54; AAC in, 92; disproportionality and, 111; from Education for All Handicapped Children Act, 55; FAPE in, 51; IEP in, 7–9, *9*, 58, 149; leadership for, 202; LRE in, 146–47; principles of, 7–9, *9*; progress monitoring and, 37; transition planning in, 178–79, *181*, 184
Individual with Disabilities Education Improvement Act (IDEIA), special transit and, 65
informative roles, in collaboration, 120
informed consent, for IEP, 8
instructional technology, in HLPs, 44
intensive instruction, 27–28; curriculum planning for, 193; in HLPs, 44; in monthly checklist, 81
intersectionality, 141
Ives-Rublee, Mia, 141

January: collaboration in, 117–27; monthly checklist for, 119, *119*; special education in, 117–27; well-being for, 127, *127*
Johnson, A. P., 163
July: leadership in, 200–204; monthly checklist for, 199, *199*; parent/guardian input in, 201; professional development in, 200–202; special education in, 197–208; well-being in, 204, *204*
June: curriculum planning in, 193–95, *194*; early childhood in, 187–92, *191*; monthly checklist for, 189, *189*; special education in, 187–96; well-being in, 195, *195*

King, Martin Luther, Jr., 143
know, want, learn (KWL chart): for disability frameworks, 135, *135*; EBPs in, 34, *35*; HLPs and, 34, *35–39*; RBPs in, *35*

Ladder of Inference, *112*, 112–13
Latino/Hispanics, in special education, 85–86
LDA. *See* Learning Disabilities Association of America; least dangerous assumption
leadership: in collaboration, 118; in July, 200–204; paraprofessionals and, 164; with UDL, 84
learning disabilities, as hidden disability, 52
Learning Disabilities Association of America (LDA), 208
Learning Media Assessment (LMA), in IEP, 62
least dangerous assumption (LDA): in EBPs, 40; for multiple disabilities, 153
least restrictive environments (LRE): accommodations and modifications for, 69–70; for autism, 148–49; collaboration and, 127, 148; consultation model for, 148; co-teaching in, 146, 148; curricular adaptations for, 70; Education for All Handicapped Children Act and, 55; in IDEA, 146–47; in IEP, 8, 57, 58–59, 67, 69–70, 147; inclusion model for, 147; for inclusive education, 130, 146; in March, 146–50, 153; MTSS for, 148; for multiple disabilities, 153; resource room model for, 147; RTI for, 148; self-contained classroom model for, 147–48; specialized schools and programs for, 149; special transit and, 65; transition planning for, 149; for UDL, 3
LEP. *See* limited English proficiency
limbic system, 88, *89*
limited English proficiency (LEP), in IEP, *61*, 62–63
literacy learning: AAC for, 95–96; intensive intervention for, 28
Little People of America (LPA), 206–7
LMA. *See* Learning Media Assessment
long-term goals, in HLPs, 44
LPA. *See* Little People of America
LRE. *See* least restrictive environments

March: deficit-based programs in, 151–53; inclusive education in, 143–50; LRE in, 146–50, 153; monthly checklist for, 145, *145*; special education in, 143–55; strengths-based instruction in, 150–51; well-being for, 154, *154*
mathematics: ADHD and, 197–98; Asian students and, 108; for Down syndrome, 31–32
May: monthly checklist for, 177, *177*; special education in, 175–86; transition planning in, 175–86, *181–83*; well-being in, 185, *185*
medical model, for disability, *136*
metacognition, in UDL, 85
Meyer, D., 17
mindfulness, 168
modifications: curricular adaptations as, 70; in IEP, 57, 67, 69–72, *72*; in transition planning, 179, *182*
Mohammad, Gholdy, 115
monthly checklist: for April, 159, *159*; for August, 15, *15*; for December, 101, *101*; for February, 133, *133*; for January, 119, *119*; for July, 199, *199*; for June, 189, *189*; for March, 145, *145*; for May, 177, *177*; for November, 81, *81*; for October, *57*; for September, 33, *33*
motivation: HLPs and, 34; in UDL, 83
MTSS. *See* Multiple Tiered Services and Supports
multiple disabilities, 48–49, 86; AT for, 93; health care plan for, 63; LMA for, 62; LRE for, 153; self-contained classroom model for, 147–48; special factors for, *61*
Multiple Tiered Services and Supports (MTSS), 148
Murawski, W. W., 29

NAD. *See* National Association of the Deaf
National Association of Special Education Teachers (NASET), 207
National Association of the Deaf (NAD), 208
National Center for Intensifying Interventions (NCII), 127
National Council on Disability (NCD) 206
National Disability Rights Network (NDRN), 205

National Down Syndrome Society (NDSS), 207
National Federation of the Blind (NFB), 206
National Spinal Cord Injury Association (NSCIA), 206
National Technical Center on Transition: The Collaborative (NTACT:C), 186
NCD. *See* National Council on Disability
NCII. *See* National Center for Intensifying Interventions
NDRN. *See* National Disability Rights Network
NDSS. *See* National Down Syndrome Society
neurodiversity: in disability studies, 138–39; in EBPs, 41
neuroplasticity, 83; in disability studies, 138–39
NFB. *See* National Federation of the Blind
nonverbal, 191
November: monthly checklist for, 81, *81*; special education in, 79–97; UDL in, 82–91; well-being for, 97, *97*
NSCIA. *See* National Spinal Cord Injury Association
NTACT:C. *See* National Technical Center on Transition: The Collaborative
nurse, collaboration with, 123

occupational therapists (OT): collaboration with, 121; neuroplasticity and, 139
occupational therapists, AT and, 92
October: IEP in, 56–73; monthly checklist for, *50*; well-being for, 74, *74*
orientation and mobility, 62, 122, *183*
OT. *See* occupational therapists
over-doing, 165
over-prompting, 165
overrepresentation, 110

parallel teaching, *124*
paraprofessionals: accommodations and, 162; collaboration with, 160–67; communication with, 162–64, *163*; contingency and, 166; education of, 161; empowerment and, 167; in general education, 162; gradual release and, 161, 165–66; IEP and, 160, 161, 163; in inclusive education, 161; leadership and, 164; scaffolding and, 161

parent/guardian input: in December, 99–102; in early childhood, 192; for IEP, 7, 58, 59–60; in July, 201; for transition planning, 179–80
The Parent Movement, 52
PBIS. *See* Positive Behavior Support System; positive behavior support systems
PBSP. *See* positive behavior support plan
performance monitoring, in EBPs, *43*
person-centered planning, transition planning and, 184–85
person-first language, 54; defined, 134; disability justice and, 131; in EBPs, 40; in February, 134–35, *135*
physical therapist (PT): collaboration with, 121; neuroplasticity and, 139
PLCs. *See* professional learning communities
PLNs. *See* professional learning networks
positive affirmations, for autism, 49
Positive Behavior Support Plan (PBSP), in IEP, 62
positive behavior support systems (PBIS), 23, *38*
positive stress, 89
poverty: bilingual education and, 102; systems thinking on, 103
prefrontal cortex, 88
prescriptive roles, in collaboration, 120
present levels section, of IEP, 59
prior written notice (PWNs), for IEP, 8
professional development, 21; in July, 200–202; for LRE, 150
Professional Era, 52
professional learning communities (PLCs), 173
professional learning networks (PLNs), 200
progress monitoring: IDEA and, *37*; in IEP, 57, 59
PRPSD. *See* Puerto Rican Parents of Students with Disabilities
PT. *See* physical therapist
Puerto Rican Parents of Students with Disabilities (PRPSD), 99
Pulrang, Andrew, 141
PWNs. *See* prior written notice

questioning: in EBPs, *42*; for paraprofessionals, 164

race: bias against, 107; segregation by, 52; stereotype threat and, 109. *See also* anti-racism; *specific races*

racial bias, 107
Rapp, W. H., 39–40, 46
RBPs. *See* research-based practices
Rehabilitation Act of 1973, 53; accommodations and modifications in, 69; transition planning and, 184. *See also* 504 plan
rehabilitation therapy: AT and, 92; neuroplasticity and, 139
relaxation techniques, for autism, 49
religion, bias with, 108
representation, in UDL, 83–84, 91, 140
research-based practices (RBPs): HLPs and, 43; in KWL chart, *35*
resilience, in EBPs, 40
resource room model, for LRE, 147
Response to Intervention (RTI), 148
retention rates for teachers, 20
Rett's syndrome, 190
Rose, Todd, 82–83
RTI. *See* Response to Intervention
Ruby's Rainbow, 32

scaffolding: EBPs and, 39; in HLPs, 34, 44; in horizontal curriculum, 193; paraprofessionals and, 161
The Science of Well-Being, at Yale University, 28
Scott, K. L., 29
SDI. *See* specially designed instruction
Section 504. *See* 504 plan
SED. *See* serious emotional disorder
self-advocacy: movement, 53, 54; in transition planning, 180
self-care: for autism, 49; in early childhood, *191*
self-contained classroom model, 147–48
self-determination, 54
self-efficacy: disability justice and, 132; in strengths-based instruction, 31, 32
self-evaluation, 21
self-reflection, 21
self-regulation: early childhood and, 191; in UDL, 83
September: monthly checklist for, 33, *33*; special education in, 31–46, *33*; well-being for, 45, *49*
serious emotional disorder (SED): behavioral plan for, *61*; inclusive education for, 143–44
service delivery statement, in IEP, 67
SETT, 94

sexuality: anti-ableism and, 138; in transition planning, 180
sexual orientation, bias with, 107, 108
shelter and develop model, 17
short-term goals, in HLPs, 44
sign language interpreters: collaboration with, 122. *See also* American Sign Language
SLP. *See* speech-language pathologist
SLP-A. *See* speech-language pathologist assistant
SMART. *See* specific, measureable, attainable, realistic, and time-bound goals
social/emotional/behavioral issues: for autism, 49; in early childhood, 191, *191*; in HLPs, 43; in transition planning, *181*; trauma-informed practice for, 86–91, *89*, *90*
social model, for disability, *136*
social workers, collaboration with, 122
special education/educator: AT and, 92; in April, 157–69; in August, 11–29; Blacks in, 85–86; character strengths of, 28–29; collaboration in, 26–27; coordinators, 123; in December, 99–115; directors, 123; disillusionment of, 128–29; in February, 131–42; first year of, 23–29, *24*, *25*; gradual release for, 21–23, *22*; history of, 51–56, *53*, *55*; as IEP caseload manager, 25–26; intensive intervention by, 27–28; in January, 117–27; in July, 197–208; in June, 187–96; Latino/Hispanics in, 85–86; in March, 143–55; in May, 175–86; in mild-to-moderate middle school resource program, *11*, 11–29, *20*; in November, 79–97; in October, 48–74; organization by, *38*; procedures of, *39*; roles and responsibilities in, 24–28; in September, 31–46, *33*; systems thinking in, 102–6, *104*, *106*, 113–15; Whites in, 86. *See also specific topics*
special factors, in IEP, 61, 61–65, *66*
specialist support staff, collaboration with, 121
specialized schools and programs, for LRE, 149
specially designed instruction (SDI): intensive intervention for, 27

special transit, in IEP, 61, 65
specific, measureable, attainable, realistic, and time-bound goals (SMART), in IEP, 57, 66
speech-language pathologist (SLP): AT and, 92, 95; collaboration with, 121; IEP and, 68; neuroplasticity and, 139
speech-language pathologist assistant (SLP-A), collaboration with, 121
speech-to-text, 93, 153
state standards, IEP and, 58
station teaching, 124
"stay put" rights, 8
stereotypes: in bias, 108; of disability, 52
stereotype threat, 109
strengths-based instruction, 146; disability justice and, 131–32; in EBPs, 40, 41; IEPs and, 41; in March, 150–51
stress, categories of, 89–90
stress reduction, for autism, 49
student input section, of IEP, 59–60
students of color: bias against, 102; disproportionality of, 138
supplemental teaching, 124
supportive roles, in collaboration, 120
systemic bias, 108–9
systemic inequality, in EBPs, 41
systems thinking, 102–6, 104, 106, 113–15

TASH, 207
TBI. *See* traumatic brain injury
teams. *See* collaboration
team teaching, 124; in LRE, 148
text-to-speech, 72, 79, 93, 94, 153
Thompson, Vilissa, 141
tolerable stress, 89
toxic stress, 91
transition planning: ADA and, 183–85; for FAPE, 178, 182; in IDEA, 178–79, 181, 184; in IEP, 60, 61, 149, 181, 182; for LRE, 149; in May, 175–86, 181–83; parent/guardian input for, 179–80; person-centered planning and, 184–85; specialist in, collaboration with, 122
trauma-informed practice: for autism, 48–49; for social/emotional/behavioral issues, 86–91, 89, 90; in UDL, 85–91, 89, 90
traumatic brain injury (TBI), 139; AT for, 176; transition planning for, 175–76

UCP. *See* United Cerebral Palsy
UDL. *See* Universal Design for Learning
underrepresentation, 110
underrepresentation due to exclusion, 110
UNESCO, 99
United Cerebral Palsy (UCP), 206
Universal Design for Learning (UDL), 2, 141, 146; AT and, 3, 79–82, 94–96, 96; accommodations and modifications in, 71–72; action and expression in, 84; complexity of learning in, 84–85; contextual influence in, 85–91, 89, 90; disability justice and, 131; for Down syndrome, 31–32; dynamic brain development in, 85–91; EBPs and, 40; engagement in, 83, 91; IEP and, 3; inclusive education and, 54; individual differences in, 83–84; LRE for, 3; metacognition in, 85; motivation in, 83; in November, 82–91; representation in, 83–84, 91, 140; trauma-informed practice in, 85–91, 89, 90

vertical curriculum, 193, 195
vocabulary, in EBPs, 42

WATI. *See* Wisconsin Assistive Technology Inventory
well-being: in April, 168, 168; for August, 28, 29; in collaboration, 120; for December, 114, 114; early childhood and, 191; for February, 140, 140; for January, 127, 127; in July, 204, 204; in June, 195, 195; for March, 154, 154; in May, 185, 185; for November, 97, 97; for October, 74, 74; for September, 45, 49
What Really Works with Exceptional Learners (Murawski and Scott), 29
Whites: disproportionality of, 109; in special education, 86
Wisconsin Assistive Technology Inventory (WATI), 94, 95
Wong, Alice, 100, 115, 141

Yale University, The Science of Well-Being at, 28
Young, Stella, 141

About the Author

Dr. Tara Mason is a Universal Design for Learning (UDL) consultant for the Center for Teaching and Learning at the University of California, Berkeley. She is passionate about working on teams focused on equitable and inclusive learning environments that uplift student voice, identity, and access to educational opportunities. She holds a PhD in special education from Texas Tech University, specializing in assistive technology, serving students with multiple disabilities and visual impairments. Her master of education (MEd) focused on curriculum and instruction from the University of Nebraska-Lincoln. Before joining UC Berkeley, she served as a faculty member directing a graduate and undergraduate special education teacher preparation program at a university in Colorado. While working in Colorado, Dr. Mason held leadership roles within the Teacher Education Division of the Council for Exceptional Children (CO-TED), and secured funding for teacher preparation grants to support paraprofessional and alternative special education teacher pipelines. Dr. Mason has an extensive background working within K–12 special education, spanning more than two decades. Her special education teaching background encompasses working in K–12 special education settings from elementary through teaching in eighteen-plus transition programs. She has also led coaching teams to support new special education teachers at the school district level. In addition, Dr. Mason has taught as a self-contained special education teacher and worked as a teacher of students with visual impairments (TSVI) at the Texas School for the Blind and Visually Impaired. Dr. Mason's research interests primarily relate to UDL, special education, disability studies, faculty development, promoting equity and inclusion, disrupting bias and disproportionality in special education, mentoring, and teacher preparation. She lives in California with her family.

Author positionality statement: Dr. Mason, who prefers she/her pronouns, is a middle-aged White woman. She was raised in a middle-class family growing up in a densely populated urban area in the Southern United States. As a young person, she attended public schools and universities, where she was primarily taught by White teachers. She has experienced privilege in multiple areas of her identity, as well as in her educational opportunities, which have positively impacted her teaching and learning experiences. During her elementary school years, Dr. Mason received special education services in speech and language, as well as reading interventions. She began her career in special education as a paraprofessional and has taught in a variety of settings, including highly restrictive school settings and inclusive general education classrooms. Dr. Mason is a licensed middle school generalist, K-12 special education teacher, early intervention specialist, a teacher of students with visual impairments (TSVI), and an assistive technology specialist.

www.ingramcontent.com/pod-product-compliance
Lightning Source LLC
Chambersburg PA
CBHW080634230426
43663CB00016B/2866